OVER A BARREL

BREAKING THE MIDDLE EAST OIL CARTEL

RAYMOND J. LEARSY

NELSON CURRENT

A Division of Thomas Nelson, Inc.

To lovely Melva

Published in Nashville, Tennessee, by Nelson Current, a division of a wholly-owned subsidiary (Nelson Communications, Inc.) of Thomas Nelson, Inc.

Nelson Current books may be purchased in bulk for educational, business, fundraising, or sales promotional use. For information, please e-mail SpecialMarkets@ThomasNelson.com.

Library of Congress cataloguing-in-publication data on file with the Library of Congress.

ISBN 1-5955-5036-4

Printed in the United States of America
03 04 05 06 07 QWK 5 4 3 2 1

ACKNOWLEDGMENTS

First, I would like to thank Mike Levitas, the erstwhile editor of the *New York Times* op-ed page; William F. Buckley Jr., editor of editors; and Priscilla Buckley, Rich Lowry, and Kathryn Jean Lopez, editors of *National Review* and NRonline. All of them had the gumption to publish out-of-the-box articles by me that presented the issues touched upon herein and ultimately set up the parameters of this book.

I am particularly grateful to Donna Carpenter, Maurice Coyle, and the other talented editors and researchers at Wordworks, Inc.— Ruth Hlavacek, Larry Martz, Cindy Sammons, and Robert Shnayerson—for their ever thoughtful, intensive, and cheery assistance with this manuscript. If I needed to jump into a foxhole, they would be among the first I would ask to join me there.

A further word of thanks to my agent, Helen Rees, who has not only been supportive, but has carried the message of the book as her personal grail. Don't get in this lady's way! Best send her to Paris

ACKNOWLEDGMENTS

where good food and wine will take a tad off the edge of her e-mails.

And my appreciation to my formidable editor, Joel Miller, for his dedication to this project, and to my personal assistant, Marianne Lehners, who has worked hard and long in helping me in this enterprise.

Thanks, finally, to my friends and family, but most especially my wife, Melva, who has suffered me through this process with love and support no matter the level of my irascibility. She read every draft, made countless insightful suggestions, and encouraged me to go on even when the going wasn't easy. More than my wife, she became my "Ruth" and my official, full-fledged muse.

CONTENTS

Introduction   ix

Part 1—The Barrel We're Over

Chapter 1   3
The Scarcity Myth

Chapter 2   25
Hysteria Premium

Chapter 3   47
Oil Poor

Part 2—How OPEC Put Us over a Barrel and
Where We Go from Here

Chapter 4   77
OPEC's Bludgeon

Chapter 5   101
Crude Squabbles

Chapter 6   127
    The Faustian Bargain

Chapter 7   145
    Tightening the Chokehold

Chapter 8   161
    Old Schemes for the New Millennium

Chapter 9   179
    Iraq's Real Victors

Chapter 10   213
    Fate Rolls the Dice

Chapter 11   223
    Spelling Doom for OPEC

Epilogue   243

Sources   247

Index   267

INTRODUCTION

In the harsh old days of Britain's Royal Navy, a sailor caught stealing extra rum was trussed over the barrel of a cannon and left to broil in the sun, waiting to be flogged.

Figuratively speaking, you and I and everyone else in the oil-consuming world are already caught in just such a predicament. Instead of a cannon, though, ours is a barrel of oil. And the people who put us there are the members of the OPEC oil cartel, profiteers who have been flogging us for years with no end in sight.

There is a mystique surrounding oil. It is a deliberate one, trumped up to make everyone thankfully accept a manipulated market with hugely inflated prices. These market machinations rob the world's consumers of literally hundreds of billions of dollars every year, both from higher energy prices as well as artificially inflated costs for just about every other kind of good. Over the past three decades, according to one U.S. government estimate, the tab has totaled a staggering $7 trillion.

These costs land disproportionately on those least equipped to bear them, the people in the developing world. Already treading a precarious path of existence, Third World countries lack the money and technology to introduce energy-efficient techniques and processes, and typically have little or no access to energy sources that can be substituted for oil. With nothing to shield them from the full brunt of rising prices, the world's poorest people are thus forced to spend more of their meager resources on food, fuel, and transport. The hole they're in just gets deeper.

For the thievery of all the world's citizens, we can blame OPEC, the Organization of the Petroleum Exporting Countries. Though OPEC's eleven member states (Algeria, Indonesia, Iran, Iraq, Kuwait, Libya, Nigeria, Qatar, Saudi Arabia, United Arab Emirates, and Venezuela) account for an estimated 40 percent of world oil production, their brazen market manipulations largely determine the price for all the rest.

Blame must also go to OPEC'S co-conspirators—non-member countries like Mexico and Russia, the Western oil companies and their minions who collude with the cartel, Western governments (including, at key junctures, the United States) that actively support the conspiracy, the media with its willingness to swallow and regurgitate OPEC's propaganda, and all of us who have stood by and passively watched this disaster unfold.

Astonishingly enough, President George W. Bush has admitted the U.S. government's complicity. Speaking of our dealings with Middle Eastern countries during a press conference early in 2005 at NATO headquarters in Brussels, the president said: "The policy in the past used to be, 'Let's just accept tyranny for the sake of "cheap" oil or whatever it might be,' and just hope everything would be okay." He added that the events of September 11, 2001, changed all that when long-held Arab hatred exploded on U.S. shores.

But what the president got wrong in his Brussels remarks is that OPEC oil has not been "cheap" for quite some time, at least not in the way free-market enthusiasts understand that term.

OPEC is a cartel of suppliers, and all cartels are inherently suspect. They earn that suspicion by joining in schemes to control production, allocate markets, and fix prices to balloon their profits.

Price fixing is illegal in this country, and the Justice Department has prosecuted any number of antitrust cases over the years (most notably, perhaps, John D. Rockefeller and Standard Oil). But U.S. courts have decided that the "foreign sovereign immunity doctrine" precludes the Justice Department from suing OPEC. Various senators have sought to override the doctrine with legislation that would subject government-owned commercial ventures, such as the state-controlled and state-owned oil companies of the OPEC members, to antitrust laws. These efforts have been derailed by a Senate provision that allows senators from oil-producing states to put the legislation on indefinite "hold," thus guaranteeing that it will never make it to a floor vote and never threaten the conspiracy.

The damage wrought by OPEC is not only economic. America's security is also at risk. In making a Faustian bargain with OPEC— selling our soul for a steady supply of "cheap" oil—the United States has squandered a great national resource: the independence that would be secured by moderating, or more intelligently providing for, our own energy needs. We have placed our security in the hands of an extortionist cartel, just to keep our industrial heart beating. Worse, the world's addiction to Middle Eastern oil means that hundreds of billions of dollars are being pumped into a region where people despise us and where too many preach and pray for our destruction.

In fact, prominent members of OPEC openly work to undermine democratic ideals in the United States and other Western countries. Millions of dollars of Saudi Arabian and Kuwaiti money go to finance schools, mosques, and supposedly charitable organizations that actively promote the virulently anti-Western Wahhabi strain of Islam and encourage Muslim citizens of Western nations to reject the principles upon which their governments were founded.

Ironies abound, not least that we supply the money that buys the textbooks and prayer books stuffed with venomous words designed to bury us. American citizens' gas money is used to pay the salaries of imams and school officials who propagate the poison.

But it isn't only hate-filled teaching and preaching that we support. The sheer volume of this torrent of funds practically guarantees that some of our dollars will wind up in the hands of people—both stateless terrorists and recognized leaders of rogue nations—who are capable of acquiring biological, chemical, or nuclear weapons, and eager to use them against us.

Indeed, at this very moment, Iran's Islamic regime is putting its oil money to work acquiring long-range, ballistic-missile capability. It is also producing enriched uranium that could be used to make nuclear weapons. Iranian leaders deny that their intentions are malignant, of course, but the CIA isn't convinced.

Meanwhile, Abu Musab al-Zarqawi, Osama bin Laden's chief murderer in Iraq, is said to be targeting American schools, restaurants, and movie theaters. *Time* magazine quotes al-Zarqawi as believing that "if an individual has enough money, he can bribe his way into the U.S."

That money—petrodollars, of course—will procure fake visas and passports and guarantee safe passage through Canada or Mexico and into the United States. In countries where life is touched by fanaticism and virtually everything is for sale, the combination of limitless wealth, seething hatred, and weapons of mass destruction is more than frightening; it can be deadly.

This book aims to awaken us all to that danger, to explain how it evolved and what it could do to the world, and to suggest ways we can escape our shameful dependence on OPEC oil and break OPEC's extraordinary grip on the world's economy. So great are the perils that we can no longer permit the unfettered consumption of oil. Our national honor and security depend on it.

But before I go any further, let me answer the inevitable questions: Who am I? How do I know what I am talking about? And why am I writing this book now?

For openers, I am not an oilman. (By the time you finish reading this book, I think that fact will enhance my credibility, not erode it.) I have spent more than twenty-five years of my professional life trading in commodities—and that's just what oil is, no more and no less than a simple commodity. Despite all the hyped-up rhetoric about its being uniquely political, strategic, scarce, and rapidly depleting, oil is merely one of the unglamorous raw materials of civilization, no different from any other.

OPEC, as I said, is a cartel, but not just any cartel; it is the world's most egregious combine and its most damaging. It blatantly violates the spirit of free trade, as well as the rules of the World Trade Organization, while being meekly thanked by its holdup victims.

I am writing this book because OPEC and its machinations make me very angry. OPEC's dealings offend my sense of fairness and justice. Like most traders I know, I take pride in playing by the rules on a level playing field. In the markets I worked in, traders who try to take unfair advantage soon find themselves frozen out. But there is a whole industry, led by OPEC, that is permitted to hoodwink the world, while governments collude in the robbery and hardly a protest gets registered. Just imagine the firestorm of indignation that would erupt if the public found out that the world's big grain exporters (say, the United States, Canada, Brazil, Argentina, and Australia) were conspiring to triple or quadruple the price of such basic commodities as soybeans, corn, and wheat. If subsidies were eliminated and growers conspired à la OPEC, grain prices, and the prices of products made from grain, would balloon. Yet oil is just as basic, just as essential, and the damage done by the OPEC oil cartel is every bit as costly to the world as a grain conspiracy would be.

This shakedown also alarms me because of the danger it poses not only to my country but to the world. I served in the U.S. Navy as a district security officer, and was given a sound but frightening education in all the basic elements of chemical, biological, and nuclear warfare. (Ironically, part of my service was spent in the federal building at 90 Church Street in lower Manhattan, a building that was destined to become the northern demarcation line of the hollowed quadrant that was once the World Trade Center.) I know what I'm talking about—more sometimes than I want to know. I know how easy it is, especially for those who are determined and willing to sacrifice themselves, to buy or steal these weapons or their equivalents, move them around the world, and use them to destroy their targets and kill as many of us as they can. We are in imminent deadly peril, and every dollar we ship off to the Middle East for oil increases the danger.

The cartel must be broken, and the United States must lead the fight. Our government alone carries the clout to stand up to OPEC and the oil interests, their powerful friends and well-entrenched allies, and the accumulated billions of dollars that bankroll their activities. The time has come for our leaders to honor their commitment to this nation by coming down squarely on the side of its people; they must defend us against the greed and destructiveness of OPEC and its minions in the oil and related industries. Anything less will be a dereliction of duty.

I have nothing to gain from OPEC's demise. If the cartel were broken tomorrow, I would receive no more or less than one man's share of the resulting rise in global prosperity.

Commodity trading has been good to me. I can indulge my fondness for travel and my passion for art, a love that began when I was a young man hanging around the Cedar Bar in Greenwich Village, listening to arguments among artists such as Franz Kline, Jackson Pollock, and Willem de Kooning. These days, *Art News* lists my wife and me among the two hundred foremost collectors of art, and I have been privileged as an appointee of President Ronald Reagan to serve on the National Council for the Arts and on museum and other art organization boards.

I found my way to commodity trading by a natural route: I originally came from Luxembourg, the son of a leather goods wholesaler with clients all over Europe. My family immigrated to the United States at the outset of World War II. I attended the Wharton School of Finance and Commerce at the University of Pennsylvania, majoring in what was then quaintly called "international commerce." Two years of my life were spent in the Navy, after which I landed an apprenticeship in commodity trading with a large trading company. From there, I started operating on my own.

Most people never give commodity trading a thought, but it is a fascinating, complex business that keeps the world running. To be a trader, you have to know a lot—what's needed where, what it's worth there, and where you can find it at what cost. You negotiate for the purchase and sale, arrange financing and letters of credit, take possession of the goods, move them to a port, charter ships or planes for the long haul, arrange to move the material from the port of arrival to the final destination, and buy insurance to cover any conceivable loss along the way. Even so, you worry until the goods are safely delivered and the check is in the bank.

Forty years ago, the commodities business was less formal than it is now. We got along on our character, our connections, and what we knew. We didn't need vast amounts of capital to get financing, or flow sheets detailing every move in every part of each transaction. We calculated our deals on the back of an envelope and made our bets. And sometimes we lost. A partner and I once loaded two tons of fresh strawberries in California, flew them to New York, and transferred them to a flight to London, where we had an eager buyer. But the plane's cargo refrigerator wasn't up to the job, so the plane landed in London with two tons of strawberry jam. Still, we survived.

I got an education in those years, and part of it came when I encountered my first cartel. In hindsight, that taught me everything I needed to know about OPEC. It was the mid-1960s, and this cartel controlled the world market in sulfur, most of which was then extracted from huge underground domes in the southern United States. Forming a joint export operation under the Webb-Pomerene Act would allow the three companies dominating the business to legally operate as an export cartel. So they formed the Sulfur Export Corporation, or Sulexco, which, in effect, had a world monopoly. Sulexco set the price and controlled the supply, and it kept the market so tight that some buyers couldn't get sulfur at all.

Few people realize how essential sulfur is, to both industry and agriculture. You can't make steel or industrial explosives without sulfuric acid; the entire "green revolution" in agriculture would have been impossible without the sulfuric acid that converts phosphate rock into phosphate-based fertilizer. And in the mid-1960s, Sulexco was saying there wasn't enough of it to meet demand, a claim that was almost surely untrue.

The sulfur domes were virtually limitless, and all the producers had to do was pump in heated water to dissolve the sulfur, pump it back out, and then separate the mineral from the water. In classic cartel fashion, Sulexco probably just decided that rather than increase production, it could make more money with less effort by fabricating a shortage and raising the price. This manufactured shortage ensured that those lucky enough to get their hands on some sulfur were grateful to Sulexco, rather than resentful over the egregiously high price.

But the shortage, though artificially induced, still meant that some people couldn't find the sulfur they needed, and they became fairly desperate to get it. In South Africa, for example, the mining industry was about to come to a halt because of a lack of explosives, which would have dealt a mortal blow to the South African economy.

Meanwhile, the French had a company producing sulfur as a byproduct of a new process to remove hydrogen sulfide from "sour" natural gas. Rumor spread in the commodity business that the South African government, worried about its mining industry, had offered to equip its air force with French-made Mystere jet fighters if the French would sell sulfur to South Africa's explosives producer, African Explosives & Chemical Industries (AECI). But the negotiations seemed to stall.

AECI was partly owned by Britain's then-monolithic Imperial Chemical Industries (ICI), so Pretoria also put pressure on ICI to deliver the needed sulfur by threatening to nationalize AECI if it didn't. Sulexco still held the upper hand, though. Based on its claim that there wasn't enough sulfur to go around, it would sell ICI only what it needed for its own use, not for AECI's. ICI was almost frantic to find another source of sulfur to prevent the loss of its AECI investment.

That source turned out to be me. I was operating at the time in western Canada, where some oil companies were experimenting with the same process the French were using to sweeten sour natural gas by removing its foul-smelling and dangerous hydrogen sulfide. So I went to a number of these companies and offered them a reasonable price for their sulfur byproduct. I put together small parcels until I had commitments for 20,000 to 30,000 tons, a major portion of what South Africa needed. Then I offered it to ICI.

It was a heady scene. There I was, twenty-eight years old, a small trader based in Canada, having a boardroom luncheon in ICI's grand London Millbank headquarters with a lot of starchy British executives in Saville Row suits. I told them I would supply AECI with sulfur, but they would have to support me in purchasing other commodities particular to the chemical fertilizer industry, including nitrogen products, phosphates, and potash. We struck the bargain, and I set up my trading business with that deal. I called my company Brimstone Export Ltd., using the biblical term for sulfur.

After that, more and more companies began using the new process to separate sulfur from natural gas, and the so-called shortage eased considerably. It soon became clear that Sulexco was going to lose its market control, because the huge amount of sulfur coming from gas was a lot less expensive than the sulfur pumped from underground domes.

That brings me to the real parallel with OPEC: For years, Sulexco put out propaganda to persuade its customers that sulfur was still in short supply and that anyone who didn't buy at full price from Sulexco was in danger of running out. It used all the tactics practiced by OPEC—writing articles, hiring "experts" to parrot the message, and feeding the press the cartel's line. The aim was to persuade the world that sulfur was strategic, that it was a fast-depleting finite resource, that its sale and movement were politically sensitive, and that high prices were beneficial because they would help Sulexco ration the precious element and make sure it was wisely used. In time, Sulexco's fiction collapsed of its own weight, but until it did, the cartel reaped enormous profits.

I never forgot that. Years later, after the 1973 Arab oil embargo enabled OPEC to gain a stranglehold on the world, I began to sense that something similar to the Sulexco fraud was being perpetrated on oil consumers throughout the world. I wrote a letter that the *New York Times* graciously published, arguing that oil was no more scarce or strategic than the commodities that make agriculture possible. By then, however, the alleged shortage of oil had already been accepted as received wisdom, reinforced by the environmental movement and various reports from so-called experts.

For a while, the 1973 embargo seemed to backfire on the cartel. There was an active push to find new reservoirs of oil and alternative sources of energy. Oil prices drifted lower. But late in the 1980s, it became clear that OPEC and the world's major oil companies had joined forces to push up the price of oil, and that the U.S. government was helping them. After the Persian Gulf War in 1991, OPEC became a major force in world markets, influencing both the supply and the price of oil with its machinations. And not surprisingly, I found myself reading the same kind of propaganda from OPEC that Sulexco had foisted on its consumers years before.

In March of 1991, shortly after the end of the first Iraq war, I wrote an op-ed for the *Times* asking, "Did We Fight the War To

Save OPEC?" It argued that OPEC was restraining global trade and imposing an unfair tax on the world economy. I suggested that since we had saved Kuwait and protected Saudi Arabia from Saddam Hussein, the least those countries could do in return was to leave OPEC and trade their oil on a free-market basis.

Yet, OPEC continued to spread its propaganda and hardly anyone spoke up in protest, least of all the cartel's friends in Washington and other world capitals.

A decade later, the United States again went to war with Iraq. The uncertainty and fears of an oil-supply crisis pushed prices to unimagined heights. OPEC happily fed the panic.

In September 2003, the cartel's chief propagandist, Omar Farouk Ibrahim, wrote a letter to the *International Herald Tribune* that reached a new level of hubris. He said the cartel was ensuring the steady flow of "a finite resource . . . at a price that is fair and reasonable," and thus doing nothing less than "fulfilling our obligations to humanity." Ibrahim went on to claim that the Western nations were "the biggest beneficiaries of high oil prices," since the oil companies were headquartered in these countries, and OPEC spent its oil riches on Western goods and investments. His brazen claim that OPEC was good for all humanity prodded me to write another piece. "OPEC Follies—The Breaking Point" was published by *National Review Online* in December 2003, after which I began writing this book.

It is heartening to consider that Sulexco no longer exists and few people even remember it. My goal is to start the process of sending OPEC along the same track to oblivion, by exposing its deceptions and corruptions, its extortionist tactics, and the pathetic complicity of its victims.

Clearly, it is no fun being over a barrel. But there is another way to look at it. The phrase "over the barrel" once also referred to a sailor's way to resuscitate a drowning victim. Victims were laid not over the barrel of a cannon, but over a wooden barrel. Rocked back and forth, they would expel the water from their lungs and gasp for life-giving air. Maybe, if we rock our oil barrel long enough and hard enough, we can expel the strangling forces of OPEC and become self-reliant once again.

Part 1

The Barrel We're Over

1

THE SCARCITY MYTH

Nothing lasts: not fame, fortune, beauty, love, power, youth, or life itself. Scarcity rules. Accordingly, scarcity—or more accurately, the perception of scarcity—spells opportunity for manipulators.

This is precisely the approach pursued by the Organization of the Petroleum Exporting Countries (OPEC), the biggest and most relentless manipulator ever foisted on the oil-addicted economies of the world. It has become a vicious cycle of boom and bust, carrot and stick, lies and deceptions. The best—perhaps the only—way to stop this devastating cycle is to rise up and thunder a simple truth: Oil is not scarce. We only fear that it is.

The fear of scarcity makes oil unique among commodities. No one loses sleep over shortages of bauxite or phosphate or molybdenum. But an anxiety approaching panic grips us at the mere thought of an oil-bereft future. Visions of dying industries, freezing houses, stalled cars, and grounded airplanes send a shiver up our collective spine. There is surely no doubt that much of the developed world would go to war—and perhaps already has in Iraq—to prevent such a future.

But worries about petroleum shortages are needless. If a shortage of anything exists, it's of truth and candor and market transparency. The fact is, the oil shortage we are warned about is a fiction. The *alleged* oil shortage, well, that's directly tied to the ability of a scheming group of oil producers to deceive consumers across the globe.

OIL RUNS OUT—OVER AND OVER AND OVER

From the beginning, the story of oil has been a continuing cycle of discovery, followed by fear of scarcity, followed by more discovery and more fear. In 1855, when people were making patent medicine from crude oil that bubbled up to the surface of the Pennsylvania earth (and touting it as a cure for everything from diarrhea to rheumatism to ringworm and deafness), an advertisement for Samuel Kier's Rock Oil instructed buyers: "Hurry, before this wonderful product is depleted from Nature's laboratory!"

Soon thereafter, when the area's first drilled well hit pay dirt just 69 feet below the surface, alarmists began predicting dry wells ahead. In 1874, the state geologist of Pennsylvania, then the nation's leading oil producer, estimated that the United States had only enough oil to keep kerosene lamps burning for another four years. As chronicled by Daniel Yergin in *The Prize*, his sweeping history of the oil industry, a Standard Oil executive named John Archbold began selling his company shares in the 1880s because engineers told him the country was nearing the end of its petroleum supply. When other experts informed him about signs of oil in Oklahoma, Archbold was incredulous, famously replying, "Why, I'll drink every gallon produced west of the Mississippi!"

In 1885, California was tagged by the U.S. Geological Society as having "little or no chance" of finding oil. In 1914, the Federal Bureau of Mines adjudged the U.S. oil supply enough to last for only ten years, and two years later, it ratcheted up the rhetoric to predict "a national crisis of first magnitude," with "no assured source of domestic supply in sight." In 1940, sixteen years beyond the designated day of doom, and apparently unfazed by its history of misreckoning, the bureau predicted reserves would now be exhausted in fourteen years.

Clearly, the oil industry was on its way to compiling a record of failed prognostications unmatched by perhaps any other industry, past or present. The prophecies, and the dearth of supporting evidence, continued unchecked.

In 1972, for example, the Club of Rome, an international consortium of prestigious worrywarts, predicted a global energy shortage that would stunt economic growth and force the world into a new pastoral age. They estimated that only 550 billion barrels of oil remained to be tapped, and warned that the world would run out of crude by 1990.

Once again, however, the doomsayers were wrong—this time because they ignored the effects of technological advances like computer-assisted imaging that raised the odds of finding new pools of oil.

Journalists Amy Myers Jaffe and Robert A. Manning pointed up the utterly incorrect analyses of the "sky-is-falling" crowd of oil forecasters. Writing in the January/February 2000 issue of *Foreign Affairs*, they noted that two decades worth of pundits' predictions for a 3.6 million-barrel-per-day decline in non-OPEC production had been given the lie by a more than 4 million-barrel-a-day *increase*. None of this is to mention that, in those two decades, the world used up 600 billion barrels of oil—more than the Club of

Rome thought even existed back in 1972. And, by the millennium, proved reserves exceeded a trillion barrels.

Though buried deep in the consumer psyche, the fear of shortages never quite disappeared. For instance, a widely used 1981 textbook on economic geology, *Economic Mineral Deposits*, again warned of an "energy gap." Authors Mead L. Jensen and A. M. Bateman predicted a 125-year-long calamity that would pinch hardest shortly after the year 2000. But, lo and behold, by 1986 a soft economy, cheating on OPEC production quotas, and increased output from non-OPEC rivals had combined to produce an oil glut that drove prices below $10 a barrel.

Nevertheless, the voices of doom persisted, even in the face of contrary facts and low prices. In 1989, one expert warned that world oil production would peak that same year, and the ensuing catastrophic crash in output would soon drive the price to $50 a barrel. As this book goes to press in the late spring of 2005, all I can say is, if nothing else, at least this fellow correctly pegged the price.

So it went, and so it goes. Similar predictions of imminent calamity appeared in 1995, 1998, and 1999, relayed in somber tones by such prestigious journals as *Nature*, *Science*, and *Scientific American*. No matter that, in the real world, oil production and, more importantly, proved oil reserves continued to rise all through the 1990s, as prices hovered between $20 and $30 a barrel. As a result, the life index of existing world oil reserves, as measured by the ratio between proved reserves and current production, has risen from twenty years in 1948 to about forty-three years at the end of 2003.

Yet the Chicken Littles continue to scratch and tremble, sometimes to the point of absurdity. In 1997, for example, widely quoted British oil analyst Colin Campbell wrote in *The Coming Oil Crisis* that peak world production was just around the corner (again).

Plunging supplies, he speculated, could bring "war, starvation, economic recession, possibly even the extinction of *Homo sapiens*."

So far, no one has trumped Campbell's ace—though it is hard to imagine a prediction much bleaker than the end of humanity. But neither has his prediction come true, and I don't believe it ever will, at least not for lack of oil.

RUNNING ON FULL

Why the persistent predictions of calamity? After World War II, an abundance of oil made possible widespread electrification, mass transportation by automobile and airplane, and the production of an array of new materials ranging from synthetic rubber to artificial fibers to plastics, fertilizers, pesticides, and detergents. Each of these dramatically changed life in the developed world.

Accordingly, oil consumption exploded. Increased oil consumption became not just the driver of economic growth, but, ironically, a consequence of it as well.

Seizing on this remarkable global transformation and keen to control its key ingredient, OPEC began training consumers— indeed, most governments around the world—to believe that oil is a much more finite resource than it really is. OPEC perpetuates the phony theory of scarcity and successfully manipulates the price of oil with the help of Mexico, Russia, and other non-OPEC producers.

Contrary to what the casual observer may believe, there is no identified fixed supply of world oil that dwindles with each passing year of growing consumption. Instead, the oil business is built on a series of gambles that the development of any given field will pay a big enough reward to justify the cost of coping with the industry's negative conditions and obstacles. A gamble is, by definition, no sure thing, and oil-well drilling is often deferred to await the lower costs, better technology, or higher prices that might increase the odds of success. The point is, even if we knew exactly how much total oil Earth holds, the number would be tangential to the issue that matters: How much oil is accessible for profitable extraction right now?

Over the long term, despite heavy production and dire predictions of oil depletion, all data show a net gain in the worldwide pool of extractable oil. Take California's Kern River field, for example. Discovered in 1899, it was declared largely depleted after forty-three years of production, with remaining reserves thought to total fifty-four million barrels. Instead, over the next forty-four years it produced more than twelve times that much, pouring out another 736 million barrels. That isn't all: Further geological examination has turned up yet another 970 million barrels of recoverable oil at Kern River.

Or how about the more recently discovered Kashagan field in Kazakhstan? Thought to contain 2 to 4 billion barrels when test drilling was begun in the latter half of the 1990s, by February 2004 the official estimates had climbed all the way to 13 billion barrels.

The Kern River and Kashagan experiences have been repeated many times the world over. During a fifteen-year span ending in 1996, for example, the estimated volume of 186 huge oil fields around the globe jumped from 617 billion barrels to 777 billion, and that was *without* additional discoveries.

Did all these fields somehow grow more oil? Not likely. What grew was know-how and the tools to drill deeper and wider. So rather than shortages, the real story of the oil industry over the past century—and most especially the past fifty years—has been one of discovery enormously enhanced by technological improvements that have lowered the cost of bringing oil out of the ground while also giving new life to fields once thought exhausted. Indeed, the recovery rate of existing oil fields has risen from about 22 percent a quarter-century ago to 35 percent today.

Consider the term *proved reserves*. A key measure of the oil world's always-fluid future, it refers, in its most general sense, to the accessible oil in a field that hard data suggests has a 90 percent chance of being pumped out. This assumes no drastic setbacks in economic, political, and technical conditions. Determining the amount of proved reserves, then, is more art than science. Geological and engineering surveys are analyzed and production from nearby wells assessed to come up with a reasonable figure. But as even Roger W. Bentley, secretary of a depletionist-oriented group of international scientists called the Association for the Study of Peak Oil and Gas, has acknowledged, "Proved reserves have been very conservative numbers, indeed. They do not reflect the total oil that has been discovered, but only that small portion for which definite plans are in place for current access."

Varying rules and methods of measurement also complicate the issue. In the United States, the Securities and Exchange Commission insists that a very narrow definition of proved and recoverable reserves be used in measuring an oil company's financial health. In Canada, meanwhile, companies are allowed to report both proved and probable reserves, which may better reflect the true potential.

Partly because of pressure from oil companies eager to attract investors, the SEC may revise what many consider to be its unnecessarily restrictive, outdated rules that were adopted in 1978 and don't properly account for non-conventional reserves, such as those found in tar sands and deep-water locations. The current SEC reporting standards are so narrow that they discourage investors and prevent financial markets from correctly assessing the results of exploration.

A Cambridge Energy Research Associates report released in February 2005, and funded by oil industry heavyweights ranging from production companies themselves to their law firms, auditors, and investors, points out that new technology like 3D seismic mapping has not only made oil in remote locations accessible and economically feasible to extract, it has also made estimates of these reserves far more accurate. If investors are to be enticed to finance production from these new sources of oil, the report adds, they need a better calculation of a company's reserves than the current SEC guidelines provide.

The problem, as critics see it, is multi-pronged. For one thing, the SEC does not allow companies to include in their reserve reports any oil at all from deposits such as those found in Canada's tar sands, even though these deposits have attracted billions of dollars of investment and are estimated to contain more oil than is buried in the Arabian desert. Never mind that gasoline derived from oil sands is already powering cars on U.S. highways.

In addition, the SEC alone uses year-end product prices to calculate reserve estimates, which, critics charge, distorts the numbers and forces oil companies to forgo many promising expansion opportunities. ExxonMobil, ConocoPhillips, and others were forced to excise from their 2004 SEC reports millions of barrels of extra-heavy oil deposits after a last-minute slide in prices made these sources uneconomical in the eyes of the SEC. The heavy-oil prices subsequently rebounded, but too late to change the annual reports.

Then there's the problem of a company's internal reserve auditors attempting to apply SEC rules that don't mesh with the policies in many of the countries where the fossil fuels are located.

Right now, though, as this and the succeeding chapter show, oil-producing nations aren't required to document anything at all, and they don't. In an attempt to remedy the confusing and often market-roiling lack of transparency, the Group of Seven (G-7) industrial nations are urging producing countries and oil companies alike to lift the veil of secrecy and share data on output and reserves. "Transparency and data is [sic] key to the smooth operation of markets," the finance ministers acknowledged in a statement issued after a two-day meeting in February 2005.

"We need more information about oil reserves," declared Gordon Brown, the United Kingdom's chancellor of the exchequer, whose county hosted the talks. Brown suggested that international financial institutions work with industry groups to devise worldwide accounting standards for oil reserves, and he also advocated that producing nations release exact figures on supply. Brown had previously issued a statement at the October 2, 2004, meeting of the International Monetary Fund saying that transparency was needed "to ensure lower and more stable prices," and that "a lack of transparency in oil markets and poor quality information contribute to volatility and uncertainties." Reliable information would relieve traders' fear of the unknown, which so persistently sends market prices spiraling upward.

In countries like Libya, where Occidental Petroleum, Marathon Oil, Amerada Hess, and ConocoPhillips are scrambling to explore—a sure sign that significant reserves are thought to exist there—and in Iraq, Iran, Kuwait, Saudi Arabia, and every other place where secrecy rules, transparency would surely deal a significant blow to the myth of scarcity.

Is it any wonder, then, that the G-7 proposal was quickly denounced by the Saudis? Ihsan Bu-Hulaiga, an economist and adviser to the Saudi government, was quoted by Bloomberg as saying: "Western nations are not dealing with oil producers as partners. Why should they have the advantage of knowing details of oil producers' reserves? Data on reserves is information, and information is power."

No one would dispute the power of information. The question is, why must the world's consumers be the victims? It's a question we should ask every time we stand at the pump and see that the cost of gas has ticked upward again.

The lack of international standards of measurement doesn't deter the "experts" from making prognostications, however. Early in 2004, the generally accepted estimate of global proved reserves was 1.2 trillion barrels. But not everyone accepts these numbers without question; it is hard not to be suspicious, particularly when the estimates come from people with a vested interest in the oil business. Apart from vested interests and standards problems, just how much credence should one put in a "global" estimate that excludes one of the globe's largest oil producers? Russia, ranked second behind Saudi Arabia and ahead of the United States, doesn't divulge its reserves— the numbers are literally a state secret. And the petroleum data that are available from the former Soviet Union are so poor as to make it impossible for an outsider to make a reasonable guess.

Then there's OPEC. Knowing the true size of the cartel's proved and probable reserves is critical to gauging with any degree of accuracy how long the world's oil will last—and the supply would not be difficult to determine. But because scarcity pays, Saudi Arabia and its OPEC brethren have reason to minimize their treasure. The Saudis alone sit on top of 80 known reservoirs, allegedly holding 261 billion barrels of proved reserves. But the desert kingdom currently taps just 11 of those basins, having opened two new fields ahead of schedule in August 2004, when fears of shortages sent prices on one of their periodic, one-way elevator rides. Reprising their well-practiced, self-serving song, the Saudis professed to be opening the new fields in order to boost their oil output and protect the world economy.

The newly opened fields are said to contain a total of 14 billion barrels, but given that they were discovered more than forty years ago, how can the estimates be considered credible? The kingdom has long since stopped exploratory drilling to ascertain how much more oil remains to be found. Most experts believe there is a lot.

Moreover, recent developments indicate that the Saudis know much more about their already proved reserves than they have been revealing. On December 27, 2004, Saudi Minister of Petroleum and Natural Resources Ali al-Naimi said, in a statement issued after opening new oil fields in eastern Saudi Arabia, that those 261 billion barrels still waiting to be pumped might actually turn out to be 461 billion barrels. "There are big chances to increase the kingdom's producible reserves by 200 billion barrels," he said. "This will come either through new discoveries or through increasing production from known deposits."

No one bothered to ask al-Naimi how he could predict with such precision the number of barrels just waiting to be discovered. Or why he chose this moment, when rumors of OPEC production cuts and higher prices were roiling the markets, to make his announcement. He gratuitously reiterated that "the kingdom is keen to ensure a balance between supply and demand and the stability of the market . . . so that producers benefit and consumers do not lose."

Never mind that world consumers had already "lost" trillions of dollars to the OPEC manipulators. The obviously calculated dispensation of significant "new" information could only reinforce the sense that the Saudis were deliberately hiding reserves. But why should the Saudis rush to divulge their secrets? Why admit to having an underground ocean of petroleum that will only weaken your leverage in the market?

Iraq is usually reckoned the world's number two depository of petroleum, with an estimated 115 billion barrels of reserves. But since its war with Iran in the 1980s, its invasion of Kuwait in 1990, its status as an international pariah barred from normal oil trade, and the destruction of wells and production facilities by insurgent groups fighting its 2003 occupation by the United States, exploration has languished and its industry has fallen into decay.

Reserve estimates aside, no one really knows how much oil lies beneath Iraq. In August 2004, the country took steps to find out when it began soliciting bids to determine the size of some of its reserves, the first time since the Iran-Iraq war that modern exploration technology will be used to size up Iraq's fields. The fields to be examined are Rumaila and Kirkuk, Iraq's oldest and its two biggest producers. Kirkuk began producing in the 1920s, and even the Iraqis realize that applying updated exploration technology there is long overdue.

Iran's situation is similar. The commonly accepted figure for its reserves is 125.8 billion barrels, but supposedly knowledgeable estimates run all the way from a ridiculously low 37 billion barrels to an astronomical 500 billion.

The entire dilemma can be summed up in one contradictory set of figures: In 1970, non-OPEC oil producers had 200 billion barrels of proved reserves among them. In the next thirty-three years, they pumped a total of 460 billion barrels. Now they say they have 209 billion barrels of proved reserves remaining. OPEC members, which supposedly had 412 billion barrels of reserves in

1970, have since produced 307 billion barrels and now claim to have 819 billion barrels in reserve. In a world where pumping billions of barrels out of the ground paradoxically seems to increase the billions still remaining, we are left to wonder where the real truth lies.

So what is the ultimate global potential? Who knows? Any answer requires crystal-ball forecasts of future developments in science and technology. All we have now is a bare framework for conjecture. Since the first well was drilled, a total of slightly over 1 trillion barrels has been pumped. Most doom-saying theorists, led by Colin Campbell and Jean Laherrère, a retired deputy exploration manager for French-based Total S.A., estimate that perhaps 2 trillion barrels of ultimately recoverable reserves (URR) are left.

Campbell and Laherrère, it should be noted, arrived at their estimate using closely held proprietary reserve figures and their own arcane formulas. Meanwhile, the U.S. Geological Survey, after making its own analysis in 2000, pegged URR at 3 trillion barrels, 50 percent more than the Campbell-Laherrère estimate.

What is more, two major discoveries of recent years—the previously mentioned Kashagan field in Kazakhstan and the Azadegan field in Iran—together account for nearly 40 billion barrels that were not included in the estimates. It seems unlikely that so much of a supposedly scarce resource would be found so quickly. Indeed, these discoveries throw the whole theory of scarcity into question.

Besides the store of conventional oil, there are, as mentioned, also reservoirs of non-conventional petroleum. Found in tar sands, oil shale, heavy oil, deep water, or polar locations, it is admittedly more difficult to tap than conventional oil, which is found in liquid form and pumped without further processing or dilution. Tar sands, for example, are really deposits of bitumen, a heavy black viscous substance that requires a good deal of processing before it can be burned as fuel oil. The sands must first be strip-mined, which doesn't cost much, but then the bitumen has to be melted out of the clay encompassing it. That can add anywhere from $10 to $15 to the price of a barrel of oil.

Nevertheless, some estimates of oil reserves already include the 1.6 trillion barrels in the tar sands of the Canadian West, now approaching economic feasibility after forty years of dogged effort. Legendary Texas oilman T. Boone Pickens is a significant investor in this area, giving credence to its growing potential. China is interested as well. In January 2005, the Chinese and Canadian governments announced preliminary agreements that are expected to lead to joint energy ventures. In addition, Enbridge Inc., a Canadian pipeline company, is working with Chinese refiners on plans for a $2 billion pipeline project stretching from Edmonton, Alberta, to the northern coast of British Columbia. Known for taking the long view, the Chinese appear to be betting that the extraction of oil from Canada's tar sands will be economically feasible by the time the pipeline is completed.

No one yet counts the equally vast heavy-oil deposits of Venezuela's Orinoco belt, which now yield 500,000 barrels a day, even though they may be technically closer to conventional oil and easier than tar sands to recover. An even larger amount of oil—estimated at several trillion barrels—is locked in the oil shale of the American West, still awaiting economic extraction.

The real cost of lifting oil from beneath the Middle Eastern sands is small, thought to be as little as $1 to $2 per barrel. That makes it risky to spend much larger sums extracting oil from the harder-to-get-at deposits. Yet, at today's high market prices, extraction is increasingly feasible.

Who is to say, however, that the Saudis and their OPEC

brethren won't suddenly flood the market by pumping more of their cheap oil if only to put this new competition out of business?

Again, recent Saudi behavior adds credence to this notion and increases suspicions about the actual size of their reserves. Abandoning two decades of strategy, Saudi Aramco, the kingdom's state-owned oil company, said in February 2005 that it would have more than 70 drilling rigs operating by year-end, compared to 34 rigs operating one year earlier.

Over the past twenty years, through all the ups and downs of the cyclical oil market, Aramco has sought only to maintain capacity, not increase it (even though, before the 1973 oil crisis, it produced a ten-year plan that projected 1983 production of 20 million barrels a day, more than double what the kingdom currently pumps). But now the G-7 is pressing for more transparency, and the cash-rich oil majors are coming under pressure to beef up their budgets to find and pump oil at a cost the industry puts at approximately $6 a barrel. It hardly seems coincidental that the Saudis have announced a big push to sharply increase their own output, which costs less than $1.50 a barrel to produce.

The kingdom's real agenda is surely to placate the G-7 and dissuade Western oil companies from using their cash windfall (together the top ten companies earned more than $100 billion in 2004) to open up exploration elsewhere in the world.

Still, technological breakthroughs and higher market prices are attracting more risk takers. Nevertheless, in the face of this trend, the depletionists refuse to quit muttering about a petrol Armageddon. As further evidence that the world is fast running out of oil, they point to the fact that announced discoveries have been diminishing in size ever since the 1970s. There may have been major discoveries since then in Iran and Kazakhstan, as well as in the Caspian Sea, offshore Africa, and the deepwater Gulf of Mexico. But none of them, the depletionists claim, is remotely comparable to the vast reservoirs in the Persian Gulf region. In fact, these naysayers flatly assert that no more major basins remain to be found.

Even in the Gulf of Mexico, Laherrère has argued, the pace of discovery is rapidly declining. He has claimed that, prior to 1980, 1,920 wildcat wells drilled in the region located a total of 723 billion barrels of oil. In the next two decades, he has said, another 1,720 wildcat wells discovered only 32 billion barrels of crude.

All this might make for a powerful argument if it were not deeply misleading. First, as mentioned earlier, Saudi Arabia stopped exploratory drilling soon after 1980, despite straddling the world's largest oil reservoir. Why? Because the Saudi princes saw no point in spending money to find reserves that would not be needed for years.

Second, Iran and Iraq also stopped drilling around the same time. This occurred not because they were trying to avoid finding more oil, but because they were at war with each other and mired in political turmoil. With the region's three biggest potential sources of discovery calling a timeout, wildcatting was stepped up in less likely places like Oman, Syria, and Yemen. Not surprisingly, the reservoirs of oil found in those countries were smaller. Even so, the odds are that the announced size of the discoveries isn't the last word on the subject. Experience shows that reserves are almost always revised upward as fields are thoroughly explored and new technology is applied to production.

The supposed dwindling pace of new oil discoveries is simply a red herring. It proves nothing about the amount of oil left to be found. While it seems unlikely that other fields as large as those in the Persian Gulf remain to be discovered, a large part of the world has yet to be thoroughly probed, and no one can rule out the possibility of equally significant discoveries at some point in the future.

BELL CURVE VERSUS PLATEAU

So let's state the facts clearly and forcefully: The world is not running out of oil, as alarmists insist. On the contrary, the industry is more likely to run out of markets long before the supply of oil peters out. So say experts like Morris A. Adelman, the respected oil analyst and a professor at the Massachusetts Institute of Technology. "Just as the Stone Age did not end for lack of stones," Adelman wrote in his 1995 book, *Genie Out of the Bottle* (paraphrasing, ironically enough, former Saudi oil minister Ahmed Zaki Yamani), "the Oil Age will not end because of the scarcity of oil. Rather, oil will inevitably be surpassed in convenience by a new source of energy in the future."

In other words, we will never use it all. We began by using up the easiest oil to find and the cheapest to produce, and we are progressing to increasingly more difficult and costly wells as the inexpensive fields are drained. Earth's last drop of oil will never be pumped, because extracting it would cost many times its highest conceivable value as fuel. No matter the scenario, a point will inevitably be reached where what remains isn't worth the cost of bringing it out of the ground.

How soon? That question generates competing answers, notably "too soon" and "stay tuned."

"Too soon" is the refrain of the rapid-depletion school, adherents to the ideas of M. King Hubbert, a Shell Oil geologist. In the 1950s, Hubbert set out to predict production trends in America's lower forty-eight states. He made the assumption that oil output would follow a classic bell curve, beginning a gradual rise in the nineteenth century, ramping up rapidly in the first half of the twentieth, leveling off as production began to match new discoveries, then plunging quickly as reservoirs were exhausted and discoveries dwindled. The final leveling-off on the far side of the bell is known in mathematics as an "asymptote," a curve always approaching but never quite meeting a straight horizon—reflecting the fact that the last drop will never be pumped.

In 1956, Hubbert predicted that oil production in the lower forty-eight states would peak in 1970. When his forecast came true right on schedule, his methodology seemed triumphantly vindicated. Campbell and his latter-day colleagues—principally Jean Laherrère, David Goodstein (a professor at the California Institute of Technology), and Kenneth S. Deffeyes (petroleum geologist and author of *Hubbert's Peak: The Impending World Oil Shortage*)—take Hubbert's theory, including his bell curve, as gospel. They are convinced that after production peaks, the curve falls just as precipitously as it rose. The depletionists don't agree precisely on the date world oil output will top out, nor on the steepness of the declining curve. But most of them say production will peak in this decade and then plunge at a rate they liken to falling off a cliff.

The other side of the debate—the side this book argues—is made up mostly of economists specializing in energy. They do not disagree that, some day, oil production will reach a maximum level and begin to decline. But they think that day is, at the very least, two decades away and probably more, and that the decline will be long, slow, and relatively painless.

It is instructive that two hundred years ago, when European dominance depended on coal, Europeans worried that their primary energy source would run out. But although Europe's coal production peaked in 1913, there are billions of tons of coal in the ground today that are still being dug out, because it is economically feasible to do so. By the same token, there are even more billions not worth digging out—in large part because oil came along.

As Thomas Ahlbrandt, world energy project chief with the U.S. Geological Survey in Denver, told *Oil & Gas Journal* in 2003: "Is there an imminent oil peak? The short answer is no. I believe in the plateau concept [a long, slow tailing-off]. The symmetric rise and fall of oil production is not technically supportable." Ahlbrandt then asked, "Why is there no accountability for these failed forecasts?" Why indeed.

Call Ahlbrandt a "straight-liner," someone who believes that the Hubbert curve analysis is simply too static to encompass all the variables of the hyper-dynamic oil market, in which constant change shapes the market as it responds to innovation and regulation.

We straight-liners point out that peak production is more often than not followed by a plateau formation or a long-term tailing-off that makes the curve asymmetrical and anything but bell-shaped. The slow plateau of gradual change, or even comebacks, is a function of improvements in drilling or refining.

Today's technology makes it possible to drill deeper and to recover more oil from a reservoir than geologists initially thought possible. New computers chart potential undersea fields with an accuracy that slashes the high cost of exploration wells. Holes can now be dug at angles in any direction, enabling companies to use fewer platforms and establish oil wells on the sea floor. Using multilateral drilling, one North Sea operator cut drilling costs by 75 percent in three years.

The slowly receding nature of the underground pools in a long-tail pattern, as opposed to the steep drop envisioned by the depletionists, is especially evident in North Sea production, which has repeatedly refuted bell-curve forecasts over the past two decades. In the Gulf of Mexico, which now produces 30 percent of U.S. crude, pumping from deep offshore wells has helped to lengthen the long tail patterns for the past thirty-five years, thus keeping production at previously unimagined levels.

The depletionists, who have joined forces in the Association for the Study of Peak Oil and Gas, tend to be ambivalent about these nettlesome facts. They claim to have developed new techniques that correct some of the more obvious flaws in the Hubbert model, and they have begun to acknowledge that the bell curve isn't invariable. As Laherrère noted at a September 2001 OPEC seminar in Vienna, "The important message from Hubbert's work ... is that oil has to be found before it can be produced." Still, they continue to use the curve in predicting future oil output.

WORRIED IN PUBLIC, COOL IN PRIVATE

One great petroleum paradox is that the industry's biggest worry has always been abundance, not scarcity. When supply far exceeds demand, prices tumble—and that spells grief for producers. "We're a cyclical business," ChevronTexaco Chief Executive Officer David J. O'Reilly told the *New York Times*. "History tells us that what goes up also goes down." Avoidance of oil gluts is thus among the industry's chief preoccupations.

Similarly, the whole point of OPEC's creation in 1960 was to safeguard member nations from overproduction and its attendant price wars, which threatened to bring down their revenues. By curbing production in major oil-exporting countries, such as Iraq, Iran, and Saudi Arabia, the cartel caused petroleum prices to balloon.

All in all, this is not the record of an industry fearful that its core resource will vanish. Quite the opposite. It is the story of an industry determined to curb supply in order to milk expanding demand at maximum prices. That means a level somewhere between inflation and extortion, but one that also carefully allows the golden goose to go on clucking.

Most of the Hubbert modelers and their alarmist colleagues work for major oil companies, energy consultants, or governments of oil-producing nations. It is in their employers' interest to keep the world in a fluctuating state of alarm over the oil supply, since looming shortages are used to justify high prices.

If the major corporations really foresaw the near-term peaking of production followed by an abrupt decline, it would also be in their interest to prepare for sharp price increases. They would be signing long-term leases on drilling rigs, investing in high-cost production technology to exploit oil shale and the like, and borrowing to buy proved reserves that they could hoard until prices went up. In fact, they are taking none of these actions. Flush with cash from record-high oil prices, they are using their bankrolls to buy back stock and pay dividends to shareholders. One can only conclude that they are far less worried than they let on.

There is objective evidence to support this conclusion. For twenty years starting in 1982, Dr. G. Campbell Watkins, an internationally recognized expert in energy policy who is joint editor of *The Energy Journal*, has kept track of all the sales of proved U.S. reserves of oil still in the ground. If the cost of finding and developing new reserves had really been rising, or if companies were expecting sharp cost and price increases in the future, the value per barrel of known reserves would have risen in anticipation. In fact, Watkins found no such price increases. Investors who bought reserves in 1982 would have lost money selling them twenty years later.

Don't misunderstand. This is no reason for comfort, and certainly not for complacency. The ongoing melodrama of the oil business, driven by the ruthless machinations of OPEC, is not just another media morsel, easily dismissed. It has a moral: The specter of scarcity should never be forgotten, especially not in times and places of seeming abundance and of political turbulence such as we find ourselves in today. Scarcity is part of the human condition and heritage, a crucial motivator for both good and ill. We know that nothing lasts, but repressing that fact is apt to leave us in thrall to whoever exploits our fears. That includes OPEC. It is time to quit flinching about an oil famine invented by fearmongers.

2

HYSTERIA PREMIUM

The date was May 29, 2004. Over a year had passed since jubilant Iraqis, with the assistance of U.S. Marines, sent a towering, twenty-foot likeness of Saddam Hussein crashing into the streets of Baghdad. Over a year had passed since President George W. Bush announced the end of major combat under a "mission accomplished" banner on the flight deck of the aircraft carrier USS *Abraham Lincoln*. Hussein himself had been caught, as Major General Raymond Odierno put it, "like a rat" in a hole less than six months before. But still the Iraqi insurgency ground stubbornly on, part of a war that seemed always to have at least as many setbacks as victories.

The world was uneasy, and the price of oil reflected that unease. It included what traders call a "fear premium," a measure of the market's worry that hostilities might disrupt supply lines and choke off a significant part of the world's oil supply. The specter of possible supply interruptions, a remote possibility that is tirelessly promoted by OPEC's public relations apparatus, hovered over trading on the New York Mercantile Exchange (NYMEX), where the price, which had averaged $20 for a decade, had soared to $35.80 leading up to the war. Then, amid expectations for a quick victory and the actual fall of Baghdad, the price slid back to $30 and below.

But zigs and zags in the months afterward had pushed the oil price steadily higher. On May 1, terrorists burst into an office in Yanbu on Saudi Arabia's Red Sea coast and opened fire. Five Western oil-industry workers, including two American engineers, were slain. Four weeks later, on May 29, terrorists struck for the second time in what had once been the safe haven of Saudi Arabia. The attacks on a Khobar office building housing major oil companies and on an upscale residential complex killed twenty-two people, including four Saudis, an American, and workers from Asia, Africa, and Europe. When U.S. oil trading resumed on June 1 after a long Memorial Day weekend, fear gripped the market. The price of oil was driven to a record high of $42.33.

The reaction to the Saudi attacks was a perfect example of how bouts of often irrational panic have come to rule the petroleum markets in the early twenty-first century. No matter how dramatic the raids and how tragic the deaths, the incidents were, in truth, minor hit-and-run skirmishes. Although the assaults were clearly intended to drive away Western workers, damage the Saudi oil industry, and hurt the U.S. economy, there was no evidence that Al Qaeda or any other terrorist group could do any real damage to the massive Saudi oil infrastructure, or seriously interfere with shipments to Western refineries. And whatever disruptions did occur would be short-lived, as the attacks proved. In fact, an Aramco oil analyst pointed out that company operations have continued without interruption since the 1950s.

More to the point, at any given moment, the world oil industry has inventories of millions of barrels of oil in every stage of production, making any glitch in the pipeline just that—a glitch or inconvenience, not a life-threatening event. Beyond that, the world's industrial nations keep 1.4 billion barrels of crude oil stashed in strategic reserves to cope with any serious disruption. That is the amount of oil needed to fill the gap should Saudi Arabia produce nary a drop for 166 days.

So rather than a fear premium, it was an hysteria premium that spawned the market gyrations. Unwarranted emotionalism continued to convulse the trading floors, thanks in no small part to the OPEC propaganda machine.

"OPEC cannot control prices," Qatari Minister of Energy and Industry Abdullah bin Hamad al-Attiya told the *New York Times*. "It cannot control the fear factor. It cannot control politics. We can only increase supply to calm the markets."

As subsequent events would show, it effectively couldn't (or wouldn't) do that, either. After the post-Memorial Day panic, the price fell back below $40, only to leap again in early July when the color-coders at the U.S. Department of Homeland Security issued a warning that Al Qaeda planned to disrupt the American presidential election. The election was still five months away; nonetheless, the price shot up more than 3 percent in a single day.

Irrationality ruled. Hysteria had traders in a headlock. There were no shortages. Inventories were actually rising. But none of that mattered. As Fadel Gheit, senior vice president of oil and gas research for Oppenheimer & Company, rightly observed to the *Wall Street Journal*, "Whether or not more disruptions to oil supply are likely to happen, it's perception that's moving the market, not inventories at all."

Less than a week later, perception bested reality once again. Shipping sources reported that a South Korean tanker had refused to load up at the southern Iraqi port of Basra because the captain was afraid of terrorists. Naturally, the NYMEX futures price jumped to $41.05 a barrel, as savvy traders wrung their hands and shook their heads over the prospect of a lone Korean tanker captain bypassing Basra and setting off a serious stampede of like-minded seamen.

How big is the fear factor in the oil markets? At various points during 2004, traders reckoned it added as much as $15 a barrel, or about 36 percent of the price. And the fear could be triggered by nearly anything, no matter how trivial the impact on world oil supplies. Prices spiked on news of an ethnic squabble that cut a pipeline in Nigeria, the evacuation of drilling platforms during a hurricane in the Gulf of Mexico, political upheavals in Venezuela, and insurgents blowing up a pipeline in northern Iraq. In each case, the flow of oil was soon restored, yet the price still slithered upward.

Two of the most telling incidents came in August. In one, an attack briefly shut down Iraq's offshore facilities, affecting less than 2 percent of the world's flow of oil for just a few hours. But it was enough to send the New York price further along its record-breaking path, that day reaching $44.34. Equally outrageous, a fire at a single BP refinery in Whiting, Indiana, pushed the New York price to another new record, $46.58. The unceasing speculation and irrational overreaction to every blip on the world screen finally drove the price for a single barrel of oil past $50 in October.

Throughout the entire year, no significant disruption in the supply of oil occurred anywhere in the world system. This indisputable fact—the equivalent of Sherlock Holmes's dog that didn't bark in the night—is key to understanding the oil markets. But hardly anyone noticed, and for good reason.

This market is the culmination of OPEC's prime strategy over the years: carefully fostering the illusion that the oil supply is incredibly vulnerable and that any kink in the pipeline can bring the industrial world to its knees. It is a shell game, with OPEC hiding the pea of truth under a series of walnuts that it switches around in an intricate shuffle to fool the untrained eye. The basic premise is transparently untrue; throughout modern industrial history, the only real interruptions in the world's oil supply have come when OPEC leaders purposely closed the spigots. Yet, as this chapter explains, the fabrication has been woven into the tapestry of conventional wisdom through years of repeated "expert" warnings, the collusion of Western governments and the oil industry, and credulity on the part of the media.

Despite the relentless propaganda, the truth to be remembered is that oil is a plentiful commodity. There are billions of barrels of it lying just below the surface of the Arabian desert, where it can be found and produced for less than $1.50 a barrel (some analysts put the cost of extraction in Iraq at closer to 50 cents).

In a free market, competition would drive the price down to the cost of extraction and production plus a fair profit. That would be a major boon for the world economy, freeing it of the burden created by the transfer of literally billions of dollars to OPEC countries. Lower prices would also speed growth and raise living standards for everyone. But the cartel keeps the price indecently high, and the OPEC nations' outrageous profits of 3,000 to 4,000 percent, based on stated production costs, come at the expense of virtually every other person on the planet. This truth makes OPEC the world's biggest parasite, feeding on the lifeblood of humanity.

OPEC wins as much by controlling production (even though its smaller members often exceed their assigned quotas) as by persuading everyone that the peril is real and could bring the world to a standstill overnight. That ought to be a hard sell, but the cartel's tactics are both crafty and effective.

SLEIGHT OF HAND

In the oil industry, the most basic facts are hidden deep from public view. In shifting them around, OPEC's hand is quicker than most people's eyes. What the industry relies on as basic data on petroleum production is gathered not from audited reports or government figures, but from networks of secret informants furtively monitoring flows and counting tankers at oil terminals around the world. The figures these spies come up with are neither dependable nor transparent. Their notorious unreliability, coupled with the SEC's antiquated and vexing policy on booking reserves, leads to endless debates about basic facts, and also to occasional sudden shocks.

The Royal Dutch/Shell Group rocked the markets in 2004 by announcing that its reserves of oil had been overstated by 23 percent. But while the Shell discrepancy, which was exacerbated by financial accounting rules, grabbed headlines and was seized upon by the depletionists as an example of eroding oil reserves, hardly anyone took note of equally startling news from Yukos: The publicly traded Russian oil giant, not bound by the government's penchant for secrecy, said its reserves had increased by 500 percent. But skeptics cast doubt on the claim, noting that Yukos was fighting to prevent a cheap sale of its assets in a tax dispute with the Kremlin. At both ends of the measuring stick, confusion prevailed.

To begin with, no one knows exactly how much oil even exists, let alone how much of it is readily accessible. The best we can do is estimate reserves, and those estimates are always subject to revision as history shows our guesswork to be limited and fraught with error. Additionally, OPEC has been careful to obscure exactly how much oil it can produce on any given day. Politics play a big part in the obfuscation, and individual OPEC members often understate their production figures to make it easier to exceed quotas.

Here's the way it works: You claim to be pumping more than you really are to inflate your baseline production figure. Then, when the cartel mandates that you cut a specific percentage from that baseline, you can appear to be going along without actually hurting your revenues too much.

But even though everyone involved in the global oil industry knows that OPEC members exceed quotas and lie about production levels, accepted wisdom in the summer of 2004 held that OPEC's production of 28 million barrels a day represented near-maximum capacity. Given that the cartel had produced more than 30 million barrels a day in the late 1970s, that assumption was, at best, dubious. Does anyone really believe that the member nations have not added to their capacity in a quarter of a century?

Nonetheless, it was taken as gospel that Saudi Arabia was the only OPEC member not pumping flat-out. Industry analysts said the Saudis, then pumping 9.3 million barrels a day, might be able to add another 1 million to 1.5 million barrels, but it would be low-quality, high-sulfur oil.

Those figures, too, are open to challenge. The Saudis tend to say whatever suits their purpose at the moment. When they are pushing for higher prices and trying to create the illusion that the oil supply is insecure, they stress their limitations. But when hysteria is getting out of hand and driving prices too high, thereby encouraging competition from alternative sources and causing political discomfort that might threaten to upset their carefully concocted plans, the Saudis embrace an entirely different point of view. Suddenly, ramping up production is simple—and even more, a gracious move meant to keep the world economy from needless disruption.

So in the summer of 2004, when hysteria-prone traders were near panic, the Saudis soothed the markets by disclosing that they were tapping new fields and raising their capacity to 12 million barrels a day, and might possibly be able to do 15 million if necessary.

Interestingly, this claim was promptly discounted by the industry, brainwashed as most participants are by the illusion of scarcity. But, in truth, the Saudis were almost surely still downplaying their real production capacity. This notion was given more than a little credence in December, when, seemingly out of nowhere, Minister al-Naimi let slip to reporters that Saudi reserves might increase by 77 percent in a "few" years. He hinted that there were "big chances" to boost producible reserves by a whopping 200 billion barrels. It is hard to imagine a supposedly dying energy source suddenly coughing up that kind of bonus.

Even among OPEC's smaller producers, capacity figures are by no means a given. This uncertainty sets the stage for the kind of three-act farce performed by cartel members before a world audience in August 2004. When the New York price hit a then-record $44.34, OPEC's president, Purnomo Yusgiantoro of Indonesia, nudged it upward by confirming what everyone thought they already knew: Saudi Arabia had some spare capacity but could not tap it right away, while none of the other members could pump another drop. "The oil price is very high, it's crazy," he told reporters in Jakarta. "There is no additional supply."

The very next day, Purnomo was back with a different story line. Now the cartel *did* have extra capacity. "OPEC continues to hold, at present, a spare production capacity of around 1 million to 1.5 million barrels a day, which would allow for an immediate increase in production," Purnomo declared. He didn't say which OPEC members had unearthed the extra barrels, nor did he explain why these anonymous donors could pump immediately when Saudi Arabia could not.

The following Monday, OPEC's official mouthpiece tried to explain things yet again: OPEC members were pumping the allowed quota of 26 million barrels per day, Purnomo said, while Iraq was kicking in 2 million barrels more, and "2 million others [were coming] from OPEC's overproduction [read: "quota cheaters"] in the field." What is more, OPEC was "ready to add another 1.5 million barrels a day."

For those paying attention, Purnomo had placed the cartel's real capacity at 31.5 million barrels a day, well above the figure it dispensed for public consumption.

The audience at this theater of the absurd was still scratching its head when yet another cast member, Venezuelan Minister of Energy and Oil Rafael Ramirez, stepped out from behind the curtain a few days later to contradict Purnomo. Ramirez insisted that OPEC was already pumping at its maximum capacity and had no way to respond to increased demand.

There was no telling who was correct. No matter. Oil industry observers and analysts, gullible as always, could reach only one conclusion: The supply buffer was obviously perilously thin.

Where did the real truth lie? We may never be able to penetrate OPEC's pronouncements, but we can look at the bottom line of experience to get a better sense of what is really going on. All through 2004, the world's output of oil rose and fell; there were disruptions large and small in Nigeria, Venezuela, Russia, the

United States, and, above all, Iraq. Consumption soared in China. Beset by mismanagement, corruption, and underinvestment, long-time OPEC member Indonesia couldn't even meet its production quotas. In 2004, the Asian nation was a net *importer*, not exporter, of oil. Yet, there was never a real shortage of oil in the world arena. Whatever the production and capacity figures bandied about by OPEC and its member states, the cartel had no problem keeping the market supplied.

More to the point, throughout it all, OPEC was amassing huge profits—the member states' oil export revenues shot up 42 percent in 2004, to more than $338 billion—while taking pains to reassure its victims that its motives were pure. Saudi Arabia's Crown Prince Abdullah has long promised that his country was "willing and ready" to pump any amount of oil "necessary to stabilize the world oil market." The new wrinkle was the war in Iraq, but right from the beginning of the U.S. crackdown on Saddam Hussein, OPEC ministers promised they would not profiteer or use oil to retaliate for an attack on the Muslim nation. If the war were to disrupt supplies, vowed Algeria's energy minister, Chekib Khelil, "We will satisfy the demand in the market, whatever the reason."

In between dispensing such soothing words, the oil barons liked to argue that OPEC was "unfairly blamed" for high prices. "People in power know that crude supplies have nothing to do with the current gasoline prices in the U.S.," Saudi Minister al-Naimi had the gall to declare to reporters during the 2004 run-up of record prices. He said the real problem was a shortage of refinery capacity in the United States—in other words, the victim was cutting its own throat. And, previously, at a September 2000 OPEC meeting, Crown Prince Abdullah had outrageously proposed that Western governments "share the sacrifice" with producers by cutting their taxes on oil.

Prince Bandar bin Sultan, Saudi Arabia's gadabout ambassador to the United States, chimed in to rebut those "politicians and media commentators [who] have attempted to score political points by misrepresenting" Saudi motives. In a *Washington Post* op-ed written during the middle of the hotly contested U.S. presidential campaign, Bandar tried to bat down speculation that the Saudis' summer pledge to increase production was part of a "secret deal" to boost President Bush's prospects. Bandar stuck to the party line: "Saudi Arabia has always stood by America and the world when our intervention was required to stabilize oil prices . . . [and] maintain strong national and global economies."

Whatever the Saudi *raison du jour*, the drill was the same: Stoke fears of insecurity when prices begin to weaken; rush in to assure adequate supplies no matter what when runaway prices threaten to hurt demand and political relationships.

Riddles, contradictions, and concerted efforts to confuse and obscure the relevant issues are the stock-in-trade of the Saudis and their OPEC fellows. In their constant obfuscation over prices, these apologists often argue unconvincingly that oil is somehow a more uniquely political commodity than, say, wheat or copper. They love to float the phony notion that the "inflation-adjusted" price isn't even all that high. In their distorted view, the real record price was reached back in 1981, when the oil price of $38 was equivalent to $72 a barrel in 2004 dollars. This is particularly exasperating double-talk that is not applied to any other commodity. The fact is, the price of anything is determined by its value in the present economy, thus no commodity's price can usefully be compared with whatever its price happened to be in some other era.

But don't think double-talk and obfuscation are solely reserved for outsiders. They are a staple of relations among OPEC members themselves. For instance, the cartel's price mechanism relies on production quotas to keep the oil price in a predetermined narrow range. But in 2004, as throughout much of OPEC's history, these quotas were a hollow fiction. Everyone knew, even before Purnomo's August admission, that most members were exceeding their pre-set limits. That meant that any sure-to-be-trumpeted increase in the formal quota would simply legalize what was already being pumped, without adding a single drop to actual production.

What was really happening? In theory, the cartel's official target price was still in the range of $22 to $28 a barrel. Below $22, OPEC would cut its production quota enough to raise the price. Above $28, it allegedly was committed to pumping more oil to soften the market and bring the price down. But even though the target was never officially changed, the price averaged $30 a barrel between 2000 and 2004. Who could doubt that member nations relished every added nickel they raked in as the market soared toward $50?

As the price charged ahead, even the Saudis seemed to abandon their well-rehearsed worrywart act about pushing the price too high, which could trigger a recession and encourage the West to look for alternate energy sources. Al-Naimi told reporters at an OPEC meeting in December 2004 that the price band was still in place, quickly adding, however, that investors, producers, and consumers all seemed to agree that $30 was a fair price. Then, with the market price over $42, al-Naimi proposed to cut the cartel's production quota by 1 million barrels a day. As if any further proof of OPEC's rapacity were needed, that move alone provided it.

A few weeks later, al-Naimi finally dropped all pretense. Speaking to a Reuters reporter at the World Economic Forum in Davos, Switzerland, in January 2005, he said, "My view is the world is not suffering. . . . The price today doesn't seem to be affecting economic growth negatively." Translation: full speed ahead toward a higher target and baseline price, the upwardly mobile market-price starting point from which OPEC calculates its price band. Saudi Arabia, OPEC's most powerful member and once the self-appointed voice of reason against hotheaded price hawks like Iran and Venezuela, was itself championing a target price closer to $40 a barrel.

Just where the new price band would eventually settle remained unclear following OPEC's late-January meeting in Vienna. Iran reportedly had wanted $30 to $40, while Nigeria proposed $45 to $55, and Libya's representative suggested $60 a barrel. The only issue not in dispute was the dramatic change in the Saudi position. Whatever it had become, it was no longer the voice of reason.

Amid all the confusion, concealment, OPEC-induced panic, and self-serving Saudi double-talk, a number of questions begged answers: How often do the OPEC producers deliver on their promises? What had become of the Saudis' new capacity of 12 million barrels (maybe even 15 million), revealed at the height of the hysteria in the summer of 2004?

No one seemed to know. Talk turned once again to cutting production quotas and raising the OPEC price band. There was apparently no need to offer soothing words. Higher oil prices (the NYMEX crude price hit $57.79 in April 2005) had apparently been cravenly accepted by consumers and governments. OPEC still had us over its barrel. Now all it had to do was sit back and collect the money.

A LITTLE HELP FROM OUR FRIENDS

But we can't blame OPEC alone for fleecing the world economy and taking an intolerable toll on our future. The oil-security shell game would have collapsed long ago were it not for the collusion practiced by the oil industry and major governments, most notably the United States.

The time has long since passed when OPEC nations were at war with the oil industry, trying to break the monopoly of the infamous Seven Sisters, the major oil companies whose treaties with desert sheiks cemented their dominance in the oil fields.

The companies discovered years ago that the high prices OPEC craved were good for them, too, fattening profit margins all along the pipeline, from the oil fields through the refineries to the gasoline pump. That's why, when crude oil prices rise, there tends to be only token protest from the industry.

The industry also prefers price "stability," even at high levels, to sharp fluctuations that could change the basic calculus of energy investment. After the first great "oil shock" in 1973, when the Arab nations embargoed oil bound for the West, the industrialized nations set up the International Energy Agency to encourage the search for new oil outside of OPEC and explore alternate energy sources. But as soon as serious investments were made in more expensive production from fields like the North Sea and Alaska's North Slope, the IEA began to fear that a return to cheap OPEC oil might make these efforts worthless, whereupon it joined the rest of the industry in becoming a cheerleader for high prices and promoting the illusion of a fragile supply.

In support of that cause, the industry gives remarkably little scrutiny to OPEC's fuzzy production numbers. When all is said and done, the supposedly independent analysts and consultants, who typically parrot OPEC's party line in the media, are mostly on the payroll, directly and indirectly, of the oil industry or those who benefit from high oil prices. So it isn't surprising that they accept, with straight faces, whatever fictions they are fed by the people who give them their consulting assignments and award them contracts.

Even the most obvious discrepancies seldom get questioned. It was a rare acknowledgement of reality when Kyle Cooper, an analyst at Citigroup Global Markets, remarked on the evident mismatch of supply and demand in the oil market in the fall of 2004. "We now are 8.3 million barrels above last year in terms of gasoline [inventories]," said Cooper. "Yet we are 50 percent higher in terms of price. I'd like someone to explain that to me."

The clear explanation was that the price had been pushed to irrational levels by cultivated panic. But, of course, no one thought to offer the truth.

On the face of things, OPEC's unlikeliest ally might seem to be the United States government. Why should Washington collude in a highway robbery that costs the American people literally billions of dollars a year? Part of the answer is the excuse that the government, like the industry, favors stability in the energy markets. It seems reasonable to question whether stability is worth the increasingly high prices American consumers must pay.

Be that as it may, we can be forgiven for suspecting that a larger part of the reason for our collusion with what can only be called an economic adversary has to do with political alliances. President George W. Bush, an oilman and the son of an oilman, has lifelong ties to the industry. In the 2000 election, which first put him in the White House, individuals and political action committees from the oil industry ponied up some $35 million in contributions, the lion's share to Bush's Republican colleagues. Over the six years from 1998 to 2004, the Center for Public Integrity reports, the oil and gas industry has showered more than $440 million on political parties and politicians, and on lobbyists whose job it is to influence those very same politicians. If you believe this has nothing to do with government energy policy, please clap for the tooth fairy; she needs your help.

Again, let's go to the bottom line: Throughout the price gyrations and near-panic in the oil market in 2004, George W. Bush refused to follow the example of two former presidents, Bill Clinton and his own father, in releasing oil from the Strategic Petroleum Reserve to damp down soaring prices. When consumer advocates urged tapping the reserve, the administration, citing genuine national security concerns after 9/11, said such an action would be inappropriate except in a major disruption of supply. There was a case to be made, however, for using the reserve to prevent high prices from damaging the nation's economic security. Instead, President Bush chose to increase the SPR from 600 million barrels right up to its newly expanded capacity of 700 million barrels, thus compounding the problem. With demand high and supplies tight, every new claim on the available stocks of oil sent prices still higher.

Apart from the impact even the release of small amounts of oil from the SPR could have had on market psychology, the president also passed up the opportunity to send an unmistakable message to OPEC: Had he suspended fresh deposits when the price rose past $35 a barrel, he would have made clear the limits of our price tolerance.

Deutsche Bank energy analyst Adam Sieminski, quoted in *The Christian Science Monitor* on June 3, 2004, spoke for many of us when he asked: "Why are we buying oil at $40 a barrel when most people think it's going back to $30 a barrel?" Of course, by failing to change the market mind-set or signal our displeasure with OPEC, $30 a barrel became nothing more than a fond memory.

What the president did was to give OPEC both a kiss and a conspiratorial wink: First, the show of affection said, in effect, we don't care how much your oil costs just as long as you let us keep buying it from you; and, second, we can rationalize paying these prices so long as we all pretend this is really the free-market price. In other words, President Bush gave OPEC every incentive to keep inflating the price.

So all through the summer and fall of 2004, our own government was adding to the demand by buying oil on the market, at prices up to $50 a barrel, to pump into salt domes in the Gulf of Mexico. Had it not been so insanely costly, this unfathomable policy might have been the stuff of comedy.

If any doubt remains that our president is solidly in OPEC's corner, consider what has happened in Iraq. After toppling Saddam Hussein and taking over his government, the United States could easily and sensibly have ended Iraq's membership in OPEC. Doing so would have removed the nation's vast reserves of crude oil from the cartel's arsenal of weapons arrayed against the West and the world economy, thereby loosening the rope around our neck.

No such luck. The Bush administration named Philip J. Carroll, a former Shell Oil executive, to head up a modest "advisory committee" to the Iraqi oil ministry. Carroll insisted that he was there only to make suggestions and claimed to have no veto power. Pointing out that Iraq had been a founding member of OPEC, Carroll said Washington had no business trying to influence that relationship.

Carroll's successor, Rob McKee, another old hand in the oil business, had no such qualms. A former ConocoPhillips executive and still-chairman of Enventure, a Halliburton drilling-supply subsidiary, McKee set to work building a strong national oil company that can go along to get along in the OPEC cartel. The state-owned assets would be operated by international oil companies, whose profit motives mesh so perfectly with the exorbitant prices forced on oil consumers by OPEC.

The April 2005 edition of *Harper's* describes how McKee turned to a select handful of "Big Oil" consultants and executives to draft a 323-page plan for Iraq's oil industry, "even if he had to act over the objections of the Iraqi Governing Council." In short order, Iraq was back at the OPEC table, gleefully helping to tighten the noose around our neck.

Just how gleefully became evident in January 2005, when Dhiaa Al-Bakka, the head of Iraq's State Oil Marketing Organization (SOMO), said Iraq would slash exports from its southern region by 10 percent. The cutback was scheduled to last five months, until the end of June. SOMO blamed insurgent attacks and bad weather for the cutbacks, but it seemed more likely the Iraqi agency was bowing to OPEC demands to cut oil production in order to tighten the market and drive slightly weakening prices higher again.

Were this just another typical move by a typically short-sighted and self-serving OPEC member, we might shrug it off. But the fact that it came from Iraq, where more than 1,500 Americans have lost their lives and thousands more have been gravely wounded, points out the utterly perverse nature of the oil situation we have helped to create. While we are spending billions of American taxpayer dollars to rebuild the Middle Eastern nation, it has joined forces with OPEC.

It is also a sad reflection on the state of our government and its allegiances that nothing has been heard from Washington about this betrayal.

MEDIA MAYHEM

In the end, no matter who promotes it, the real reason for OPEC's success is the fiction of oil insecurity. But that doesn't discount the role played by the world's news media in cementing the myth. Far from it. With rare exceptions, the media have swallowed the myth whole and broadcast it with gusto.

In the summer of 2004, for example, when the market price stood well above $40, the *New York Times* ran a lengthy dispatch empathizing with OPEC as the cartel, in the newspaper's view, tried in vain to bring enough oil out of the ground to force the price back below $28 a barrel, then the high end of OPEC's ceiling. It was the OPEC party line and conventional wisdom taken at face value.

Beating the drum yet again, the paper followed up early in 2005 with another sympathetic piece that concluded: "Many of the issues that have vexed the oil industry in 2004 are expected to recur. Cheap oil increasingly looks like a thing of the past. . . . While demand has steadily increased each year, the industry's exploration efforts have not kept pace in new discoveries. . . . There is no cushion left in the system to weather a potential blow."

In yet a third piece, when NYMEX prices were edging toward $60 a barrel in mid-March, and just after OPEC had offered up its traditional 500,000-barrel "quota" increase, the *Times* opined that, "for OPEC, the situation is paradoxical since the group is uncomfortable with today's high prices. . . . But there is not much OPEC can do. Its 11 members are pumping close to 29 million barrels a day and do not have much more production capacity left to tap."

Nor was the *Times* alone in its fanciful assessments. Many publications hewed to the cartel's line. In January 2005, for instance, the *Wall Street Journal* duly reported OPEC drivel clearly designed to prepare the world for still higher prices. A *Journal* story asserted, "China's rising demand would increase dependence on the group in 2005. However, [OPEC] added that it would be able to meet global demand."

Sticking to script, OPEC had bad news ready to counter the good. The ultimately reassuring report from headquarters was followed by Venezuela oil minister Rafael Ramirez's warning that the cartel would waste no time in tightening the spigot if need be. And just in case a reader had dropped in from Mars and didn't know that oil supply levels were precarious, the *Journal* reporter ended her dispatch with the obligatory pipeline bombing in Iraq, a strike threat in Nigeria, and, incredibly, news that fog had closed the Houston ship channel. Would rain in Spain be cause for worry next?

Occasionally, a reporter got the story at least partly right, as in this dispatch from the *Journal* noting that, "to some extent," the oil market was "confusion by design."

But the media weren't altogether to blame. Journalists depend on their sources, and without reliable, audited, official statistics, they have no better idea of production capacity and security than anyone else. What is more, the people they usually talk to in the industry tend either to believe the myth themselves or to be part of the conspiracy. Journalists normally consult a source's detractors to assure credibility, but, in this case, even the opponents have fallen prey to the fallacy. Environmentalists and consumer advocates are among the firmest believers in the insecurity of the world's oil supply.

Ultimately, what members of the media seek are riveting stories, and the threat of imminent supply disruption will always trump a tale of business as usual. Why break your pick getting at the truth when the conventional wisdom is so much more accessible and interesting?

For the rest of us, though, the price of living in the shadow of fiction and deceit is intolerably high. Every glittery bauble and stretch SUV in Saudi Arabia represents wants and needs unfilled for those of us who spend good money for a cheap, plentiful commodity whose price has been artificially inflated. What we need is to admit the obvious, apply a dose of calm, rational thinking, and begin treating oil as a commodity like any other. At that magic moment, OPEC's power will evaporate.

3

OIL POOR

Nigeria is big, and it is diverse. Stretching across an area of West Africa that dwarfs California twice over, its 137 million inhabitants represent more than 250 ethnic groups and speak scores of languages. They reside in climates ranging from equatorial in the south to tropical in the mid-section and arid in the north. They live and work in a land that contains a wealth of renewable and non-renewable resources; rubber, tin, columbite, iron ore, coal, lime-stone, lead, zinc, and natural gas are all abundant. Yet, despite its many natural blessings, one resource alone rules Nigeria's economy: oil.

Nigeria is the world's sixth-biggest oil producer and a major member of OPEC. It is also the second most corrupt country in the world, according to Transparency International, an anti-corruption watchdog based in Berlin. Financially, politically, and morally, oil is strangling Nigeria. How can a gift of nature cause such destruction?

As night follows day, so oil persistently fuels corruption in the poorly governed states where it is now most likely to be found. Initially, oil is hailed as a panacea for poverty. It is no panacea. Quite the opposite. In oil-boom states from Chad to Angola to Nigeria, sudden wealth typically erodes initiative, weakens institutions, invites crooks, and entrenches despots. Oil is the Pied Piper of Third World hopes. A poor country that discovers petroleum under its barren land is like a lottery winner who squanders his windfall and crashes six months later. Nothing is more disorienting than the illusion that you have struck it rich for life.

Oil ultimately turns into a toxic substance, a curse to those nations "blessed" to sit atop it. A country sitting on vast oil reserves has no incentive to put its human talents to work creating anything new, much less doing mundane chores like cleaning the streets or picking up the garbage. For those dreary tasks, one imports labor. All the rulers of an oil-rich country need do is rent out the premises to foreign drillers and then cash their colossal checks for as long as internal combustion engines shall ferry the human race.

The plague decimating Nigeria is the result of an overabundance of oil, but the condition goes by the more general name, "resource curse." It affects resource-abundant nations outside the OPEC circle, of course, but the devastation becomes even more horrific when the power and influence of the wholly corrupt oil cartel is injected into the mix.

The combination of a weak domestic government and outside manipulation by an influential and self-serving force like OPEC prolongs and intensifies the suffering of a country's less fortunate citizens. OPEC is all about sustaining OPEC. That means maintaining the injurious status quo at whatever cost, a status quo that allows the cartel to continue robbing the world economy and keep its gang of thieves firmly in control in each of its member nations.

Consider the effect the resource curse has on a country's leaders. There is no need to tax anyone, no need to protect property rights, no need to worry about accountability or pay even the slightest attention to the ordinary citizenry (the only exceptions being the usual few hotheads plotting revolution).

For their part, the untaxed find little reason to complain. They need not do any work if they live in one of the earthly paradises staffed by poor Filipinos or Pakistanis brought in as virtual indentured servants. Those few citizens who do grumble, perhaps irked by the elite's self-indulgence, have no real way to make the government answer for its failings.

In the end, all the oil remains firmly in the hands of a few unchecked rulers, who, aided by OPEC, inevitably abuse their power. It seems unavoidable, a basic paradigm of human existence. When a country runs on a single resource, or suddenly discovers one, and this treasure is controlled by a select few, the winners spend huge amounts of time and money eliminating rebellious losers and making sure that nothing like a free press, dissident political party, or independent judiciary gets in the way. Should it be deemed necessary to hold an election, if just for appearance's sake, the incumbents in an oil state are sure to win, since they control not only patronage and the police, but also who gets to vote (relatives, party hacks, state employees) and who doesn't (critics, ethnic outcasts, women).

A neglected and ill-functioning economy, massive corruption, and human pain inevitably follow when oil is in abundance and the policies of OPEC hold sway. This chapter surveys the devastation wrought by too much oil and the money it attracts, using Nigeria, Venezuela, and Saudi Arabia (OPEC members all) as sad examples. But every OPEC nation displays the symptoms of the same disease.

Indeed, Josef Joffe, the publisher of *Die Zeit* and a research fellow at the Hoover Institution, has described Saudi Arabia as a "pious kleptocracy." And if not all its OPEC brethren exhibit the same degree of piety, they are all well and truly kleptocracies. Dishonesty, bribery, and immorality of every sort are, as the pages ahead reveal, the oozing sores of a society awash in oil wealth.

POISONED BY OIL

Countries that should be rich by virtue of their oil wealth are, in fact, poor. A well-known 1995 study by economists Jeffrey Sachs and Andrew Warner, both Harvard professors at the time, discovered that some of the biggest economic breakdowns in recent memory came in countries where oil and other natural resources are plentiful. Of ninety-seven developing countries studied, Sachs and Warner found that the bigger a natural resource's role in a country's economy, the lower the country's rate of economic growth. At its simplest, the explanation boils down to too much of an ostensibly good thing distracting a nation from nurturing the other parts and pieces needed to support a productive society and economy.

To understand the curse of oil, it helps to look at the evolution of modern development theory as it pertains to economic and political advancement in non-industrialized nations. In the 1970s, the experts, taking their cues from the astounding success of Europe's Marshall Plan, sought to help poor countries by financing their physical infrastructures (dams, roads, power plants). Such hardware, it was thought, would work quickly to shore up fledgling governments in newly independent nations. Then, in the 1980s, with little in the way of progress against poverty to show for the many billions of dollars spent, the global policy wonks switched to a model known as the Washington Consensus. Here, the idea was to promote generous economic incentives to attract foreign private investment, the benefits of which would, in turn, seep down to the masses.

When neither approach proved to be the lifeline that could save sub-Saharan Africa from inexorable decline, nor explain why Asian countries, notably China, followed a very different model and blossomed, development theory took yet another turn. Now the experts have discovered the importance of all the intangible assets that sustain markets and save them from damaging swings: the traditions of trust, reliable contracts, property rights, honest courts, social loyalties, and so on, all the things noticeably lacking, whether by coincidence or design, in the OPEC nations.

It is the longtime presence of such checks and balances, it turns out, that allows a democratic country to take sudden oil wealth in stride, as the U.S. did in the late nineteenth and early twentieth centuries. It is their absence in less-developed countries that can turn an oil windfall into a cyclone that sweeps away every incentive for healthy growth and development, leaving only tyrants, crooks, and paupers. In the OPEC nations, we see the consequences of such corruption writ large.

History suggests that human and social assets are better indicators of national success than natural resources. In the 1500s and 1600s, "poor" little England and Holland outdid mighty Spain, despite all the gold and silver its conquistadors had stolen from New World indigenes. In the early 1900s, Japan, rich in culture, poor in resources, readily defeated Russia, an autocracy with huge natural resources but a tottering political system. In our time, tiny Singapore, with no oil but blessed by an educated and skilled population, has greatly overshadowed oil-rich Nigeria and Venezuela, both of which are wallowing in political and economic chaos.

According to a 2003 study financed by financier-philanthropist George Soros, growth in resource-poor countries began to rapidly outrun growth in resourch-rich countries starting in the 1970s. By no coincidence, 1970 marked the upsurge in world oil discoveries that have since bedeviled their beneficiaries.

Just why oil wealth seems to corrupt and impoverish nations is a question with multiple answers. The boom-and-bust cycle of natural resources is one explanation. Global prices for oil, copper, natural gas, and the like traditionally fluctuate according to which way the global economic winds are blowing. Problems arise when the governments of resource-rich nations spend their windfalls and more, only to find themselves strapped for cash and forced to make drastic cutbacks when prices retreat. Even if official corruption is not draining off funds from health, housing, and education measures designed to lift the masses, the unreliability of resource income makes lasting gains difficult, if not impossible, to achieve.

Economists also cite "Dutch disease" when explaining the resource curse. Named for the malign effects of natural-gas discoveries in the Netherlands in the 1960s, it broadly refers to the destructive consequences of rapid increases in a country's income. This theory holds that a sudden boom in oil, or any other resource from gold to coffee, causes a jump in foreign revenues that inflates a country's currency and crowds out other economically valuable activities. In a country awash in natural resource money, everything begins to cost more, including labor. Starting up a factory, say, to make shoes for Nike or Reebok, becomes economically unviable. High labor costs would make the shoes produced too pricey to compete in a global market.

Rising prices also make it harder for domestic producers to sell their goods; they simply can't hold their own against a flood of cheaper imports in the home market. And with capital and labor mostly siphoned away into the booming resource sector, existing manufacturing and domestic farming begin to shrivel. This decreases technical skills, management know-how, and on-the-job training. Growth fades in just about every area except bankruptcies and jobless workers.

Entrepreneurial drive itself withers because no other wealth-creating mechanism seems as easy and attractive to tap as the prevailing natural-resource industry. So instead of spending time trying to invent new products or come up with other novel ideas to generate new wealth, people are focused on trying to get their hands on some of the existing resource lucre. The most common way is by getting a job in the industry or, as in Saudi Arabia where few citizens work in the private sector, by procuring a government sinecure that is indirectly supported by oil money.

To understand the debilitating effects of such a mind-set, one need only think of the immense wealth created by railroads, automobiles, and computers, none of which was there before someone did the hard work of invention.

When a single resource rules, economists become particularly worried that the loss of opportunities to "learn by doing" will stifle the development of people's skills, thus inhibiting long-term growth potential. If a country's manufacturers can't even get into the competitive race, the experts argue, how can they ever gain the experience needed to stay and win?

Economists put great store in manufacturing because it develops the finance, production, marketing, and distribution skills needed for success in many other areas of global business. An economy based solely on raw-material export, on the other hand, gets back little knowledge from abroad and is not exposed to the ongoing technological and theoretical innovations that propel the modern world of business to ever-greater accomplishment.

Not to be overlooked in the search for answers to oil's corrupting influence is the inherent power of abundant natural resources to stymie a country's desire and ability to construct strong, workable political institutions. Typically, natural resource wealth is controlled by an elite group that selfishly opposes democratic reform, or by state-run monopolies that foster bureaucratic incompetence and invite official corruption because of the huge sums of money flowing from the booming resource. Having no reason to tax its citizenry and no incentive to safeguard property rights in order to generate new sources of wealth, governments can rule without restraint. When there is no one to answer to, muscular and democratic political institutions cannot take root.

Nowhere is the toxic fallout of a natural resources boom more apparent than in the OPEC nations, all of which began to rake in enormous sums in the 1970s. In the decade following the organization's decision to ignite an explosion in oil prices, the price of a barrel of oil tripled to $30. While consumers suffered, the OPEC nations spent recklessly on government boondoggles, which are detailed in the chapters ahead. As political power became concentrated in the hands of a few, political problems, civil wars, worsening poverty, and corruption became the order of the day.

One of the founders of OPEC, Venezuela's Juan Pablo Perez Alfonso, who famously labeled oil "the devil's excrement," sensed early on that oil wealth would be fraught with danger. Nigeria, though certainly not the only country drowning in a cesspool of oil, so completely reflects the sad and sometimes appalling effects of the curse as to make it a prime case in point of Perez Alfonso's prophetic wisdom.

NIGERIA SICKENED BY A DIET OF OIL

In its first thirty-five years as a petro-power, from 1965 to 2000, Nigeria took in roughly $350 billion of oil revenues. Yet, during that same time, the number of poverty-stricken Nigerians living on less than a dollar a day soared from a dispiriting 36 percent to an alarming 70 percent.

Long ruled by generals who failed to diversify the economy, Nigeria saw its domestic industry collapse; capacity utilization rates plunged to 30 percent from 75 percent. The agriculture sector crumbled as well, transforming a former food exporter into an importer. The environment was degraded by oil pollution. As non-oil business plunged, so did the average Nigerian's purchasing power; per-capita gross national product stood at only $320 per year in 2003, putting Nigeria in the bottom tier of World Bank rankings.

What is more, violence has flourished and crime has run rampant over the decades. Since the late 1960s, disputes over controlling Nigeria's oil have triggered ten coup attempts (six successful), the assassination of two national leaders, three decades of military dictatorship, and a civil war that killed a million people. Carjackings and kidnappings are commonplace today, as are daylight muggings and robberies.

An especially brutal mix of poverty, crime, and acceptance of, or at least indifference to, malefaction among the Nigerian populace allows for a thriving international trade in people—young people, that is, mostly young girls recruited for prostitution in Europe, Saudi Arabia, and neighboring African countries.

Beholden to "sponsors," who charge them thousands of dollars for the privilege of working outside the country (some victims are duped into thinking they will be working in legitimate jobs or going to school), the girls sometimes find their way back home. Not all are welcomed with open arms, however. Parents have been known to berate a daughter for escaping her captors, preferring instead that she keep prostituting herself until she can repay her sponsors and then bring home extra cash that will make her a neighborhood somebody. Nigerian children also fall prey to domestic trafficking, in which impoverished parents readily send their girls and boys into slavery.

Right now, oil so dominates Nigeria that it is almost the sole medium of power and wealth. The country is divided between those in the oil business—whether buying, selling, or stealing—and everyone else. Nigeria professes to be a democracy, but in its elections, corrupt politicians raise campaign funds by hiring armed thugs to snatch and sell crude oil from pipelines. An estimated 7 percent of the country's daily output of 2.5 million barrels disappears this way. The proceeds are used not for television campaign commercials, but for buying weapons and goons to intimidate voters.

Oil provides 90 percent of Nigeria's foreign-currency earnings and two-thirds of the federal government's revenues. This flood of cash evaporates, however, long before it reaches the masses, leaving nothing but toxic fumes. Most of the money lubricates the corrupt practices of the godfathers of Nigeria's 36 state governments and 774 local governments. Those in power blithely raid the public treasury to maintain their iron grip. They consistently squander oil revenues on patronage schemes, buying off political opponents, hiring armed gangs to beat up stubborn rivals, and funding such absurdities as the huge Ajaokuta steel plant. This boondoggle ran up a tab of more than $5 billion over twenty-five years before ever producing a single ton of steel.

A full member of OPEC since 1971, Nigeria is one of the world's oil giants. Yet its inflation rate (now 20 percent) is rising so fast that millions of people can't afford to buy the oil they need for cooking and heating. Many Nigerians have taken to stealing from pipelines, and many lose their lives in fires and explosions as a result.

Already rent by ethnic and religious conflicts, Nigerians have become increasingly enraged at their oil-induced poverty. In May of 2004, hundreds died in sectarian massacres that were exacerbated by oil inequities. Christian mercenaries butchered Muslims, who then slaughtered Christians in return. Alarmingly, many politicians inflame such religious and ethnic grievances to win votes, sparking fears that another Rwanda might be in the making. Such danger-ously irresponsible behavior is perhaps inevitable in a country whose kleptomaniac leaders have thus far pocketed at least $100 billion of its oil revenues.

In what might be seen as a bit of poetic justice, the crony capi-talism major oil companies have so long practiced in league with OPEC and the corrupt leaders of the countries in which they operate is coming back to bite them. Royal Dutch/Shell, for instance, which initiated exploration in Nigeria a half-century ago and today gets about a tenth of its oil production from the West African nation, is being pushed to the brink by the pervasive violence. Despite its admittedly "less than perfect" efforts at community building, the company finds itself battered by the effects of crime, corruption, ethnic feuding, and poverty—all part and parcel of the oil curse it helped to spawn.

President Olusegun Obasanjo, who may or may not be a reformed sinner in a distinctly dishonest society, was once a cheer-leader for the alleged blessings of oil in a poor country. No longer. In a recent public blast at Nigeria's deteriorating condition, which was reported by the *International Herald Tribune*, Obasanjo cried out, "Oil and gas have blinded us. Oil and gas have taken us away from the values we used to know. Oil and gas have brutalized us."

VENEZUELA GAGS ON THE "DEVIL'S EXCREMENT"

When Venezuelan's former oil minister, Juan Pablo Perez Alfonso, predicted that oil would bring ruin, people scoffed. After all, he uttered his famous forecast when petroleum production was filling Venezuela's coffers with unimagined wealth.

But now, in a striking and oft-repeated economic paradox, Venezuela and most of OPEC's other ten members also suffer, to a greater or lesser degree, from the Nigerian syndrome, the oil curse. Fabulously rich in oil and natural gas, their societies have become distorted, ruled by a privileged few at the expense of the ever-poorer many.

In Venezuela, for example, poverty has almost doubled since 1970, with 80 percent of national income going to business owners and only 20 percent to ordinary workers. And in the decade between 1988 and 1998, the number of Venezuelans with twelve years of education who were living below the poverty line jumped from 2.4 percent to a shocking 18.5 percent.

In the Lake Maracaibo area, which boasts one of the world's largest concentrations of oil, a growing contingent of unemployed oil workers tries to cope with rapidly escalating living costs. It is a losing battle. Venezuela, like most of the world's resource-dependent economies, suffers from the Dutch disease.

The South American nation struck oil in the first decade of the 1900s. But it took more than five decades under the rule of two dictators, one military junta, and assorted legally elected presidents before Venezuela evolved into a relatively affluent country. In the early 1960s, Venezuela was a functioning democracy with the highest per-capita income in South America.

Now, Venezuela is a cauldron of anger, corruption, national labor strife, attempted coups, and quasi-civil war, thanks to the inevitable fight over the control of its suddenly exploding oil wealth that began in 1973. The struggle has sapped the country's political and economic institutions, allowing strong-armed factions to take over, and leaving it with a lower per-capita income than it had in 1960.

The current president, Hugo Chavez, is an anti-globalist who insists that he is the champion of the poor. Yet he has nevertheless made clear that he is willing to play politics with the country's oil, no matter how the tug-of-war harms the economy and the country's citizens.

With estimated reserves approaching 1 trillion barrels (including the extra-heavy oil in the Orinoco belt), Venezuela had long been considered a reliable and relatively close source of oil for the United States. Chavez shattered that assumption in 2002 and 2003, when a series of strikes erupted to protest his efforts to control and manipulate the oil sector.

Eventually, 18,000 workers at the state-owned oil company were thrown out of work, and the production, refining, and export of oil came to a standstill for three months. Some 200 million barrels of oil and gasoline did not make their way onto the world market, and neither the Venezuelan economy nor its citizens were allowed to benefit from a potentially huge injection of export earnings.

The price of oil goes up and down, and the economy goes with it. But never before had Venezuela's oil shipments been halted completely, and never before had a Venezuelan leader willingly cut off his country's lifeline simply to impose his political will.

Then there is Chavez's controversial arms buildup. The former army-paratrooper-turned-politician has decided to spend hundreds of millions of Venezuela's petrodollars not on badly needed social programs, but on high-tech military equipment. Plans include the purchase of twenty-four multipurpose combat planes from Brazil, at a cost of $170 million, and 100,000 assault rifles and military helicopters from Russia. Chavez reportedly has also been negotiating a $4 billion purchase of Russian-built MiG fighter planes.

No one disputes that Venezuela has the right to modernize its military, but observers like Miguel Diaz, a senior analyst at the Washington D.C.-based Center for Strategic and International Studies, question the scale and timing of the purchases. Noting that Chavez's political career began when he led two unsuccessful coup attempts in 1992, Diaz worries that the always provocative leader may be "inclined to follow through on his often-repeated threat to arm his supporters for the purpose of intimidating the opposition."

Others fear that he may be planning to arm leftist rebel groups in neighboring Colombia. Given that the number of Russian rifles Chavez is buying exceeds the number of legitimate Venezuelan soldiers, these fears are not unfounded.

But whatever Chavez's real motives, one thing is clear: For all the talk about revolutionary social policies and development that doesn't leave the poor behind, nothing much has changed for the ordinary Venezuelan who is still mired in poverty and unemployment despite the nation's enormous oil wealth.

As for the mood of the people, the cyclical swings that typify an unstable industry like oil have engendered a boom-and-bust mentality. The people have grown used to a government that behaves in schizophrenic fashion, spending wildly when times are good and abruptly pulling back when oil prices sour. The trouble is, many government programs can't be turned off and on at will, so the state is periodically forced to live beyond its means on borrowed money, tax hikes being out of the question. Venezuelans balk at paying any taxes, since the state is thought to be awash in petrodollars. As one former Venezuelan president famously remarked, "In Venezuela, only the stupid pay taxes."

Venezuela offers a broken-record replay of the stories that have spun out across the oil-producing Third World ever since OPEC began to tighten its grip on consumers and squeeze out maximum profits for member states. Venezuelans struggle in a fun-house economy that makes citizens of a richly endowed country dependent on government handouts and imports from abroad. The nation produces little in the way of exportable goods other than oil, and allows its fertile land to lie fallow while foodstuffs are shipped in from foreign fields. Hobbled by a simplistic belief that God put the oil under their feet because he wanted them to be wealthy, many Venezuelans simply expect their government to redistribute the nation's existing riches. It follows that hardly anyone is interested in trying to create new wealth. As the public sector expands, the private sector shrinks. It is a deadly combination.

SAUDI ROYALS THREATENED BY TERRORIST TIES

No country has reaped more riches from oil than Saudi Arabia. In fact, it is fair to say, no other country even comes close. Yet, despite its massive wealth, Saudi Arabia is poor in innovation, poor in initiative, and poor in self-reliance. Increasingly, its citizens are just downright poor, as an exploding population vies for what little is left after the famously extravagant Saudi princes indulge their every whim.

In an oligarchy, the few rule the many. In the Saudi oligarchy, more than 100 male descendants of founding patriarch King Abd al-Aziz hold sway in senior government positions over the other 22 million Saudis. All told, some 7,000 male descendants of the prolific king receive government stipends.

The royals have long held the view that they own Saudi Arabia and its enormous stores of underground wealth. They can do with it as they please. Viewing the Saudi people as mere subjects, the ruling class metes out benefits from the oil riches in the form of royal charity. In the beginning of the great oil boom, average Saudi citizens received education and health-care benefits. Many received government sinecures.

In the 1980s, however, as the population began to expand sharply and oil prices fell back, economic troubles germinated. With nothing but oil supporting its economy, the government eventually slid into deficit and could not keep up with the demand for public-sector jobs and entitlements. Spending by the ruling elite continued unchecked, of course, leaving the Saudi people to suffer the consequences of a bloated bureaucracy, gross fiscal mismanagement, and a dysfunctional, largely noncompetitive, private sector dominated by the royal family and its cronies.

Economic problems are just the beginning. Despite archives of photos showing smiling Saudi Arabian princes being feted by fawning U.S. government and oil industry figures, Saudi Arabia has one of the world's most repressive regimes. Women are second-class citizens. Religious freedom is nonexistent, which the U.S. State Department belatedly recognized in a 2004 report. "Non-Muslim worshippers risk arrest, imprisonment, lashing, deportation, and sometimes torture," the report said, but even devout Muslims are not safe if they choose to practice something other than the state-sponsored Wahhabi brand of Islam.

Wahhabism is an extremist Sunni sect that urges the faithful to commit acts of violence against non-believers. The ruling Saudi princes have spent tens of billions of dollars exporting their intolerant, violent religion around the world. But now, as its benefactors have belatedly discovered, even they are not safe from Wahhabi fanatics.

Started by Ibn Abdul Wahhab in the mid-1700s, Wahhabism dictates strict observance of the prophet Mohammad's teachings based on a literal reading of the Koran. Among its precepts are the punctual performance of public prayer; modest dress, especially for women; and prohibitions against music, dancing, and the consumption of alcohol or tobacco. Many of Ibn Abdul Wahhab's teachings are similar to those of other fundamentalist sects, but where they differ is in the leader's insistence on conformity under pain of death. One of the sect's most infamous adherents is Osama bin Laden.

For their part, the Saudis consider it a sacred duty to propagate the faith because Islam began in their country. Islam's two holiest sites, Mecca and Medina, are located in Saudi Arabia. Thus, the ruling family has helped create a tangled web of government-sponsored and private charities that aim to make puritanical Wahhabism the prevailing doctrine in the Islamic world. Thousands of mosques, Islamic centers, schools, and colleges have been financed with Saudi oil money. Reams of Wahhabist propaganda have been distributed. Much of the missionary work has been directed at the United States and Europe, where Islam is not the predominant religion and where nonbelievers are considered fair game by devoutly militant Wahhabists. Deadly terrorist attacks in France, Spain, the Netherlands, and the United States have all been attributed to Muslim fundamentalists.

The activities at Germany's King Fahd Academy have drawn special notice. At this white-marble structure built with $20 million donated directly by its namesake Saudi king, Muslim students hear calls for violence against non-believers and are versed in the glories of martyrdom as servants of Allah. Originally founded in 1995 on the pretext of educating the children of Saudi diplomats posted to Germany, the school wasted little time in reaching beyond its mandate to bring the children of German-born Muslims under the influence of its dangerous theology. Indeed, the school defiantly ignored German law to recruit local children.

Parents of the students at King Fahd Academy, many of whom have themselves been accused of links to terrorist organizations, defend their academic choice as nothing more than an effort to educate their children according to their cultural beliefs, in the manner normal to schools in Saudi Arabia. No doubt, they are being absolutely truthful, which is what makes the situation so frightening.

There are schools like King Fahd Academy in numerous countries, where malleable young minds are being inculcated with beliefs that call for the destruction of the infidels. This includes anyone who doesn't practice Wahhabism, including even other Muslims. School curriculums in institutions run by members of this extremist sect are almost wholly devoted to religious teaching, at the expense of math and science and the humanities, thus ensuring that hatred of the West and all it stands for will be dominant for generations to come.

The Saudis claim that the problem is not with the religion but with those who wrongly interpret it. They insist they have tried to stop the diversion of missionary funds to terrorist causes.

Ironically, since the first Gulf War, the royals themselves have begun to feel threatened by the zealots they have financed. Extremists have accused Saudi rulers of desecrating holy ground by bringing in the infidel Americans to defend them against Saddam Hussein. Internal discontent over government policies has been rising, and Islamic militants have killed scores of people in bomb-ings and shootouts.

Saudi Arabia's ruling family has apparently decided that idle, and increasingly poverty-stricken, hands are the devil's workshop. It is now directing more of its recently escalating oil windfall into new job-training programs and other initiatives designed to put people to work. The efforts center around ejecting foreign workers from jobs that Saudis could do, including positions in the building and food trades and computer-related work.

Yet, even as they grapple with massive unemployment, poverty, subpar housing, and insufficient social services, many citizens seem unwilling or unable to take advantage of the available opportunities. Long conditioned to having others do the work for them, or perhaps trained for more skilled jobs that do not exist in the Saudi economy, they are reluctant to take on what they consider to be demeaning labor. Meanwhile, nothing has been done to reform the private sector, where people of privilege operate through monopo-lies that largely exclude the average Saudi citizen and, because they are protected by Islamic law, pay no taxes on their earnings.

A few insiders are concerned enough about the growing discon-tent to push for economic and social reforms. *Okaz*, a Saudi news-paper, printed an article in 2002 that called for drawing "the sword of conscience in the face of the lazy and the crooks." But it is hard to imagine that the ruling princes, who believe the country's treasure is theirs to squander, will easily give up their control.

FUNNY OIL MONEY TURNS UP AT RIGGS BANK

A select few may take command of oil wealth, destroy all rivals, and sell petroleum for as much as the market will bear, but these toll keepers do not act alone. Their corrupt behavior is aided and abetted by toll payers, notably the multinational oil companies that notoriously compete for extraction rights by buying off the toll keepers. At least thirty-four such companies paid to recover the Angolan government's oil in recent years, but all we know is that they paid. How much, to whom, and for what are secrets to which even the companies' auditors, much less their stockholders, are not privy.

Such is the way in a murky world that laughs at the notion of transparency and is under no legal pressure to divulge the massive bribes that presumably win drilling rights in corrupt oil-producing countries like Nigeria. The estimated $100 billion skimmed by Nigerian officials to date was not manna rained down from heaven. Uncovering shady deals is tough, but not impossible.

If George Soros has his way, it may get easier. As part of his campaign to address the rampant corruption associated with natural resource extraction, Soros and his Open Society Institute are promoting an international "Publish What You Pay" initiative that would force publicly listed oil and mining companies to divulge details of their payments to governments.

"Sadly, U.S. oil companies have thus far resisted," the institute's Thomas Palley noted in an article posted on the organization's Web site. "[They claim] that corruption is a government problem. The reality is that corruption is a systemic problem."

Unless and until the established system is changed, perhaps the most promising route is to trace the toll keepers' stash, which is presumably deposited in safe hideaways outside their own not-so-safe countries. Which brings us to the Riggs National Bank of Washington D.C., a capital institution that counts Abraham Lincoln and Jefferson Davis among its past depositors.

In more recent times, Riggs has drawn attention because of the large shadow cast by its controlling stockholder and sometime chief executive officer, Joe L. Allbritton. A charming Mississippi octogenarian and patron of the arts, Allbritton's five-foot stature belies his towering presence on the Washington social scene, as well as his ownership of a sizable personal fortune estimated at $500 million.

Riggs itself is pint-sized as banks go, but its less-than-dazzling balance sheet did not dampen Allbritton's enthusiasm for its global cachet: The bank specializes in serving Washington's foreign embassies and U.S. consulates worldwide, a mission that fit like a glove on the hand of Allbrittton's social ambitions. For some thirty years now, Joe Allbritton has helped keep Riggs close to Washington's diplomatic and political elite, the black-tie-and-champagne crowd he favors.

Its longtime social prestige notwithstanding, however, Riggs has lately proved an embarrassment to anyone closely associated with it. Banking regulators, congressional investigators, and federal agents have all been searching its records for evidence of terrorist financing, money laundering, payment of bribes to oil executives, and collusion on the part of a bank examiner-turned-bank employee.

Allbritton himself is not considered culpable, except perhaps for having paid more attention to the bank's social glitter than to its depositors' transactions. Indeed, Riggs's relaxed attitude about banking rules and red tape was a major drawing card for wealthy clients.

Not everyone appreciated the bank's tastefully discreet manners, as it turned out. In July 2004, federal regulators, disturbed at the bank's laissez-faire policies, publicly rebuked Riggs for neglecting to follow rules aimed at stopping money laundering. Federal officials handed Riggs a record $25 million fine, while continuing to investigate its role in alleged money laundering by the former Chilean dictator General Augusto Pinochet and by officials of Equatorial Guinea. These revelations were particularly embarrassing for Riggs, coming as Pinochet, who ruled Chile from 1973 to 1990, awaited trial on charges involving human rights abuses.

It turns out Riggs's involvement with Pinochet goes back to 1979, far longer than originally suspected, when the bank began helping him move his money through accounts hidden from regulatory scrutiny.

In January 2005, Riggs admitted criminal negligence in the money-laundering schemes and agreed to pay an additional $16 million fine. Federal prosecutors called it the largest criminal penalty ever imposed on a bank of Riggs's size. Continuing investigations against individuals were expected to produce indictments.

Another major Riggs client used to be Prince Bandar bin Sultan, the highly connected Saudi ambassador to the United States. Before September 11, 2001, Riggs bankers merely beamed when the prince and other Saudi diplomats routinely withdrew a few million dollars on their way to weekend parties in London.

After the terrorist attacks, things changed. The FBI's suspicions that Saudi money might have bankrolled the hijackers led to scrutiny of Riggs accounts controlled by Bandar and his wife, Princess Haifa.

No smoking gun has been found as yet, but Bandar's and his wife's subsequent banking activities raised eyebrows. After a series of very large and very quick deposits and withdrawals in the prince's personal accounts, Riggs officials finally bestirred themselves to ask Bandar what he and his wife were up to. He refused to answer. The Saudis no longer bank at Riggs, a decision each party says it arrived at first.

As the global monetary mess continued to unravel, it was probably only a matter of time before blue-chip oil companies, a corrupt

African oil kingdom, and an enormous sum of suspicious money would enter the picture.

In 2004, congressional investigators began delving into Riggs accounts held by the notorious dictator of Equatorial Guinea, Brigadier General Teodoro Obiang Nguema Mbasogo. A Senate panel was particularly curious to know why Simon P. Kareri, the Riggs executive who handled the bank's Equatorial Guinea accounts, personally dragged a sixty-pound suitcase stuffed with $3 million of plastic-wrapped $100 bills into a Riggs branch bank for deposit. Kareri refused to answer, invoking the Fifth Amendment.

Until February 2004, Riggs managed $360 million deposited by the poverty-stricken West African country most notable for oil strikes and human rights abuses. The tangled skein of shady deals, sloppy oversight, and money laundering started to take shape a decade earlier, the Senate committee said, when Riggs began opening and managing more than sixty accounts for the country, its officials, and assorted family members.

Operating like a Swiss bank on the Potomac, asking few if any questions, Riggs, the panel found, "turned a blind eye to evidence suggesting the bank was handling the proceeds of foreign corruption."

At their peak, Equatorial Guinea's accounts at Riggs, largely stocked with royalties from oil production, are said to have totaled as much as $700 million, which would have made it the bank's largest customer.

Equatorial Guinea has been the wholly owned property of Brigadier General Obiang since 1979. He began his association with Riggs in 1995. Taking personal banking to new heights (or, rather, lows), Riggs opened a slew of accounts for Obiang and his relatives, set up shell corporations for them, and lent a helping hand when the general and his wife desired to stash $13 million of cash in their Riggs accounts. In addition, some $35 million of government oil money made its way, via Riggs-sanctioned wire transfers, into "private" company accounts, at least one of which Obiang is thought to have controlled.

The United States had been on the outs with Obiang since the mid-1990s, but diplomatic relations were resumed in 2003 by a Bush administration hoping to secure oil supplies outside the Middle East. Even before the resumption of formal ties, however, American oil companies like ExxonMobil, Amerada Hess, and Marathon Oil had poured some $5 billion into the oil-rich nation just since oil was discovered there a decade ago. According to the *Los Angeles Times*, among other things, payments went to buy protection from a company owned by Obiang's brother; to lease buildings from other relatives, including a fourteen-year-old landlord; and to pay college tuition costs for scores of students from elite families.

ExxonMobil, a major player in the region, was the point man in some of Obiang's dubious dealings, supplying cash as part of a profit-sharing arrangement with the dictator's regime in exchange for drilling rights. Naturally, ExxonMobil can't discuss the details of the deal; it is confidential. All the company will say is that the contract requires it to pay Equatorial Guinea income taxes, oil royalties, and something called "legal obligations."

The deal provided much of the money in the regime's Riggs accounts, which were officially described as government treasury funds requiring multiple signatories, but which, in practice, were apparently controlled by Obiang.

The fact that a government would keep its treasury funds in a private bank abroad, or that a ruler would have exclusive control over a national account, should have raised red flags at Riggs.

It didn't, at least not until September 2003, when federal investigators ratcheted up their investigation. In reviewing its accounts, Riggs executives discovered that a company called Otong, controlled by General Obiang, had opened a Riggs account through which the company passed millions of dollars from suspect sources.

Riggs examiners questioned Kareri, the executive who oversaw all the bank's Equatorial Guinea accounts. Kareri said Otong's big money came only from foreign accounts elsewhere that Obiang closed, transferring the funds to Riggs for safekeeping. That explanation fell flat with Riggs officials, who suggested the money was derived from bribes or political graft involving American oil company executives.

In January 2004, Kareri's bosses at Riggs caught him in a peculiar impropriety. He allegedly asked Obiang's son in Washington to give him money to buy a car. The son reportedly handed over a signed but undated check for $40,000, leaving the payee line blank. Kareri is said to have changed the value of the check to $140,000, filled in the payee line with the name of a friend, and then managed to have the funds sent to his wife. Riggs subsequently fired Kareri.

Meantime, Riggs officials uncovered more unusual transactions in which Equatorial Guinea oil money was switched to offshore accounts for unknown reasons. Asked to explain, Obiang came to Washington to meet with Riggs officials, but then took offense at their questions and walked out. Riggs finally closed all of its Equatorial Guinea accounts, blaming the whole mess on the departed Kareri.

The investigations continue, but so does the corruption. The U.S. State Department acknowledges that Equatorial Guinea's oil wealth is not being used for the public good. Obiang still rules the country, although plots against him abound. Under Obiang's leadership, law enforcement in Equatorial Guinea is said to include chopping off ears, smearing naked bodies with substances attractive to stinging ants, and murdering by beating.

Perhaps the worst thing about oil wealth is that it seems to corrupt the minds and hearts of all complicit parties—government officials, oil companies, banks, and even entire countries and cultures. A black sticky substance pumped out of the ground provides a self-justifying excuse for valuing easy money over creativity and vital work, over true enterprise, over democracy, and even over life itself. And as the 2004 scandal over the Oil-for-Food program showed, it has corrupted everything from the United Nations on down. (The ignominious Oil-for-Food program is discussed in detail later in this book.)

ACCURSED BY OPEC, BUT TOO BLIND TO SEE

It is hard not to conclude that oil and its corruptions have had a profoundly enervating affect on too many countries, particularly Muslim ones. Instead of freeing young minds, male and female, to thrive in the modern world, these countries often seem to cultivate stagnation and inspire resentment against progress. Arabic cultures that once pioneered key mathematical and scientific concepts now seldom invent or patent anything. They don't even bother to trade with one another.

The West may yearn to end its dependence on OPEC oil, but, in many ways, the OPEC nations are even more destructively dependent. The terrible irony is that countries seemingly blessed with reservoirs of underground wealth can become so completely addicted to a resource-based economy as to end up impoverishing their cultures and their people.

Unlike China, Japan, or Korea, which grow in spite of their need to import oil, the true wealth of OPEC petro-economies spirals downward in spite of their richly abundant resources. Their oil dependence deadens minds, kills initiative, and numbs hopes. It leaves millions of people furious at—though well-funded by—the West, yet unable to look inward at their own strengths and weaknesses, and unable to summon their talents to meet the West on a level playing field. For them, oil dependence is an abiding curse, the ultimate corruption, and OPEC is the master evildoer, the terrible genius that is choking the life out of its members.

Part 2

How OPEC Put Us over a Barrel and Where We Go from Here

4

OPEC'S BLUDGEON

History is littered with the ironies of revenge. The narcissistic tyrant becomes easy prey for the courtier's stab in the back. The avenging victim of injustice becomes a brute himself. The early communists derided capitalists as so greedy that they would willingly profit from their own hanging. As Vladimir Lenin sneered, "We will find a capitalist who will sell us the rope." (Though it didn't exactly turn out that way.)

All these forms of vengeance and more are at play in the bizarre story of OPEC, a Leninist script in which the oil cartel drapes a hangman's noose around the global economy's neck and the world not only cheers but actually collaborates in the economic equivalent of assisted suicide. If OPEC now has the strength and means to choke the life out of our economy, it is only because we supplied the rope, along with instructions on how to use it.

It will take several chapters to explain just how the world's nations managed to become hostage to the market manipulations of eleven contentious oil producers, most of them Middle Eastern. This chapter tracks the cartel from its obscure origins in the vast Arabian desert through the first "oil shock" in 1973. It is a convoluted tale of twists and reverses, advances and declines, culminating in the emergence of a new global force with power over billions of lives.

Starting as a grab bag of Third World countries, sheikhdoms, and emirates, OPEC came together only when its members joined in smoldering resentment at the diktats of the Seven Sisters, as the biggest oil companies collectively had come to be known.

OPEC gradually remade itself from a pawn of the corporations into their partner, and, finally, their unchallenged master. By the end of this chapter, the reader will see how over the last four decades, oil has been transformed by OPEC into a bludgeon it wields to become a major player on the world's political and economic stage.

The long saga has its roots in the nineteenth century, when the British Raj (Great Britain's rule of the Indian subcontinent) dominated the Middle East to secure its routes to India. In those days, the barren tribal kingdoms and sheikhdoms were of little importance, their rulers surviving only on what they could skim off their subjects' meager income from fishing, pearl diving, camel herding, and regional trading.

Before World War I, it was the British resident in the Persian Gulf, an imperial official comparable to a Roman proconsul, who largely dictated the terms of the first oil "concessions" giving the major companies exclusive rights to find and pump oil. As was so often the case when oil was involved, fear played a part in Britain's dealings. The British government decided to revamp its naval fleet to run on oil rather than coal. Top government officials (most notably First Lord of the Admiralty Winston Churchill) wanted to make sure the Royal Navy would not be caught short in its burgeoning naval arms race with Germany.

With the resident's backing, the world's major oil companies held a distinct advantage over their host governments in the Middle East. The concessions were designed to benefit mainly British and British-based multinational corporations, whose officials wrote contracts on their own terms and set up an interlocking network of national and regional operating companies in which the local governments had no share at all.

The Iraq Petroleum Company (IPC), for example, was a holding and operating business jointly owned by the Anglo-Iranian Oil Company (later British Petroleum and now BP), Compagnie Francaise de Petrole (now Total), Royal Dutch/Shell, Standard Oil of New Jersey (now Exxon), and Socony-Vacuum (later Mobil, now part of Exxon). The other members of the group that would come to be called the Seven Sisters were Gulf, Standard Oil of California (now Chevron), and Texaco (now part of Chevron). That actually adds up to eight; the list of "seven" depended on who was doing the listing.

Partnerships and percentages in the operating companies varied from country to country, but the major players had shares in concessions all over the Middle East. They were often joined by another partner, Calouste Gulbenkian, the legendary oil field operator known as "Mr. Five Percent" for his ability to cut himself in on such deals. Gulbenkian, the son of an Armenian oilman, got his start when he took the lead in forming the Iraq Petroleum syndicate to drill for oil when Iraq was still part of the Ottoman Empire. The syndicate tapped gushers and Gulbenkian clung like a limpet to his partners, shrewdly insisting that any exploration anywhere in the former Ottoman Empire must be conducted through IPC itself.

But for all its wealth of oil reserves, the Middle East remained a backwater until after World War II. Then, with the Cold War emerging from the still-smoldering ashes of that great struggle, U.S. strategists feared the stricken nations of Europe would fall into the Soviet camp.

Using the Marshall Plan, Washington decided to accelerate Europe's economic recovery by using a modern, oil-based model to rejuvenate the continent's industrial base. Obtaining the needed oil meant building up the oil industry in the Middle East, the only region of the world with then-known reserves cheap and plentiful enough to fuel Europe's modernization.

Washington pushed the major international oil companies to move aggressively into the region and, with U.S. and British diplomatic backing, concessions were expanded and rapidly developed in the postwar years.

This strategic decision paved the way for the golden age of oil. From 1948 to 1972, world oil production would mushroom by 500 percent, and no one would benefit more than the Seven Sisters.

The key to the Sisters' lucrative arrangement was the so-called "posted price" of oil, an arbitrary per-barrel fee named for the sheet that was literally posted at a producing field. The posted price was set unilaterally by the big producers. They used it to market the oil output to their own refineries and parent companies, as well as to determine what they owed in taxes and royalties to the governments or rulers of the areas from which they pumped the crude.

Naturally, the Sisters kept the posted price low. This maximized their profits from both ends. By paying a cheap price for the raw materials acquired from the host governments, and then padding the prices of the refined products they produced downstream and sold to consumers, the Sisters created huge margins that fattened their bottom lines. Later, when a free oil market did develop, the true market price took into account differences in quality and accessibility. It often would vary widely from the one posted by the Sisters.

For each barrel pumped from its pool of reserves, a host country received royalties and taxes totaling 50 percent of the posted price, minus half the cost of finding and pumping the petroleum. Middle East oil was exceptionally cheap to locate and produce. Industry wags liked to say that if you just poked a straw into the Saudi desert, oil would come out. At the time, it cost just 20 cents a barrel to produce Mideast oil, versus 80 cents a barrel in Venezuela and 90 cents in Texas. So at the longstanding posted price of $2.04 a barrel, a host government received 92 cents and the oil company took $1.12.

At first, it seemed like a winning proposition for all parties. The majors profited handsomely while a torrent of revenues transformed sandy sheikhdoms into centers of opulence. Architects designed striking monuments and built modern cities, while water from new desalination plants irrigated gardens, flowed from fountains, and created oases of green golf courses in the desert. Middle Eastern potentates and their vast retinues emptied barrels of oil money in the shops of London, Paris, and New York. Back at the palace, meanwhile, armies of migrant laborers—Egyptians, Indians, Pakistanis, and Palestinians—tackled the menial work that suddenly wealthy natives could now afford to avoid.

From the beginning, though, the arrangement chafed. It was the major companies alone that determined the posted price of the oil, and the host countries had a stake only in the upstream drilling and pumping part of the crude oil industry. The Seven Sisters, meanwhile, had their own separate downstream refining and marketing networks that let them gear production to ultimate demand in the countries where the products were sold. By keeping the posted price of drilling and extraction operations low, they made sure that most of the profits emerged later in the refining and marketing end. If the host governments wanted additional revenue (and they did) the only way to get it was to pump more oil.

Even that decision, however, was not one the individual producing nations had the power to make. The Seven Sisters had the right to allocate production to favor one government over another. The interlaced corporate structure of the operating companies meant that the Sisters could concentrate production in whatever country they chose, effectively playing one government off the next and dictating the flow of income to the hosts.

Restive voices began to grumble that oil barons in faraway places were draining the wealth and controlling the destinies of proud oil-producing nations. As the boom of the 1950s spread, two men in particular became vocal critics of the Seven Sisters: Abdullah Tariki and Juan Pablo Perez Alfonso, the oil ministers of Saudi Arabia and Venezuela, respectively. Their discontent would ultimately strike a chord among the rulers of the other oil-rich countries, and lead to the creation of OPEC.

THE SISTERS BEGIN TO LOSE THEIR GRIP

The deal the majors had promulgated was too good to last. Independent oil companies looking for new sources of crude oil began playing by their own rules, offering better terms for concessions than the Sisters gave. A limited free market sprang up for buying and selling oil beyond the Sisters' control. Most important, a giant new player stepped out from behind the Iron Curtain to enter the game.

Russia had been a pioneer and early leader in the oil industry.

The world's first oil well was drilled in 1846 at Bibi-Aybat near Baku, fifteen years before drilling began in Pennsylvania. The Bolshevik Revolution in 1917 and the subsequent confiscation and nationalization of privately owned oil fields brought the industry to its knees. The bloody birth pangs of the Soviet Union and the struggle for power within the Communist Party kept Russian oil output below pre-revolutionary levels for more than a decade. In 1930, Josef Stalin, having largely consolidated power, moved to reverse the infrastructure damage and decay.

But it was World War II that really kicked Soviet oil production into high gear. After the war ended, its enormous investment began to pay off in major discoveries in the Volga-Urals region. By the late 1950s, Soviet oil exports were beginning to become a major factor in international markets, particularly in Europe. Moscow was aggressively undercutting prevailing prices to woo new customers, stoking fears among the Seven Sisters that they would be plunged into economic turmoil. The Central Intelligence Agency was prompted to warn that the Soviets were "a force to be reckoned with in the international petroleum field."

In 1960, the Soviet Union would displace Venezuela as the second-largest oil producer in the world, behind only the United States. Its production that year equaled 60 percent of all the oil pumped in the Middle East.

With a world economy much less thirsty for oil than it is today, it did not take long before there was far more petroleum sloshing around the marketplace than buyers ready to consume. Discounting was so fierce that, at one point, a barrel of oil could be bought at a Soviet port on the Black Sea for half the price posted by the Seven Sisters. Further exacerbating the situation, the United States stepped in to protect its own domestic producers from a flood of imported oil in 1959, when Dwight Eisenhower slapped limitations on imports by presidential proclamation.

The Mandatory Oil Import Program's quotas sharply limited access to the world's biggest market. As Robert L. Bradley reminds us in his book *The Mirage of Oil Protection*, Eisenhower expressed misgivings about the program, citing the "tendencies of special interests in the United States to press almost irresistibly for special programs" that conflicted with the idea of increased world trade. The quotas nevertheless remained in place until 1973, when Richard Nixon scrapped them in favor of yet another form of protectionism, higher tariffs on oil imports.

Amid fierce and growing competition, the Seven Sisters' dominance began to wither. Between 1950 and 1960, they lost one quarter of their share of world refining capacity and one sixth of their share of world production volume to rivals.

To keep their markets, the Sisters had no choice but to match the competition's discounts. Under the agreements with their host governments, however, the Sisters still had to pay royalties and taxes based on the predetermined posted price, not oil's real market price. Given the depth of the free-market discounts, the Sisters found themselves surrendering 60 percent or even 70 percent of their actual revenues to the host nations, instead of the 50 percent less half the production costs called for in their concession agreements. Accustomed to taking a heftier share of the revenues, the Sisters were not prepared to tolerate their demotion for long.

THE SISTERS MAKE A BAD BET

Given the grumbling in producing nations about Western exploitation, the Sisters knew it would be politically risky to lower the posted price. Nevertheless, early in 1959, British Petroleum took the gamble. It slashed 18 cents, or nearly 9 percent, off its long-standing posted price of $2.04 a barrel. The other major oil companies followed suit.

Ultimately, the move backfired. In hindsight, it's clear that the Sisters were providing rope for the hangman: Their ploy to maintain their revenues and profits at the expense of the host governments sowed the seeds of anger and resentment that eventually sprouted into OPEC.

Predictably, the host governments reacted with outrage. Abdullah Tariki and Juan Pablo Perez Alfonso, the Saudi and Venezuelan oil ministers, began actively looking for ways to assert their independence and burnish national pride. They knew each other only by reputation, but after the Sisters reduced the posted price, the two were united in their determination to play a larger, more rebellious role in the unfolding oil drama.

Even before the price cut, an Arab oil congress had been scheduled to open in Cairo in April of 1959. Here, Perez Alfonso and Tariki would finally meet face to face. Perez Alfonso was attending merely as an observer, but he was armed with texts that outlined Venezuela's oil legislation, translated into Arabic for easy comparison with the concession contracts of the Middle East.

His go-between with Tariki was Wanda Jablonski, then a reporter for *Petroleum Week*, who used her charm, style, independence, and encyclopedic knowledge of what was happening and who mattered to make herself into an influential player in the decidedly male-denominated oil industry. Tough and sardonic, she wisecracked and needled her sources to get scoops on every important story in the postwar industry. Her reports made for indispensable reading, particularly after she founded her own newsletter,

Petroleum Intelligence Weekly, in 1961. Hands down, Jablonski was the most important journalist in the industry.

Neither custom nor convention stopped her. In the 1950s, for instance, she was one of the first journalists of either sex to tramp through oil fields in the Middle East, Latin America, and Africa. On a trip to Saudi Arabia to interview King Saud, she found herself lodged in the ruler's harem. As related by Daniel Yergin in *The Prize*, Jablonski wrote a friend that it had been "a perfectly gay 'hen party.' . . . Forget what you've seen in the movies, or read in the *Arabian Nights*. None of that fancy, filmy stuff. Just plain, ordinary, warm home and family atmosphere—just like our own, though admittedly on a considerably larger family scale!"

It was also on this trip that she met Tariki, an angry young man who voiced his extreme displeasure with California Standard, Jersey Standard, Mobil, and Texaco, who were the American owners of Aramco, the Saudi holding company. Struck by Tariki's determination and dedication to changing concession policies in the Middle East, Jablonski pegged him as someone who would be a key player.

At the conference in Cairo, Jablonski introduced Tariki to Perez Alfonso. The two formed an almost instant bond forged by a shared mission. Young turks from different corners of the globe, they quickly agreed that Cairo presented the perfect opportunity to hold secret talks with a few of their colleagues about what they perceived to be the growing menace of the sisterhood. They invited delegates from Kuwait, Iran, and Iraq to a private boating club on the Nile in Maadi, a southern Cairo suburb near the hot springs resort of Helwan. Held in the off-season, the meeting at the club drew no particular attention.

From the outset, there was little chance the five men could form an official pact. The Iranian delegate advised that he lacked the requisite authority from the Shah to commit his country to any agreement. The Iraqi representative, much like Perez Alfonso, was nothing more than an observer, since Saddam Hussein's new regime was boycotting the conference as a consequence of a feud with Egypt's Gamal Abdel Nasser. Nevertheless, the group reached a gentlemen's agreement that included recommendations to their governments on how to level the playing field in the increasingly cutthroat oil game.

The recommendations that came out of the secret Maadi talks outlined a common front against the Seven Sisters. Suggestions included creating an advisory body that would help to defend the oil price structure with unified action, and a bid by all of the governments to gain a share of the lucrative downstream refining and marketing business. This would be achieved by forming national oil companies, adding domestic refining capacity, and building integrated marketing structures. The group also urged the governments to junk the companies' unilaterally imposed 50-50 split of posted-price revenues and insist on at least a 60 percent share.

Observers for the Seven Sisters also attended the main Cairo meeting, which, on its face, produced little of importance. British Petroleum's Michael Hubbard wired a report back to London assuring his superiors that political issues had taken a back seat, unaware, of course, of the Maadi gathering.

Hubbard also told his chairman that, even though Wanda Jablonski had helped arrange for him to talk with Tariki, nothing substantive was accomplished because the Saudi minister wished only to harangue Hubbard about the inequities of the system. The clear implication was that Tariki was incapable of discussing the economics of the business. Tariki, however, had worked and studied in Texas, and knew full well the inner workings of the industry.

Those acquainted with him said he hated being patronized by what he perceived as arrogant Westerners whose knowledge of the oil business was, at the very least, no greater than his. He no doubt dreamed of the day when he could finally give them their comeuppance.

AN OPEN SPIGOT SINKS OIL PRICES

In the months following the Cairo conference, the recommendations presented by the rebel group gained little traction with the producing countries. The turmoil in the marketplace meanwhile intensified as more oil flowed and market-price discounts deepened. The Sisters became alarmed when Soviet crude began to make significant inroads with their primary customers in Western Europe. In fact, Enrico Mattei, head of Italy's state-owned energy company, was openly buying Russian oil. American statesmen fretted that Soviet Premier Nikita Khrushchev was using oil as an economic weapon in the Cold War. "Khrushchev has threatened to bury us on more than one occasion," said New York Senator Kenneth Keating after the Soviets succeeded in doubling production between 1955 and 1960. "It is now becoming increasingly evident that he would also like to drown us in a sea of oil if we let him get away with it."

The Sisters understood they had to fight harder if they were to survive the discount war. Their posted price was still the basis for splitting revenues with the host governments and was a drain on their declining income. The benefits they had gained by reducing the fixed posted price in 1959 were being eroded by the continuous discounting of the real market, or spot, price. Yet most of the group argued that it would be folly to cut the posted price again. They feared fueling the already considerable and lingering anger of their Middle Eastern hosts over the previous cut. But in New York, Jersey Standard's new chairman, Monroe "Jack" Rathbone, scoffed at such timidity.

Rathbone was supremely self-confident, brusque, and not much interested in other people's opinions. He had proved himself both smart and gutsy when, as a young engineer in Baton Rouge, Louisiana, in the 1930s, he developed the catalytic cracking process. He persuaded the federal government to sink hundreds of millions of dollars into this process to produce better-quality aviation fuel, despite having only tested the process in a small research unit. Fortunately, it worked, and Rathbone was credited with revolution-izing the refining process to make fuel that gave the Allies an edge in World War II.

During his early years in Baton Rouge as general manager of a Jersey Standard refinery, Rathbone had earned his spurs fending off the demagogic attacks of Governor Huey Long. Headstrong and self-assured, he zoomed rapidly to the top of the company hierarchy.

By 1960, his opinion of the oil-producing countries was, to put it bluntly, condescending. Unwilling to waste time consulting with people about whom, at that time, he knew little and cared less, Rathbone was now insisting on another cut in the posted price, with no conception of how it would be received by the host countries.

Howard Page, Jersey Standard's Middle East negotiator, tried to argue with Rathbone. He even brought in Wanda Jablonski to explain the realities of Arab nationalism to the board of directors. Rathbone dismissed this woman, friend to Arab sheiks and Texas wildcatters alike, as too pessimistic. He had just been to the Middle East himself, he said, and had heard nothing that sounded as threatening as Jablonski made out. Mindful of the protocol, and having experienced for herself the extreme courtesy and generosity typically shown to guests, Jablonski shot back that Rathbone had been treated to a display of Middle Eastern manners. But it was clear to her at least that he had no clue what his hosts were really thinking.

Page won the board's backing for making a cut only after first consulting the Middle Eastern governments and working out some kind of compromise to share the pain. Rathbone overruled them. He decreed that Jersey Standard would cut the price his way, with no consulting or dickering. On August 9, 1960, Rathbone made good on his promise: Jersey Standard knocked another 14 cents a barrel, or about 7 percent, off the posted price. With varying degrees of foreboding, the other majors followed Rathbone's lead.

Predictably, Rathbone's unilateral action was met with shock and indignation in the Middle East. The lack of consultation or even advance notice of the price move added further insult on top of the grievous injury the offended governments were already feeling. The Maadi conspirators made hurried plans to meet in Baghdad to assess the situation.

Well aware of the blunder by the Seven Sisters and brandishing the telegraphed invitation in his Caracas office, Perez Alfonso could barely contain his glee. He gloated to his aides that the alliance he so wanted was now inevitable. Though Alfonso would later grow disenchanted with oil, in 1960 he brimmed with enthusiasm for the possibilities he thought it afforded Venezuela.

The major international oil companies, meanwhile, were about to meet a countervailing force that, given their five decades of swagger, they hardly could have contemplated.

Scarcely a month after Rathbone's blustering move, representatives of the five countries that collectively produced 80 percent of

the world's oil—Iraq, Iran, Kuwait, Saudi Arabia, and Venezuela—
gathered in Baghdad.

The four-day conference in September 1960 gave birth to the
Organization of the Petroleum Exporting Countries. Though it was
destined to be one of most important developments of the twentieth century, at the time it drew scant notice. OPEC's formation,
for instance, received only oblique mention in the back pages of the
New York Times.

The group's mission, simply, was to defend the price of oil and
win a bigger share of petroleum revenues. OPEC would insist that
the major companies consult with its members on pricing matters,
and it would work for a system of regulated production that allowed
each member country to adjust supply to demand and that distributed revenues fairly. Most importantly, the members pledged themselves to solidarity should the companies try to divide them.

A SOB FROM THE SISTERS

The formation of OPEC amounted to open rebellion, and the
Seven Sisters tried to damp it down with groveling contrition. But
their public show of repentance at a later Arab oil conference was
nothing more than crocodile tears. The reality, according to Iran's
Fuad Rouhani, OPEC's first secretary general, was that the companies still did not take the organization seriously. At first, Rouhani
said, they behaved as if OPEC were a desert mirage, a figment of
the producers' overheated imaginations.

Whatever his previous misgivings about high-handed treatment
of the host countries, Jersey Standard's Howard Page later admitted
that his company gave little credence to the oil producers' cartel.
From Rathbone down, Jersey Standard's managers thought it would

never work because the notoriously quarrelsome members of the group would never be able to maintain a united front. Nor were the oil companies the only ones giving short shrift to the new alliance. Two months after OPEC was founded, the CIA wrote a report on Middle East oil that barely mentioned the organization.

In fact, for the next decade, OPEC seemed like anything but a major factor in the industry. True, its membership more than doubled, but the members frequently quarreled and feuded. Some dropped out. Saudi Arabia and Venezuela, both under new leadership, allied themselves with the United States, relegating firebrands Tariki and Alfonso to the sidelines.

Whenever they could, which was often, the Sisters ducked negotiations with OPEC. They preferred to deal directly with the countries that had awarded them concessions. Amid all of this, there was no change in marketplace realities: Both demand and supply continued to mushroom, and intense competition was the order of the decade.

Although events at the time served mainly to strengthen the hand of the major oil companies, OPEC could still count some real accomplishments and practical gains in its first years. The cartel, in fact, benefited the companies and the producing countries alike. All sides had a stake in price "stability" and "orderly markets." These code words, when translated into day-to-day reality, meant a drain on the pockets of the world's consumers to the benefit of the producers. The real difference after OPEC came onto the scene was that the oil-rich countries began to demand a bigger role in decision making, along with a bigger share of the revenue pie.

Their demands began to be met during the 1970s, thanks largely to Libyan Colonel Muammar Qaddafi. In September 1970, he forced the independent Occidental Petroleum Company to increase the posted price and lower the production of Libyan crude. Cutbacks in the output of the high-quality and much-in-demand Libyan oil tightened supplies across the market, opening the way for OPEC to make changes as well.

In 1970, following Qaddafi's showdown with Occidental, OPEC negotiated a technical change in the tax-and-royalty formula used by the oil companies, increasing its share from just under 50 percent of the posted price to a minimum of 55 percent. At the cartel's conference in Caracas in December, members decided to use their power to push for a rise in the posted price itself. After several rounds of talks with the major companies, OPEC won an increase of about 35 cents a barrel, to $2.18. The camel's nose was under the tent.

Ominously for the world's consumers, the new agreement promised an additional increase every year, supplemented by an adjustment for inflation. A later amendment would call for yet another price adjustment to compensate for any devaluation of the U.S. dollar, the currency in which world oil prices are determined. The tables were finally turning. The posted price would now be determined by OPEC, not the Seven Sisters, and now the price of oil would be pegged to both the rising costs of other goods and services and to the vagaries of the U.S. dollar.

In retrospect, it is easy to see that OPEC's first decade was a watershed. To be sure, the burgeoning free market for oil substantially increased competition and eroded the profits of both the cartel's member nations and the major oil companies. Nevertheless, OPEC had established itself as a unified power in the industry, a power that could negotiate and win on its own terms.

Just as important, the world oil market was changing, and to the cartel's advantage. The industrial world was no longer awash in oil.

Demand had continued to increase at a rapid pace and was now outstripping new production capacity in almost every country except Saudi Arabia. Every OPEC producer was being allowed to pump without restriction to meet the growing demand. But with oil prices still low, there was no economic incentive for U.S. producers to explore for additional reserves that, inevitably, would cost more to bring out of the ground than it cost to import oil from the OPEC members.

This was only one example of shortsighted U.S. policy that helped turn OPEC from a minor player into an 800-pound gorilla. By failing to devise a consistent U.S. oil policy, the U.S. government became an unintentional co-conspirator in making OPEC a dominant force in the world economy. Mesmerized by low, low prices, we didn't notice that our own self-reliance was being stripped away.

One American policy decision after another worked to strengthen OPEC, thus adding staves to the barrel that OPEC would one day put us over. U.S. policymakers had earlier encouraged the multinational companies to move into the Middle East. Now these companies were being forced to scale back their profit ambitions. The import quotas instituted by President Eisenhower in 1959 had been meant to protect domestic producers. By the 1970s, instead, they locked the Sisters out of the U.S. market and put more downward pressure on world prices. To show support for the Shah of Iran, considered a key ally, Washington refused to publicly denounce his aggressive bid to lower production and double the posted price to $11.65 a barrel, thereby further undermining the multinationals. And Washington's Middle East policy, especially after the Six-Day War of 1967, routinely antagonized the Arab producing countries.

All that was needed to bring the OPEC monster fully to life was a crisis of potentially major proportions. The world's first oil shock, triggered by the Yom Kippur War of 1973, would provide the defining moment.

OPEC'S WHIP HAND

The war that began on October 6, 1973, offered dramatic proof of OPEC's nascent power. Spurred on by the Soviet Union, Egypt's President Anwar al-Sadat and Syria's President Hafez al-Assad took Israel almost completely by surprise with their sudden assault on Yom Kippur, the holiest day in the Jewish faith. Israeli forces reeled. Having miscalculated how much equipment would be needed to fend off an enemy heavily armed with Soviet weaponry, Israel began rapidly running out of supplies. In a secret letter to U.S. President Richard M. Nixon, Israeli Prime Minister Golda Meir warned that her country was in danger of being overwhelmed. When Syrian forces began to fall back, the Soviets undertook a massive re-supply of goods and equipment for both Syria and Egypt, and urged other Arab nations to join the attack. In the then-prevailing parameters of Cold War tit for tat, Nixon and Secretary of State Henry Kissinger arranged for a similarly massive re-supply of armaments to be airlifted to Israel.

As it happened, just as the war broke out, OPEC was again holding talks in Vienna to increase the posted price of oil. Rising world demand for oil had the industry pumping flat-out with almost no capacity to spare, and the soaring spot price had long since eclipsed the OPEC posted price. While OPEC was holding its talks, market prices spiked again on fears that the war in the Middle East would cause disruption throughout the region. Just so, it was another shot heard 'round the world when OPEC made known its latest price demand: The group wanted a staggering increase of 100 percent, which would have boosted the posted price well above the spot-market level.

Worse yet, President Nixon received a message from the chairmen of the four U.S. owners of Aramco—Jersey Standard, Texaco, Mobil, and California Standard—warning that any show of American military support for Israel would risk inciting a serious oil shortage. The Arab "oil weapon," long feared and much discussed in American councils of government, was being hauled out into the open. If Nixon failed to heed their warning, the executives predicted, the United States might be shut out of the Middle East and replaced by other interests—Europe, Japan, perhaps even the Soviets.

The realpolitik of the Cold War, however, dictated Nixon's decision to come to Israel's aid in the face of the Soviet-supplied onslaught. The help from the United States enabled Israel's troops to halt the Arab offensive and mount a counterattack, but the cost was high. Arab leaders read the incident as a deliberately dramatic show of American policy in Middle Eastern affairs, not merely a proxy skirmish between two competing superpowers. Once again, they saw an insult piled onto an injury, further stoking their growing fury.

Although the talks in Vienna ultimately broke down, tabling the proposed 100 percent rise in the posted price, officials from the key nations—Saudi Arabia, Iran, Kuwait, Iraq, the United Arab Emirates, and Qatar—reconvened shortly afterward in Kuwait to take action, with or without OPEC. The six nations issued a decree raising the posted price by a whopping 70 percent, to $5.12 a barrel, which matched the latest market price in the panicked world arena. Now OPEC—or its main players, at least—had completed the metamorphosis from subservient minion to reigning master. It was in full charge of the posted price, free at last from policy decisions made by the Seven Sisters. According to *The Guardian*, Ahmed Zaki Yamani, who in 1962 had supplanted Abdullah Tariki as the Saudi oil minister, gloated in Kuwait City: "This is a moment for which I have been waiting a long time. The moment has come. We are masters of our own commodity."

OPEC'S SURPRISE ATTACK

But the war was still ongoing. Whatever its show of market muscle so far, OPEC had yet to use the full measure of its clout in the oil market. Following the price-setting action in Kuwait, the delegates from the six Middle Eastern nations stayed behind to discuss future plans. The repercussion most feared by industry if the U.S. openly backed Israel was for Arab states to nationalize facilities owned by American companies. But now the Arab leaders couldn't agree on what to do. The sticking point was Saudi Arabia's new leader, King Faisal, who wanted to consult with President Nixon before doing anything drastic. Accordingly, Faisal sent Nixon a mildly worded letter, and a delegation from several Arab states paid a visit to Washington.

Cordial discussions left the Americans hopeful. Kissinger explained to the visitors that the U.S. airlift only incidentally concerned Israel and its enemies. He stressed pointedly that it was primarily a Cold War response. Nixon chimed in to offer Kissinger's services in mediating the dispute, assuring the Arabs that they could work with the secretary, soothing any concerns over his Jewish background. In the Rose Garden afterward, the Saudi minister of state was suave and gracious. The Americans heaved a sigh of relief.

The very next day, however, the Arab oil ministers, meeting in Kuwait and led by Saudi Arabia, agreed on a surprise strategic wallop. They wouldn't nationalize the U.S.-owned companies; rather, they would withhold Arab oil from the companies' customers. States the Arabs considered friendly would continue to be supplied. Those viewed as unfriendly would be punished progressively in 5 percent monthly increments—their oil supplies would be cut by 5 percent in October, 5 percent in November, and another 5 percent every month thereafter until the Arabs were satisfied that the miscreants had mended their ways. A secret clause decreed the worst treatment for the United States, even steeper cuts that would lead to a total embargo on shipments from every country signing the decree.

It was a shrewd plan, designed to split the industrial countries and force them to compete with each other for available oil, while encouraging them to make secret deals to placate the Arabs. For all the recurrent talk of an oil weapon, it was nationalization, not an embargo, that had concerned oil executives. The Seven Sisters, like everyone else, were surprised by the news.

The embargo was decreed on October 17. Two days later, Nixon unveiled a $2.2 billion military aid package for Israel. He explained that it was designed to restore military parity and encourage the warring parties to negotiate.

Unable or unwilling to grasp the bigger geopolitical picture, Arab leaders saw the aid package as further evidence of U.S. favoritism toward Israel, and took steps far more drastic than the limited 5 percent monthly cutbacks they had announced. Libya promptly announced an immediate halt in all oil shipments to the United States. Saudi Arabia and the other Arab producers followed suit a short while later. The total embargo on Arab oil shipments, first imposed only on the United States and the Netherlands, was later extended to Portugal, South Africa, and Rhodesia (now Zimbabwe).

OPEC was now firmly holding sway. As the next chapter reveals, however, the embargo was not the only oil shock it would administer to the world. Nor would it be the worst.

5

CRUDE SQUABBLES

With the oil embargo of 1973, OPEC suddenly acquired unexpected power. Once patronized, its exotically costumed leaders were now courted and resented, flattered and despised. Apparently outflanked and outwitted, Western oilmen reacted like colonial rulers aghast to find the natives in charge. To OPEC members, it was hugely satisfying.

But OPEC's new power proved fleeting. Unable to curb their fighting and bickering, the members soon squandered their advantage. They misjudged the economic forces they had loosed on the world and the new competition their success made viable. In short order, a petroleum glut crushed prices, shook the foundations of the cartel, and reshaped the oil-production landscape. OPEC survived, but only because of yet another misguided move by the West. In the name of "stability of oil supply" and to help the U.S. oil industry, Western interests forced an end to the price war. Not for the last time, the rope tossed out in rescue would wind up around our own necks.

The embargo, aimed primarily at the United States, shook the whole world. Even though the oil shock lasted just a few months into 1974, it was still an enormous blow to the industrialized economies. No one had ever expected it, so no one was prepared. Just six years earlier, when Israel's Six-Day War rattled world oil markets, excess U.S. stocks proved to be the critical factor in meeting demand and stabilizing prices. In the intervening years, however, rocketing world demand for oil had forced the United States to move from protecting its domestic market against imports to using every drop of its own production capacity to cover demand. Furthermore, President Nixon had slapped price controls on domestic oil in March 1973 as part of his plan to stem spiraling consumer price inflation in the United States. In the absence of price controls, U.S. exploration and production might well have increased. As it was, 1972 marked the peak in production from the giant oil reservoirs of Texas. For the first time ever, with no more readily available spigots to open, the United States could not compensate for a shortage of oil from abroad by pumping more oil at home, and thus could not soften the embargo's impact on world markets.

Technically, the embargo failed in its stated goal of keeping oil from the United States. Oil being a fungible commodity, non-OPEC suppliers happily stepped into the breach when the Arabs refused to sell to the United States. In addition, "Arab unity" proved to be a contradiction in terms. Some of OPEC's fractious members quickly started surreptitious oil sales, and the embargo sprung leaks.

For example, Iraqi delegates had advocated even tougher economic warfare at the Kuwaiti gathering, then left in a huff after their ideas were rejected. Declaring Iraq unbound by the agreement, Saddam Hussein actually increased production. He explained his defection by assailing the regimes of Saudi Arabia and Kuwait, claiming that they were too close to the United States. Non-Arab Iran, where the Shah was hungry for revenues, also stepped up production to take advantage of the skyrocketing prices.

All told, the defectors managed to soften the embargo's impact by 600,000 barrels a day. Nevertheless, as the fateful year of 1973 drew to a close, the loss of world petroleum supplies totaled 4.4 million barrels a day, about 14 percent of all internationally traded oil at a time when world consumption was rising by 7.5 percent a year. In the thick of the crisis, however, no one could be sure how much oil was lacking; the uncertainty produced panic in the markets. Inevitably, market prices rose to then-historic highs, topping $12 a barrel in 1974, or quadruple the price prevailing in 1972.

FEAR AND PANIC IN THE INDUSTRIALIZED WORLD

Uncertainty and confusion fed the panic. How long would inventories last? Would the Arabs include more nations in their embargo? Would they go ahead with the threatened monthly incremental cutbacks? In the end, it wasn't actual shortages that drove prices into the stratosphere, but fear of them. Buyers became so nervous over the prospect of being caught short of oil that they were willing to pay almost any price—and each day's price increase fed the certainty that tomorrow's quote would be even higher.

In the United States, the retail price of a gallon of gasoline jumped by 40 percent, and there were real shortages. On any given day, a filling station might be forced to close shop after putting up a sign announcing that it had no gas. At stations that still had gas to pump, lines of waiting cars sometimes stretched for a mile or more. Patience dwindled, anxiety thrived, and hoarding worsened. Fearful drivers kept topping off their tanks, lengthening already long lines and burning nearly as much fuel in waiting as what they came to buy. Equitably minded station owners worked out rough rationing systems. Motorists with license plates ending in even numbers, for instance, might be allowed to buy gas on Mondays, Wednesdays, and Fridays; odd numbers could buy on Tuesdays, Thursdays, and Saturdays.

As the crisis ground on, government officials mostly fumed and blustered at OPEC members, issuing vague warnings of dire steps that might have to be taken if the embargo continued. In fact, according to diplomatic documents recently declassified in Britain, the Pentagon drafted a contingency plan for the 82nd Airborne Division to seize the oil fields in Abu Dhabi, Kuwait, and Saudi Arabia. But the plan came to naught, partly because it was exposed beforehand by U.S. media and, equally important, because Secretary Kissinger remained calm. As he would explain two years later, getting rid of the Saudi ruling family and upsetting the political balance in the Middle East would only open the way for potentially more dangerous leadership that might derail U.S. economic objectives.

The psychological impact of the embargo shook the foundations of the developed world. The end of an era of plenty seemed at hand. Economists warned of lost growth, recession, inflation, international monetary crises, and stagnation in the developing world. The Club of Rome doomsayers were hailed as prophets. Their prediction that economic growth would be stymied by a global energy shortage—we were supposed to run short of oil by 1990 and natural gas by 1992—seemed to be right on schedule.

An obscure economist named E.F. Schumacher, author of *Small Is Beautiful: Economics as if People Mattered*, which providentially appeared just in time for the embargo, was virtually beatified in the press. Schumacher's notion that a civilization built on renewable resources (forestry, agriculture) is far superior and more sustainable than one built on non-renewable resources (oil, coal, etc.) gained added credence in the economic and psychological turmoil engendered by the oil embargo and the ensuing fear of life-altering energy shortages.

This turmoil roiled nearly every spot on the planet. The hard-won gains in Western Europe's recovery from World War II seemed imperiled by the fallout from the embargo; when the West German government tried to allocate oil supplies, it was besieged by industries clamoring for higher quotas. Japan's growing confidence as an economic power foundered on the realization that it all depended on a string of tankers continuing to ply the waters from the Persian Gulf to the Sea of Japan. Fearful American housewives hoarded the supplies they had lacked in World War II, starting panicky runs on common household items.

Suddenly, everything seemed up for grabs. People questioned whether the U.S. superpower was weakening, whether the West was in permanent decline, whether Russia might win the Cold War. Fears arose about the stability of the international trade and monetary systems. With OPEC in the driver's seat, new assessments were being made.

Though OPEC was often called a cartel, in truth it did not technically qualify as one. In a cartel, two or more companies in an industry collude to reduce competition and fix prices so as to increase profits. A cartel, by definition, must be able to restrict the supply of a commodity reaching the marketplace, as De Beers, the South African diamond producer, has been able to do in its market through near-monopoly control of the supply of rough stones. Since OPEC never developed a workable mechanism for regulating its production—its own charter forbade it from interfering in the sovereign members' decisions—it could only jawbone its members to push up prices. When the Arab producers had tried to put an embargo on their oil during the 1967 war, they quickly backed down as increased U.S. production pumped enough petroleum into the market to actually lower the spot price on oil for immediate delivery.

This time, though, things were different. Soaring market prices were lining producers' pockets with record revenues even as output was being cut back. Now, everyone could see the merits of curbing production. And none other than the recently converted Mohammad Reza Shah Pahlavi had become OPEC's most fervent advocate for higher prices and lower production, not just for the duration of the embargo, but for all time.

Fiercely determined to turn his country into a modern industrial giant, the Shah constantly searched for ways to fatten his oil revenues so as to provide the investment funds needed to boost Iran's economy. Previously, however, he had scoffed at the notion of curbing OPEC's output in order to raise the posted price of oil, convinced that it would never work. But in an apparent eureka moment, the Shah had had a stunning change of heart and mind.

He couched his argument in a new, pretentious conservation theory. Speaking at an OPEC meeting in late December 1973, the Iranian monarch described oil as "noble fuel" and argued that it should be replaced by other sources of energy whenever possible. Oil, he said, should be saved for more important purposes, such as the manufacture of petrochemicals. And to the Shah's way of thinking, a commodity with such a noble purpose should carry a noble price as well.

At OPEC's year-end meeting in 1973, with the market price for oil still hovering at around $6 a barrel, the Shah pushed to make the posted price $11.65, more than doubling the $5.12 agreed on by the delegates in October. In only three years, the posted price had rocketed from $2.18 a barrel to $11.65, a more than fivefold increase. In the context of the times, it was an extraordinary jump. The Shah came up with that number after conducting an investigation of the cost of alternative fuels. The Saudis led the opposition, arguing that OPEC's actions should be seen as politically motivated, not simply a grab for more money—as if the House of Saud itself were somehow motivated by something other than the vast wealth and lavish lifestyles its underground stores of black gold bestowed.

The disingenuous prattle from the Saudi rulers was perhaps the genesis of the myth that OPEC is concerned about the economic vitality of the consumer countries. That idea, to put it mildly, is rubbish, a consistent fabrication of Saudi/OPEC public relations that has long deluded global leaders and numerous figures in the oil trade. As noted in Chapter 2, though, the scales may at last be falling from some eyes, following the Saudis' January 2005 admission of support for a sharp rise in the stated target price of OPEC oil. Make no mistake: The Saudis and all the other OPEC producers have always been united behind one goal, and that is to sell oil at the highest possible price to the largest possible market. At best, the Saudis' concern for global economies extends only so far as the ability of those nations to keep buying Saudi oil. Like the mafia, the oil producers don't want to put their customers out of business, because they want to continue getting a check every month from those they extort.

The Saudis had also voiced fears that a huge oil price boost might spur a real search for alternative sources of energy that could lessen demand for the vast Saudi reserves, making them less valuable. Ahmed Zaki Yamani, the Saudi oil minister and a lawyer by trade, argued for raising the posted price only to $8 a barrel. Yamani was poised, articulate, and charismatic, but in the end, the Shah's new vision prevailed. Two days before Christmas, Yamani stunned the industrial world by announcing that world oil prices were about to skyrocket. At the beginning of 1974, the price for a barrel of oil would be pegged at $11.65, or more than 300 percent higher than it had been only six months before.

In short order, Richard Nixon named William Simon to be the federal energy czar, he lowered the national speed limit to fifty-five miles per hour to save fuel, and he also ordered up rationing coupons (although they were never used). Nixon instituted "Project Independence," a drive to cut energy demand and increase domestic output in order to free the U.S. of foreign oil dependence. Exemplifying the behavior he wanted from Americans, the president turned down White House thermostats and doused the flood-lights after 10:00 P.M. Patriotic citizens and businesses followed his example, with many eliminating holiday lighting and dialing down winter thermostats to a chilly 68 degrees.

The president also wrote to the Shah, predicting a global economic disaster and asking him to reconsider the price increase. But the Shah was adamant, lecturing the industrialized world about the end of the era of cheap oil. New energy sources must be found, he said, gratuitously adding, according to the *Middle East Economic Survey*, that "those children of well-to-do families who have plenty to eat at every meal, who have their own cars . . . will have to rethink all these privileges . . . and they will have to work harder."

In the next few months, as the United States moved to promote a settlement and new political relationships in the Middle East, the embargo continued. Henry Kissinger twice journeyed to Saudi Arabia for discussions with King Faisal, whom he would later describe as soft-spoken and given to making somewhat inscrutable comments. Nothing came of the talks.

Nixon next courted Egypt's Anwar Sadat. Sadat, a one-time hawk who now thought that both the war and the embargo had served their purpose, favored ending the embargo. Sadat had already signed a cease-fire accord with Israel, but his ally, Hafez al-Assad of Syria, had continued the assault. With Saudi help, the Americans began negotiations with Syria concerning Israel's withdrawal from Syria's Golan Heights, talks that enabled Sadat to tell his Arab allies that Washington was working for a new political reality in the Middle East.

As the months wore on, the embargo came to resemble a sieve rather than a stopper. With so much oil leaking through the porous wall of Arab unity, Faisal finally decided that the embargo had served its purpose, and on March 18, 1974, the Arab producers moved to end it. Syria and Libya dissented.

Kissinger soon worked out a deal on the Golan Heights, and the "peace process" was in train. Richard Nixon paid a triumphant visit to Egypt, Israel, Saudi Arabia, and Syria, and was cheered deliriously by millions in Cairo. For the Egyptians, it seemed the dawning of a new age. Once suffering under the sway of the Soviet Union, they were now basking in the glory of the first-ever visit to their country by an American president and the renewal of diplomatic ties broken off during the 1967 war. Dreams of renewed prosperity filled the air and invigorated the happy crowds. This amazing scene occurred while, at home, Nixon was sinking ever deeper into the Watergate morass.

In terms of OPEC, what mattered most, however, was that the oil weapon had been used to even more devastating effect than its advocates could have predicted. The oil industry itself and the relations between producers and consumers had been reordered, while economic and geopolitical realities were transformed, not just in the Middle East, but throughout the industrialized nations as well. The realization that oil could be used as a means of coercion now hung over the world like the sword of Damocles.

OPEC: MASTER OF THE UNIVERSE

OPEC's age of influence had finally dawned. The eleven nations that formed the cartel were now the putative masters of the universe. Diplomats hung on the results of the group's periodic meetings; international journalists shouted questions as the members emerged from their limousines to glide across hotel lobbies, and their cryptic answers made headlines around the world.

The new order brought forth by OPEC was one in which its members actually controlled the destiny of other nations; their actions could dictate prosperity or recession. Never before in history, Kissinger wrote, had such a weak group of nations been able to force such dramatic change in the way the rest of the world lived. What is more, by establishing sovereignty over the commodity that helped fuel world commerce, the producing nations had completely turned the tables on the Seven Sisters. As in the timeless tale, *A Thousand and One Arabian Nights*, the king had become a beggar and the beggar a king. Symbolically, the Vienna office tower once known as the Texaco Building, which had become OPEC's head-quarters in 1965 when it moved from Geneva, Switzerland, now bore the cartel's name in big bold letters.

If there was foreboding in the industrialized world, there was euphoria in the Middle East. The Arab nations had avenged the insults and defeats imposed on them over centuries. Riches would bring power and influence. Nomads who not long before had been eating locusts in the desert would now bask in the blessings of wealth and technology. And with astonishing speed, the Arab nations sprouted the emblems of luxury—grand cars, towering buildings, great hospitals, proud universities, and lush villas in the desert oases.

Ironically, OPEC's triumphs, like those of the Sisters before it, had planted seeds that would take root and sprout into a thorny problem. Although no one had yet noticed, what the Saudis feared when they argued against instituting a large price increase was coming to pass. Prodded by the oil shock, the West was exploring furiously for new oil deposits, building energy-efficient homes, seeking alternate fuels, taxing oil products at higher rates (especially in Europe), and forcing automakers to design more fuel-efficient cars. Each of these measures would limit the growth of the market for OPEC's petroleum.

The world's appetite for oil turned out to be price-sensitive after all. In Europe, where oil consumption had been growing at 8 percent annually, oil use actually fell, from 15.2 million barrels daily in 1972 to 13.5 million barrels two years later. Although consumption later stabilized at a higher plateau of about 14 million barrels daily, the decoupling of petroleum from economic growth had begun. Oil would continue to be a factor, of course, but no longer would its overall consumption automatically increase in lockstep with GDP growth. Smarter, more efficient energy usage was, in effect, increasing supply. It would take another decade to prove out, but around the world, less and less oil was needed to support any given level of growth.

The four years from 1974 to 1978 were a time of complex cross-currents, both in the world at large and within OPEC. The Shah, ambitious to turn Iran into an industrial superpower virtually overnight, before its projected oil reserves ran out, craved ever-rising oil prices. He quarreled continuously with the Saudis, whose vast reserves dictated a strategy of long, slow exploitation that would keep the world hooked on oil.

There was still no real mechanism for regulating output. Most of the member nations were pumping at or near their presumed capacity, with only Saudi Arabia functioning as the swing producer and adjusting production to world demand. The Saudis relished being able to make this grand gesture, but they also resented the curb on their revenues.

Throughout the region, petrodollars were proving a mixed blessing. The new riches disrupted traditional values and customs, tilted the social balance, and sparked friction between the new rich and those left wanting. While some gladly embraced glamorous foreign novelties, others bewailed the loss of custom, tradition, and social order. Americanization, it seemed, bred a resentful anti-Americanism.

In Algeria, the mounting discontent turned into a twenty-year civil war between the nation's rulers and insurgents who called themselves the Party of God but wanted mainly the bounty of oil. Saudi Arabia's royal family tried to buy off its restive critics or pretend they didn't exist—a pretense that would grow more and more hollow and dangerous as the years passed. In Iraq, Saddam Hussein brawled his way to the top and used oil money to foster state terrorism, wreaking havoc both in the region and around the world.

But it was in Iran that the backlash had its most dramatic impact. Although the Shah worked tirelessly to turn his country into his envisioned "Great Civilization," there was growing resentment against him and the small group of wealthy elite who benefited from his extravagance. Meanwhile, the political corruption and social upheaval spawned by petrodollars were feeding a conservative religious movement that sought a return to the principles of fundamentalist Islam. A scowling, burning-eyed prophet, the Ayatollah Ruhollah Khomeini, led the movement from his exile in Iraq and France. As more and more of the new middle class created by the oil boom discovered its Muslim roots and flocked to Khomeini's banner, the Shah's position grew more precarious.

Reporting from Saudi Arabia, the U.S. ambassador informed his superiors that top Saudi officials considered the Shah to be a megalomaniac and mentally unstable. Later, a *New York Times* report by Seymour Hersh would quote a CIA analyst as saying much the same thing, but the warnings went unheeded in Washington. As Hersh described it, the assessments ran "contrary to U.S. policy." Yamani is also said to have predicted, quite accurately as it turned out, that a brutal, anti-American government would most likely follow if the Shah were deposed.

For their part, the Western industrial powers, led by the United States, didn't necessarily want low oil prices so much as stable, predictable ones unthreatened by crises and shock (a policy that would serve as cover for OPEC's future excesses). In fact, as noted in Chapter 2, the International Energy Agency (IEA), formed by the industrialized nations in 1974 to try to prevent future oil shocks, feared that a major drop in oil prices would jeopardize investment in high-cost alternative energy ventures and such promising oil operations as the Alaskan North Slope and the North Sea reservoirs. To safeguard these interests, the IEA actually discussed setting a floor price for oil. Washington even flirted with a long-term deal to trade U.S. wheat for Soviet oil. But talks broke down over Henry Kissinger's insistence on a lowball price for the oil and a high level of publicity for the deal as a way to humiliate OPEC.

Within OPEC, the United States lobbied consistently in support of Saudi Arabia and against raising the posted price. To pacify the Shah, Washington sold Iran huge quantities of sophisticated weapons. By the mid-1970s, fully half of all U.S. arms sales were to Iran. The strategy seemed to work, at least when it came to the oil price: OPEC made two relatively small increases that raised the price to $12.70 a barrel in 1977.

Below the surface calm, however, new currents were developing. OPEC, which produced 65 percent of the free world's oil in 1973, still accounted for 62 percent of it five years later. But global exploration and development triggered by the oil shock were beginning to pay dividends. Major new rivers of oil were about to flow from the North Slope, the North Sea, and Mexico's Reforma oil field. Within a few years, non-OPEC nations would out-produce OPEC.

Nevertheless, even as pumping from the three newest sources rose to nearly 7 million barrels a day, the overwhelming consensus in the industry was that another crisis was inevitable. Given what was assumed to be a still-critical need for oil to fuel economic growth, the experts predicted that demand in the second half of the 1980s would again outstrip supply, with the resulting energy gap triggering another oil shock.

As it happened, the experts were wrong. The decoupling of energy use from economic productivity, a trend that had begun in the mid-1970s, picked up speed in the 1980s for a variety of reasons. Not least of these was the developed world's transition from manufacturing to service and information industries, which tend to run on less energy. Then, too, global governments stepped in with taxes and regulations designed to encourage fuel efficiency and energy conservation. In the United States, for example, the Corporate Average Fuel Economy (CAFE) law boosted new-car fuel economy by more than 40 percent between 1978 and 1987. Accordingly, U.S. oil use dropped by 17 percent at the same time its GDP was rising 27 percent.

Like many other people, however, Sheikh Yamani, the Saudi oil minister, believed the experts. He began arguing that to cushion the shock, OPEC should switch from trying to foster price stability to instituting a series of small, regular price increases. Even some in Washington were inclined to go along, reasoning that small, predictable increases were better than sudden, massive shocks.

Ironically, Yamani and his allies were again at odds with the Shah, who had had yet another epiphany and now argued *against* higher prices. Money, he had decided, was not the cure for what ailed Iran, but its cause. Taking a page from Perez Alfonso's book, the Shah concluded that Iran's oil boom and the flood of petrodollars were creating chaos, waste, inflation, corruption, and political and social tensions that actually threatened his regime. He was right, but his latest insight came too late to save him. In December 1978, Iran erupted in mass demonstrations that finally forced the Shah to flee to the West on January 16, 1979. A few weeks later, Khomeini returned triumphant to establish an Islamic theocracy in Iran.

THE SECOND SHOCK—AND A FREE-FOR-ALL

It was the unforeseen events in Iran, not any market shift or economic trend, that set off the world's second oil shock, and it was to prove even more disruptive than the first. But just as during the shock six years earlier, the worst damage resulted not from lack of oil, but from panic.

California, America's most populous state and often a bellwether for the nation, was the first to experience oil-shock difficulties. Early in May 1979, for instance, gasoline stations began curtailing their hours because of fuel shortages. Long lines materialized, accompanied by sporadic violence. The *Los Angeles Times* reported that one gas station attendant was beaten with a baseball bat, while another required fifty stitches to close a wound administered by a disgruntled, beer-bottle-wielding customer. Thieves hijacked a Shell Oil tank truck after pulling a gun on its hapless driver.

Hoarding was widespread, occasionally with tragic consequences. In a three-week period, Los Angeles fire officials blamed forty-four fires and four deaths on poorly stored gasoline or siphoning accidents. A number of large organizations were accused of worsening the crisis by stockpiling millions of gallons of fuel.

Mounting tensions prompted a dozen California counties to inaugurate gas rationing on May 9; motorists were restricted to alternate days at the pump. Before the month was out, President Jimmy Carter followed up with an executive order empowering other states to regulate gasoline sales until September 30, 1979.

As shortages spread to other states, so did anger and suspicion. In mid-June, a *New York Times*/CBS News Poll found that 62 percent of those interviewed did not believe the crisis was real. Some even harbored convictions that U.S. companies and the federal government were in league to hold back gasoline. Paul Fieler, a postal clerk in Cincinnati, voiced that common skepticism when he was quoted as saying: "You can't say that they don't play hand in glove, footsie and patsie, with one another."

Iran's exports of 4 million barrels a day were sharply curtailed by the outbreak of revolution, although exports to the United States would not officially end until almost ten months later on November

4, 1979, when Iranian students stormed the U.S. embassy in Tehran and took scores of Americans hostage. President Carter then halted all shipments of oil from Iran, and Iran, in turn, canceled its contracts with the United States. Shortly after the disruptions began, however, the other OPEC producers stepped in to pick up some of the slack, leaving a worldwide shortage of about 2 million barrels, or less than 5 percent of overall daily demand. Nevertheless, a scramble among the world's oil players to avoid getting caught short again intensified the market disruption. Long-term contracts were unilaterally canceled. Spot trading, in which the agreed-on price is for immediate, or nearly immediate, delivery of the commodity purchased, became dominant. Governments responded with conflicting signals, and the OPEC members, comfortably ensconced in the catbird seat, shook down their customers and manipulated supplies to push prices even higher.

The whole international system of fixed, posted prices for oil seemed on the verge of collapse. But there was another, even greater force at work: Many feared that the new power of Islamic fundamentalism might spread throughout the region. For a while, concern about the reach and grasp of the Iranian imams captured Washington's attention. But once the hostages were safely released (on January 20, 1981, the day Ronald Reagan was inaugurated) the threat seemed to fade from consciousness and an aura of complacency set in. Sure, the U.S. periodically slapped another economic sanction on Iran as extreme anti-American propaganda and covert activities aimed at exporting the revolution continued undeterred. The United States, as we now know all too well, would come to regret its complacency.

The immediate effect of the uproar in the oil market was to push up inventories. At any given time, several billion barrels of oil are stockpiled and in inventory around the world to ease the flow from the well to the refinery and to guard against shortages. Because inventories are expensive to maintain, no one holds more than is needed—at least in normal times. But in the panic of 1979 and 1980, buyers at every level of the marketplace assumed that tomorrow's price would be higher than today's—and worse, that they might not be able to buy tomorrow at any price. It ran in the face of accepted wisdom to buy and store more of a commodity when its price was going up, but irrational behavior was the order of the day, from executive suites to celebrity mansions.

Some companies were actually holding oil in supertankers. This is a hugely expensive proposition because of demurrage, the charge assessed when a vessel overstays its allotted time in port for loading or unloading its cargo. Most tankers are chartered, and every charter contract sets out a predetermined number of days for unloading cargo. Staying overtime subjects the tanker to demurrage, which can run to many thousands of dollars. Companies using supertankers as storage vehicles during the second oil shock were paying the additional charges.

The potential rewards, however, were also great. As prices went up, the value of the cargo shot up. Thus, traders who anchored loaded supertankers with tens of thousands of tons of oil offshore at major trading ports like Rotterdam, the Netherlands, were more than willing to incur the cost.

The most notable of these was Marc Rich. Rich had long been making a fortune in the oil trade. Throughout the 1970s, he used his ties to the Iranian royal family to buy cheap oil which he then sold for whatever the tumultuous spot market would bear, a price high enough to give Rich a tidy pretax profit exceeding $350 million in 1976 dollars. When the Shah was overthrown, Rich, without missing a beat, changed partners and continued his trading with the new Khomeini regime and its radical followers. It was those transactions, made illegal by the U.S. restrictions against Iran, that later led to Rich's conviction for dodging domestic oil-price controls. (Rich, who fled to Switzerland in an attempt to escape prosecution, received a controversial pardon from President Bill Clinton in his final hours in office.)

Prior to the Iranian crisis, Rich had had the good luck—or foresight—to sign contracts for inexpensive Nigerian crude oil. By the late 1970s, he reportedly controlled as much as 50,000 barrels a day of Nigerian production. That's how Rich came to have oil-filled supertankers incurring demurrage charges as they sat outside Rotterdam while the second oil shock roiled the markets. As the price climbed, Rich, an acknowledged trading wizard, increased his profits exponentially by docking his tankers and periodically selling the oil.

One avid customer was Atlantic Richfield Company (Arco), which found itself in desperate straits in 1979 after the Iranian revolution and subsequent U.S. embargo stripped the company of 200,000 barrels of oil, or about one-fourth of what it needed to keep its refineries producing at full tilt. To fill the gap, Arco signed contracts with Rich that required the payment of hefty premiums atop the official posted price of Nigerian oil. In a twelve-month period, Arco paid many millions in such premiums, company officials later told the *Washington Post*. Arco also paid a $315 million fine for its part in colluding with Rich to sidestep U.S. price controls, although its participation in the illegal maneuvering was categorized as unintentional.

All told, the rush to build inventories added an estimated 3 million barrels a day to normal world demand, which was already 2 million barrels higher than the available supply. Inevitably, the outsized demand again drove prices heavenward. In the final reckoning, the posted price would soar from about $13 a barrel to a new record of $34 in January 1981.

The OPEC producers couldn't contain their natural urge to take advantage of panicked consumers. As Daniel Yergin recounts in *The Prize*, Shell Oil got a telegram from an oil minister one morning invoking *force majeure* to cancel a long-term contract to supply a daily quota of oil. *Force majeure*, which literally means "greater force" but is commonly translated as "act of God," is invoked to excuse one party in a contract from liability when an unforeseen, unavoidable, and uncontrollable event, such as a war or natural disaster, makes it impossible to carry out the agreed-to obligation. That afternoon, a second wire arrived from the minister, offering the same amount of oil at a spot price 50 percent higher than the contract price. Shell took it.

The oil minister's actions were disgraceful, but typical of the way the OPEC members operate. Where was the act of God? It was nonexistent. Pure and simple, this was a breach of confidence and a breach of ethics, not to mention an outright breach of contract. The oil minister pulled off a daylight robbery because he knew he could, and because Shell couldn't do a thing about it.

Even after spot prices fell back in the spring of 1979, when Iranian oil started to trickle back into the market, OPEC continued to milk the market for every penny it could get. Member nations unilaterally cut back production to keep the price up. When OPEC met officially in March, it gave its members permission to tack on whatever surcharges and premiums the traffic would bear. Obviously, this free-for-all did nothing to allay buyers' fears. The prevailing sentiment was buy now, no matter the price; otherwise, you'd regret it when the quote went higher tomorrow.

Saudi Arabia swam against the OPEC tide, insisting that it would stick to the posted price of $18 a barrel. But when only the United Arab Emirates followed their lead, the Saudis feared they were losing control of the situation. Back then, the Saudis were acutely aware that an overly voracious pricing policy could have political consequences.

Sheikh Yamani led a one-man crusade for conservation and price moderation, to little effect. Even Western leaders and analysts, whose countries had to bear the brunt of rising fuel costs, didn't seem as intent on encouraging their citizens to conserve energy as did Yamani. He stood practically alone in sounding the alarm, predicting that confidence-sapping oil price increases would lead to serious, long-lasting competition in the form of alternative fuels.

The panic sparked by the fundamentalist revolution in Iran was compounded in November 1979, when militant Iranians took more than sixty Americans hostage in their assault on the U.S. embassy in Tehran. In response to the growing tension on the world's political stage and President Carter's embargo on oil exports to the United States, spot oil prices spiked repeatedly, erasing record after record.

When the OPEC members next met, the Saudis reprised their voice-of-reason role and suggested that everyone agree to abide by a posted price of $24. No dice. Iran immediately jumped ahead to $33; spot prices had continued to climb and were now running at over $40 a barrel.

With no end in sight to the price spiral, Yamani warned that the inventory buildup would eventually end, and when it did, the excess stores would be dumped onto the market. The resulting glut would trigger a price collapse, thereby decimating the members' revenues.

Few of the Saudi oil minister's colleagues agreed with him. In fact, most openly derided both Yamani and his unpopular notions.

Marathon discussions failed to produce an agreement, and after the meeting, several members joined Iran in raising their posted prices to $33.

A few months later, in April of 1980, the Carter administration's ill-fated Desert One raid to rescue the hostages sparked yet another bout of hysterical buying in the jittery oil market. Gloom settled over the industrialized countries after OPEC's long-range strategy committee recommended that the posted price should be raised every year by 10 to 15 percent. That strategy would lead to oil at $60 a barrel in five years. Clearly, the pundits concluded, the world oil economy was in massive danger, and the mood in the United States and Europe reflected that grim assessment.

DIRE PROPHECIES BECOME REALITY

Prices averaged $32 a barrel when OPEC met again in June of 1980. Yamani, whom a Venezuelan delegate once described as "a charming genius," still couldn't convince his colleagues of their folly, although his dire prophecies were becoming reality. With inventories bulging, companies had no place left to store their excess petroleum stocks. Meanwhile, a recession was plainly developing in the industrialized nations, pulling down both demand for oil and its spot price.

By September, several worried OPEC members had agreed to cut production by 10 percent to support the price. Then, as OPEC's ministers gathered in Baghdad to plan a glorious celebration of the organization's twentieth birthday, war broke out. Saddam Hussein sent Iraq's troops across the border into Iran in a dispute over control of the Shatt al Arab, a waterway that both countries needed for access to the Persian Gulf. The war dragged on for eight years before ending in a United Nations-mandated cease-fire. It foreshadowed Saddam's grab for Kuwait in 1991, which in turn triggered the first United States invasion of Iraq.

With Saddam's foray into Iran in September 1980, more than 3 million barrels a day again vanished from the oil market, and the spot price jumped to a then-record $42. In December 1980, OPEC reached a split-decision, two-tiered price structure: $32 for Saudi Arabia, $36 for everyone else.

Meanwhile, non-OPEC production was rising. Iranian and Iraqi oil would soon reappear in the market. In order to defend its posted price, OPEC had to cut its own production, which meant accepting a lower share of the world oil market. At the same time, buyers, fed up with the high prices, began to tap into their massive inventories. As Yamani had predicted, OPEC was beginning to harvest the fruits of its ill-considered pricing and production strategy.

Finally, in 1981, OPEC announced a unified posted price of $34. This was, in effect, a price cut for most of the members. The posted price would go no higher for a decade. OPEC found itself pinned down by its own declining market share and the lower prices offered by its non-OPEC competitors. By 1981, OPEC's annual production had plummeted by 26 percent from the 1979 level, to 22.5 million barrels a day.

The year 1982 provided no respite. Non-OPEC nations outproduced the cartel by 1 million barrels a day. Soviet exports were rising, and spot prices were running as much as $8 a barrel below OPEC's posted price. Now it was payback time for the oil companies. They, not the OPEC producers, were reneging on long-term contracts and playing the spot market. The choices were stark. OPEC could either cut its posted price to match the competition, or cut production to firm up the price. Fearing that another price cut would undermine their long-term gains, weaken their posted-price structure, and sap their political and economic clout, the OPEC nations reluctantly took the last step to becoming a true cartel. In March 1982, OPEC set a collective production limit of 18 million barrels a day, a whopping 42 percent below the 31 million barrels it had produced just three years earlier in 1979. (Today, almost a quarter of a century later, OPEC is producing 27.1 million to 29.1 million barrels a day, with no perceptible decrease in proved reserves. In fact, OPEC members now claim to have nearly twice as much oil in reserve as they had in 1970, and this after producing at least 300 billion barrels in the intervening years. Clearly, the numbers OPEC distributes for public consumption just don't add up.)

Each member nation was assigned a daily quota, and Saudi Arabia was to act as the swing producer, adjusting its output to keep the price steady. The quotas were supposed to be a temporary measure while the market recovered, but the market price kept heading lower.

In March 1983, after twelve days of wrangling in a London hotel, OPEC cut its posted price by 15 percent, to $29 a barrel. The collective production quota was reduced to 17.5 million barrels a day. OPEC had now made itself the world's swing producer, propping up global oil prices at the expense of its own market share. It had come full circle from its glory days in the 1970s. No longer did buyers worry about getting supplies. Now it was the oil producers who worried about losing access to markets. Buyers who once competed to pay premium prices now expected huge discounts. Instead of "black gold," oil had become just another commodity with too much product chasing too few buyers. The glut seemed semi-permanent. The situation looked bleak for OPEC.

OPEC's troubles only deepened when the New York Mercantile

Exchange opened an oil futures contract in 1983, hammering the final nail into the coffin of dictated prices. Now the price was being set on a minute-by-minute basis in thousands of independent transactions around the world, instantly reported and transparent to all players. OPEC's quota system was in a meltdown, with overpumping rampant and member countries defying efforts to verify their production figures.

By 1985, amid a still-soft economy and a weak market for oil, booming non-OPEC production had cut the cartel's market share to just 37 percent. Saudi Arabia, the swing producer's swing producer, was pumping only 2.5 million barrels a day, or one-quarter of its presumed capacity. Its oil revenue, which peaked at $119 billion in 1981, had dwindled to $26 billion four years later. The Saudis were forced to impose actual austerity measures, with pay cuts as deep as 30 percent for government workers, teachers, and hospital employees.

However, austerity in corrupt oil-dependent societies seldom if ever affects the ruling elite. In Saudi Arabia, the royal family felt no pain. The *Wall Street Journal* reported in 1985 that the Boeing Company was hard at work converting a 747 into a flying palace for the country's new leader, King Fahd. The plane was designed to mimic the Gothic architecture of the king's new palace, with arches, chandeliers, ceiling mirrors, gold-plated hardware, a three-story elevator, a medical room equipped with a surgical table, and a communication system that outperformed the system installed on Air Force One.

Frustrated by their falling revenues, the Saudis rebelled and adopted a complex new pricing structure worked out by Sheikh Yamani that let them cut prices and increase production. Predictably, their OPEC brethren jumped in feet first and prices collapsed: By the summer of 1986, benchmark light crude was selling for $8 a barrel. Within a twelve-and-a-half-year span, the OPEC producers had ridden a round-trip roller coaster that brought the price virtually back to where it started.

Looking outside their own house for the villain, the OPEC nations declared war on the non-OPEC producers, vowing to "secure and defend" the OPEC market share. What those words really meant was no-holds-barred, cutthroat competition. To steal away market share from the non-OPEC producers, the cartel jacked up its production and hacked away at prices, undercutting the outsiders in hopes of forcing them to fall in line price-wise. "Join us or die" was the message.

Of course, the heavy-handed OPEC approach triggered another full-fledged oil shock—this time on the downside—and it was the producers and traders who felt the pain. The futures contract price on the New York Mercantile Exchange (NYMEX) plunged to $10 a barrel, while actual spot prices in the Persian Gulf fell to $6. OPEC had increased its tangible production by only 9 percent, expanding the free world's oil supply by no more than 3 percent. But in an age of greater market volatility, it was enough to spark a sellers' panic. Exporters scrambled for markets and buyers jockeyed for ever-lower prices. The free market was calling the shots.

But not for long. As had so often happened during OPEC's tumultuous existence, the cartel would be rescued by its victims. But, this time, the consequences for OPEC's ever-willing protector would prove particularly threatening.

6

THE FAUSTIAN BARGAIN

It's an ancient story of misplaced values. Faust, a German school-teacher cum fortune teller and magician, allows his pride and thirst for power to tempt him into making a fateful pact with the devil. In this sixteenth-century German legend, Faust is first rewarded with twenty-four years of pleasure and power, after which Mephistopheles, the supreme spirit of evil, carries the suddenly repentant schoolteacher off to suffer an eternity's worth of pain and sorrow for his prideful mistake.

From this ageless classic comes the term *Faustian bargain*, which describes a pact made for present gain without sufficient regard for future cost or consequence. George H. W. Bush made just such a bargain when, as vice president under Ronald Reagan, he arranged with Saudi King Fahd to rescue the oil industry. By giving OPEC a reprieve and stifling competition, Bush helped to saddle world consumers with a bill for literally hundreds of billions of dollars—money that was transferred from rich and poor countries alike into the coffers of the OPEC producers. And it was all done under the guise of protecting the domestic oil industry. In essence, the United States became OPEC's cheerleader and protector. With the American government on board, OPEC oil producers had little to fear politically.

But for anyone not part of the oil game, Bush's efforts were a disaster. Here was the mother of all crony capitalism. Oil industry constituents inside the United States and out hijacked the national interest of an unsuspecting nation (ours). Henceforth, our government would pay close heed to the opinions and well-being of the Arab states in the Gulf, rationalizing actions fraught with hypocrisy by cloaking them, as discussed in earlier chapters, in terms like *stability, security of supply,* and *finite resources.*

WASHINGTON RIDES TO THE RESCUE

In hindsight, the seller's panic and ensuing price plunge of 1986 was the world's last best chance to get the OPEC monkey off its back. The cartel was in tatters, its power vanquished. If its former victims hadn't come to its rescue, OPEC surely would have faded into history without the oil-buying nations ever having struck a blow. They could have just sat and watched as OPEC destroyed itself. Instead, a helping hand was extended, one that came from Washington no less.

For consumers and their advocates, the selling panic of 1986 was an answered prayer. The doomsday crowd, it seemed, had been mistaken: Oil was cheap and abundant, and the once-fearsome oil weapon was nothing more than a cardboard sword. Cheap oil would cut costs across the economy, and lower retail prices would mean faster growth and higher living standards for everyone. Betokening the bright promise, filling stations mounted their own retail price wars, and the only gas lines to be found were in Texas, where one entrepreneurial dealer came up with a unique loss leader: a one-day promotion offering gasoline absolutely free.

As far as the oil world was concerned, however, there was nothing either welcome or amusing in the situation. Chaos was the operative word. Even the industrialized countries discovered that rock-bottom oil prices were a mixed blessing. The higher-cost, non-OPEC producers were suffering—some North Sea oil fields were losing money on every barrel pumped because the market price had fallen below production costs. But it cost so much to mothball production platforms that their owners kept them going.

In the oil industry, there are fixed costs and variable costs. Someone drilling a well pays for the fixed costs of equipment, lease purchases, royalties, taxes, and interest—say, $100,000 a year—whether or not the well ever produces a drop of oil. So a driller with a producing well may decide to keep pumping even at a loss as a way of bringing in revenue to defray at least some of those fixed costs—so long as he can also cover his variable costs.

But, of course, producers can't hang on forever in the face of loss-making economics. A group of non-OPEC producers tried, and failed, to start a dialogue with OPEC. In the United States, where production costs were rising rapidly and total production was plummeting, oil companies reacted to the crisis with massive cuts in spending, particularly for exploration and new production. The Texas oil business virtually collapsed; deep recession gripped the Southwest.

In Washington, President Ronald Reagan single-mindedly championed the free market and rejoiced over low prices at the pump, telling audiences in South Carolina in the summer of 1986, "Thanks in large measure to our decontrol of oil, we've seen energy prices tumble, including the price you pay for gas. Isn't it good to pull into the station today and watch the gallons on the pump add up faster than the dollars?" But the domestic oil and gas industry and its backers in Congress were all clamoring for some sort of action to reverse the price collapse.

Leading the charge was then-Congressman Dick Cheney, who, representing energy-rich Wyoming, championed a new tax on imported oil. He declared in October 1986, "Let us rid ourselves of the fiction that low oil prices are somehow good for the United States."

What was good for the United States, Cheney's reasoning went, were higher prices in the domestic oil industry. Cheney failed to say a thing about the billions of dollars his proposed import tax would remove from the pockets of U.S. oil and gasoline consumers, who might have found cause to question just how good Cheney's tax plan was for their region of the country.

The backers of a tax argued that continued low prices might permanently cripple the domestic energy industry, and bring a chronic flood of imports. A weakened U.S. energy industry was perceived as a threat to national security and American leadership of the free world. To safeguard domestic oil, President Eisenhower had imposed import quotas back in the 1950s. Now, the industry was seeking a tariff on imports to level the playing field.

Cheney's plan and ones like it were criticized by other lawmakers as snake oil that would lead to factory closings and put hundreds of thousands of people on the unemployment line. The late Republican Senator John Heinz of Pennsylvania said at the time that the legislation would cost his state's consumers another $1.3 billion a year in energy costs and would send inflation spiraling higher.

Years later, when the Cheney plan was revisited by Democratic congressmen in the spring of 2004, Illinois Senator Richard J. Durbin said the proposal, had it not been defeated, would have cost consumers $1.2 trillion over the intervening span of years. What really happened proved much worse.

The industry plea for some kind of tariff had found a receptive ear in Vice President Bush, himself once an independent Texas oilman. When none of a variety of relief proposals for the oil industry made it through Congress, Bush began to press for coordinated production restrictions by the Gulf oil producers. Bush aimed to shift their focus from market share to supporting higher prices.

The vice president had long planned a visit to Saudi Arabia and the Persian Gulf states to discuss mutual national concerns, oil among them. But his actual departure in April 1986 came in the wake of the price collapse and the resulting turmoil.

Ever since the first oil shock in 1973, OPEC and its allies had been imposing what amounted to a tax on the industrialized world's consumers. Now, the price collapse, reflecting real market forces, was repairing the damage, shifting $50 billion back to the consuming nations in 1986 alone.

Vice President Bush, who set out to reverse the flow back to the producers, initially drew fire from the free-market White House. At a news conference just before flying off to Saudi Arabia, he said, "I think it is essential that we talk about stability and that we not just have a continued free fall, like a parachutist jumping out without a parachute." When that remark caused a spike in the spot oil price, a senior official in the Reagan administration acidly retorted that "poor George" had got it wrong; all things considered, falling oil prices helped the U.S. economy, and the best policy was to let the market do its thing. "It's a gaffe," the official said. "George is a Texas, pro-oil guy, but that is not administration policy."

But even while denying any change in its free-market policy, the White House sent conflicting signals when President Reagan himself insisted at a press conference that he and the vice president were in agreement, but that oil prices should be "settled in the open market." Earlier that day, the president had told the American Society of Newspaper Editors that the plunging prices were a boon for many Americans, but were hard on domestic oil producers. And he just hoped that the "whole thing will stabilize very quickly."

Energy Secretary John Herrington further beclouded the administration position when he advised in a speech that the Saudis needed "to be aware of the dire straits the American oil and gas producers are in." That, in turn, prompted Congressman Philip Sharp, a leading House Democrat from Indiana, to accuse Herrington of trying to "talk up" the oil price "by urging the major player in the OPEC cartel to return to the tactics which have caused our economy such great damage in the past."

Bush was undeterred by the sniping, including an anonymous administration official's comment that the vice president was "off the reservation," and a *Detroit News* editorial headlined: "Bush to Michigan: Drop Dead." At a news conference aboard USS *Enterprise* in the Gulf of Oman, Bush shot back: "I think this [support for the U.S. oil industry] is administration policy. I think I'm correct. I know I'm correct. Some things you're sure of. This I'm absolutely sure of."

Among the things he knew for certain, he told a group of U.S. businessmen at a breakfast meeting in Riyadh, was that, at some point, "the national security interest of the United States says, 'Hey, we must have a strong, viable domestic industry.' I've felt that way all my political life, and I'm not going to start changing that at this juncture. I feel it, and I know the president of the United States feels it."

At a dinner with several Saudi ministers, Bush warned Sheikh

Yamani that continued low prices would only turn up the heat in Congress for a tariff on imports. He added pointedly that the administration would find it hard to resist.

Yamani, who was widely regarded as the shaper of Saudi, and therefore OPEC, oil policy, took Bush seriously. Whatever the White House was saying for public consumption, he reasoned, surely the vice president of the United States had to be delivering the real message. Nevertheless, the *Boston Globe*'s Robert Healy reported that Bush carried a letter from the president to King Fahd stating "the president's desire to maintain a free market and an unwillingness to intervene in the oil markets." (In reality, the whole dispute was moot, because, as Healy went on to note, "there is no free market for world oil, and there probably never has been. . . .") Whether Bush overstepped his brief, or what might have happened had Reagan dispatched an emissary who spoke the party line, are questions for the ages.

A FAUSTIAN BARGAIN WITH THE SAUDI KING

Bush later was called to a private midnight meeting with King Fahd, after a day in which a Saudi tanker had been attacked by Iranian gunboats. The meeting was ostensibly about security in the Gulf and U.S. arms for Saudi Arabia. Oil was mentioned only in passing, according to official reports. But administration officials later told the *Wall Street Journal* that Bush had repeated his statement that national security demanded a strong domestic oil industry. He also told the king that "Saudi interests and U.S. interests aren't identical with regard to oil pricing." The king agreed that stability would be good, but, according to the *Journal*, neither Bush nor the king mentioned a desired price level.

Eventually, Bush and the Saudi ruler settled on the notion of cutting back production and boosting oil prices by 50 percent to a target of $18 a barrel. The Faustian bargain had been struck, and its repercussions would be felt not only by American consumers paying higher prices to protect the domestic oil industry. Consumers around the world would feel the pain, all with Washington's imprimatur.

Bush's trip triggered a long debate within OPEC, as well as the methodical evolution of a new concept: a "target price" for oil. The original rationale was that the price should be high enough to give the producing nations sufficient revenue for their support, but low enough that consumers could live with it, too. And it should be competitive with alternate energy sources, reducing the pressure to move away from oil or impose draconian conservation measures. Such a price would have to be enforced by quotas, which had proved problematic in the past. But perhaps the recent chaos had taught OPEC's truants a lesson about the dangers of cheating. If so, quotas might now be effective.

In the months that followed the vice president's visit, a consensus emerged that the "right" price would be one that fell within a range of $17 to $19 a barrel. Not coincidentally, this was right in line with the price brokered in the meeting between Bush and the king.

In the years since, OPEC has adjusted the range to target a price somewhere between $22 and $28 a barrel, but even that is now being reevaluated. In January 2005, OPEC members seemed set on widening the price band, with suggestions ranging between $30 and $60 a barrel. The Saudis appeared to be favoring a $40 level. Any mention of maximizing OPEC profits is studiously avoided in the cartel's public statements about these negotiations. Discussions are typically described in terms of keeping markets well supplied and offsetting currency depreciation and inflation.

Iran, still at war with Iraq in 1986, was initially a stubborn holdout on the issue of quotas. With war damage keeping it from raising its oil production, and higher prices its only option for bringing in more revenue, Iran was against the whole idea of price moderation—through the imposition of quotas or by any other means. Iraq, meanwhile, would have no part of any pact that included Iran.

But at an OPEC meeting held in Geneva in August, Sheikh Yamani had a surprise visit from the Iranian oil minister. He astonished Yamani by pledging Iran's support for the new system after all—but with a major caveat: Neither Iran nor its enemy Iraq would be forced to cut their oil outputs, while Saudi Arabia, Kuwait, the United Arab Emirates, and Qatar would carry most of the burden of reducing the cartel's production in order to stop the price bleed. The Saudis and their allies accepted the Iranian deal, giving in because they believed Iran was winning the war against Iraq, which would make it a power to be reckoned with in the Persian Gulf. An oil analyst in New York told the *Wall Street Journal* that he had detected a "subtle shift in power . . . within OPEC," with the Iranians wielding more influence and the Saudis becoming more submissive.

For Yamani, whose price-war strategy was designed to regain OPEC's dwindling share of the world oil business by boosting production, it was the beginning of the end of a twenty-four-year run that had made him the man the king turned to in matters of oil. Yamani was unceremoniously dumped a few months after the Geneva conference. Iran was accumulating power, and Yamani was the main obstacle blocking its way to higher oil prices. That and a push from Saudi royal family members resentful of his influence was all it took to retire Yamani and his perfect Oxford English from the corridors of power within OPEC.

And so it was agreed. OPEC would set its target price and enforce it with production quotas. But the OPEC members insisted that some major non-OPEC producers support the new structure as well. Several signaled that they would comply. Mexico vowed to cut production. Norway announced it would slow its rate of growth. Even the Soviet Union offered to reduce its output by 100,000 barrels a day.

By the end of 1986, the new, albeit shaky, structure was in place. After its implementation, the quota system repeatedly seemed to be on the verge of collapse. Iraq temporarily seceded from OPEC, declaring itself unbound by OPEC's numbers. Many non-OPEC producers refused to take part. As for the Soviets, it was impossible to verify that Russia was living up to its commitment. At one point, the price fell to $15 a barrel. Nevertheless, the basic structure would stand for three years, despite its rickety foundation.

If not actually happy, nearly everyone was at least reconciled to the arrangement and its outcome. Drivers filled their tanks with more expensive gasoline, a reality that OPEC and its anointed analysts tried to camouflage with sweet talk about how the price compared "on an inflation-adjusted basis."

The spinners rightly assumed that consumers could be cajoled into emptying their pocketbooks so long as some arcane method of measurement reassured them they were lucky not to be paying even more. In exchange for losing the benefit of very low prices, consuming nations won the assurance that their investment in high-cost oil fields would be protected, and that decreased dependence on imports would make them less vulnerable to another crisis. Even the Reagan administration seemed to have been converted. A

lower oil price might well generate higher growth and lower inflation, the president's men reasoned, with a touch of cynicism. But if
the domestic oil industry could make a living at $18 and stop
pushing for a tariff, the White House could sit idly by and boast
that it was letting the market work. Of course, what was really
working was the cartel, but the voters would hardly know the difference.

FADING ROMANCE

For the oil industry, the 1980s ended and the 1990s began with a
somewhat less colorful cast of characters than that featured in the
1970s. The whispery King Fahd of Saudi Arabia suffered a debilitating stroke in 1995 and was replaced by his pragmatic regent,
Crown Prince Abdullah. The Shah of Iran, Venezuela's brooding
Juan Pablo Perez Alfonso, and the Armenian Calouste Gulbenkian
("Mr. Five Percent"), were long gone. The suave, tailored Ahmad
Zaki Yamani and the oracular Henry Kissinger had both been side-
lined by political reverses. Wanda Jablonski had long before printed
her last scoop. But if the new characters were less flamboyant, the
events they set in motion were no less significant.

Oil's image was beginning to match reality. It was increasingly
viewed as a commodity like any other. Far from running out, proved
reserves of crude oil had actually risen by 50 percent between 1984
and 1990, from 670 billion barrels to around 1 trillion.

But as usual in the oil world, the newly emerging impression
would be distorted by events. Below the tranquil surface, the market
was tightening. On the brink of the global economic boom of the
1990s, total oil consumption by 1989 had recovered to equal its high
point of a decade earlier, though supply growth was thought to be

lagging. Production at the operating wellheads in the non-OPEC fields of Alaska, Mexico, and the North Sea had already peaked, and Russian production had crashed. Before its collapse, the Soviet Union had out-pumped even Saudi Arabia, hitting 12.5 million barrels a day in 1988 (most of it from what is currently the Russian Federation). By 1996, however, Russia was producing just half that amount, a drop deemed to be not easily reversible. Joseph Stanislaw and Daniel Yergin of Cambridge Energy Research Associates opined in *Foreign Affairs* that Russia would need to invest $50 billion in its dilapidated facilities just to maintain its reduced level of production, and another $50 billion to $70 billion in new technology to regain its 1988 capacity.

The global "security margin"—the gap between in-place production capacity and demand, which had been high enough in the 1980s to allow the world to weather the Iran-Iraq war—appeared to be dwindling fast. With each passing month, the world economy seemed more vulnerable to the kind of event that would give OPEC a new opportunity to squeeze the West. On August 2, 1990, that event occurred. Iraqi strongman Saddam Hussein shocked the world by massing 100,000 troops along his country's border with Kuwait.

As usual, Saddam was playing a devious and many-layered game. On one level, in the wake of the Iran-Iraq war, he was trying to rebuild his nation while Iran was preoccupied with its own internal political turmoil. Meanwhile, he was carrying on a border dispute with Kuwait over a large oil field and two strategic islands. But what is less well known is that he was also mounting a challenge to Saudi Arabia for the leadership of OPEC.

Saddam's million-strong army, the biggest and best-equipped in the entire Middle East, already sparked fear in the region. Saddam had used chemical weapons to subdue rebellious Kurds in northern Iraq, and he made his menace loom even larger by nurturing suspicions that he was developing biological and nuclear weapons as well. Now he meant to use his muscle to displace the Saudis and their steady oil price strategy, push the OPEC price up, fatten his treasury, and become the dominant force in the Middle East.

Saddam's victim was shrewdly chosen. Kuwait, a reliable Saudi ally, was widely disliked within the cartel. With huge proved reserves of oil, it consistently exceeded its production quota, driving prices down. Saddam (who felt free to ignore Iraq's own quota whenever it suited him) said his troops were on the border to enforce OPEC discipline and Kuwait's quota. Many of the member governments quietly applauded.

In answer to the threat, Kuwait and another chronic quota exceeder, the United Arab Emirates, grudgingly agreed to stop overproducing. OPEC predictably responded by quickly voting to raise its oil price from $18 to $21 a barrel.

The West reacted to the increase with naïveté. Many opined that OPEC had learned to restrain its greed by only increasing the price by 10 percent. The Pollyannas also pointed out that the higher price would enable more production from Mexico and Russia, and would help OPEC producers, notably Saudi Arabia, invest in additional production capacity.

Best of all, they said, these developments showed that energy was no longer a problem. The West had learned that oil would not run out, and that if there were a crisis, conservation and alternative sources could ease the pinch. James Flanigan of the *Los Angeles Times* echoed the sentiments of the day when he wrote, "Energy no longer frightens us. We know it's not about to run out, that conservation can dramatically affect its prices, and that if prices rise too fast—or some dictator threatens an embargo—we can use alternative energy forms. In short, we learned something in the 70s that will stand by us in the 90s."

Flanigan was right to disparage the myth of scarcity. Unfortunately, the world was not as convinced as it let on. Its false confidence would be exposed shortly when Saddam Hussein, as he had intended all along, ordered his troops across the border to overrun his hapless neighbor. It took mere days for Iraq to conquer and annex Kuwait.

The oil markets went into a frenzy. At the urging of the United States, the United Nations declared an embargo on Iraqi and Kuwaiti oil. Nearly 5 million barrels a day disappeared from the world markets, a lost river of crude equivalent to the volume that disappeared during the crises of 1973 and 1979. As in those instances, users all along the line rushed to build inventories. Prices spiked to $40 a barrel, twice the pre-invasion level. It was, many commentators suggested, the worst crisis in OPEC's history.

The cartel's other members indignantly united against Iraq, declaring their loyalty to their customers and scrambling to pump enough added oil to make up the deficit and fend off an economic crisis in the industrialized world. Not, mind you, that OPEC was doing us any favors. The producers' interest was in selling as much oil as possible, at the highest feasible price. But, led by the Saudis, they knew that a recession in the West would not be good for their own well-balanced blend of greed and political realism.

What is more, just like Kuwait had been, most of the OPEC nations in the Middle East were virtually defenseless against their more aggressive neighbors. They needed to protect their borders, and they needed the coalition of developed countries to do it. As always, the parasite needed a healthy host, so OPEC latched onto the oil-hungry nations. By December, all OPEC members were pumping flat-out; the Saudis alone raised their output by 3 million barrels a day, making up three-fifths of the lost oil. The market was fully supplied.

But markets are not always rational. Even though there was plenty of oil in the pipeline, anxiety, hysteria, and the expectation of war propped up prices. When Saddam threatened to move on to Saudi Arabia and destroy its entire oil industry, the hysteria incited another wave of panic. Again, traders and consumers rushed to build up inventories even as prices kept rising. What would happen if a full-scale war broke out? Could George H. W. Bush's coalition stop Saddam Hussein from smashing the Saudi wells, pipelines, refineries, and port facilities? Would tanker skippers shy away from the Persian Gulf? Would shipping insurance rates skyrocket? Would Saddam use biological, chemical, or nuclear weapons? What if Israel got involved and the whole Middle East erupted? Could crude reach $200 a barrel?

THE CALM AFTER THE DESERT STORM

On January 17, 1991, the day the U.S.-led coalition forces started bombing Iraq, the price of oil abruptly dropped from $40 to about $30 a barrel. The pullback in prices was triggered by President Bush's day-earlier decision to tap the U.S. Strategic Petroleum Reserve in the first emergency drawdown since the reserve was established in the aftermath of the 1973–74 oil embargo. The U.S. Department of Energy was prepared to release as much as 33.75 million barrels from the 600 million-barrel-plus reserve, but only half of the emergency drawdown was actually used. Traders and customers alike had concluded that the Saudi wells were safe.

Besides, the oil recently added to inventories was a costly burden, so consumers decided to use it rather than buy more. The price continued to fall.

After thirty-nine days of bombing Iraq, troops launched from Saudi Arabia swept north and chased the fleeing Iraqi army toward Baghdad. The ground war lasted just four days before Saddam capitulated. By the time his troops pulled out of Kuwait, not even the lakes of spilled crude and hundreds of burning wells left in their wake could scare the West's oil users, traders, and speculators. They drove the price below $18. The market was temporarily but effectively in glut. For the next five years, oil traded in a range of $15 to $20 a barrel. The entire Gulf War crisis turned out to be a hiccup on the price chart.

Nonetheless, there were lingering economic, environmental, and socio-political consequences. Extinguishing the more than 600 oil-well fires started by Saddam's troops took almost eight months, for instance, and cost $1.5 billion. The United Nations Compensation Commission later determined that Iraq owed $2.8 billion for the disruption of Kuwait's oil operations, in addition to the $3.2 billion it owed to individual victims of the invasion.

Two years passed before Kuwait was pumping crude again at its pre-war rate of 2 million barrels a day, but it took six years before the United Nations-sanctioned Oil-for-Food program would bring Iraq's oil back to the world market following the world body's imposed embargo. Yet OPEC and non-OPEC producers easily managed to cover the wartime shortfall, and they continued to meet global supply needs while Kuwait rebuilt its industry and Iraqi crude remained embargoed. Had the world stopped to think about it, the notion that oil was in short supply might have come into question once again. But the pre-war market upheaval had breathed new life into the old myth.

Over the intervening half-decade, OPEC's victims had twice come to its rescue. First, they saved the cartel's lunch when low prices threatened to break its grip on the world's oil consumers. Later, they went into battle to save two of its most powerful members, Saudi Arabia and Kuwait, from the brutal clutches of Saddam Hussein. But the story wasn't over. There would be more oil shocks, more internal dissension, and still more help from the ever-willing victims in the years to come.

7

TIGHTENING THE CHOKEHOLD

The worldwide average cost of finding and producing one barrel of oil is only $5—a seeming pittance until you compare it with Persian Gulf oil, which is so easily obtainable that it seems to leap from the ground. At the time of the first Persian Gulf War, the Saudis, who had long since recouped all investment in needed facilities, reportedly spent only 50 cents to produce each barrel of oil. By 1999, despite having spent $2.5 billion to develop its Shaybah oil field, Saudi production outlays still lagged far behind the rest of the world. In a November 1999 speech to the Houston Forum, Saudi oil minister al-Naimi pegged his country's "all-inclusive" cost of production at less than $1.50 per barrel. As for the cost of discovering new reserves, he boasted that Saudi Arabia spent "less than 10 cents per barrel," while prospectors elsewhere were paying nearly $4.

In normal commodity markets, sellers would start there, add the infrastructure cost and the expense of transporting and marketing the goods, and take a profit, which would be determined by competition with other producers. In a totally rational world, the world's cheapest oil would be used up first, and customers would turn to more costly sources only when the least expensive ones dried up. In effect, this was what the Seven Sisters did when they controlled the market. The only difference was that the Sisters dictated prices from the well all the way through the refinery to the retail gasoline pump, and allocated the profits as they saw fit.

When OPEC members finally nationalized their own oil in the early 1970s, they were an oligopoly controlling the world's biggest pool of crude, but they had little control over prices. It was only when they learned to set and enforce quotas on each member's output that OPEC producers could become a real cartel, able to reduce oil flow in order to increase its value and drive up prices.

If and when enforced, production quotas empowered OPEC to supply the world market with just a little less oil than it could absorb at any given time. This created the impression that oil was scarce when, in reality, it was practically bursting out of the sand. OPEC's spigot-turning power enabled its member countries to issue grave warnings about oil shortages while charging prices far higher than a free market would permit. That egregious margin was and is a permanent drain on the world economy.

For most of the period this chapter covers—from the end of the first Gulf War through 1999—OPEC's members worked against each other, making the target price a moving object. All the same, as the chapter title suggests, the run-up to the millennium brought a major victory for OPEC, tightening the cartel's chokehold on the industrialized nations of the world and raising its extortion power to new and frightening heights.

SAUDIS MAINTAIN THE UPPER HAND

A decade after Desert Storm, despite all assurances to the contrary, the Gulf War had not so convincingly proved America's might as to make its repeated use virtually unnecessary. Neither had the war guaranteed the overthrow of Saddam Hussein or the re-election of George H. W. Bush.

It did, however, maintain the status quo in the Persian Gulf. Lieutenant General James Terry Scott (retired), director of the national security program at Harvard's Kennedy School of Government, told the *Boston Globe* in 2001: "It precluded Iraq from dominating the Persian Gulf, the oil production, and the populations. So the gain is 10 years of relative stability in the Gulf." And, he might have added, another ten years of Saudi preeminence on the world oil stage.

For its part, the victorious Bush administration focused on cementing its ties with the supposedly grateful Saudi regime. Some years before, when the Saudis were fearful of Iran and the Soviet Union, then-oil minister Yamani had gone to the U.S. State Department with a simple, startling offer: If the United States would guarantee to protect Saudi Arabia, the kingdom would serve as America's oil reserve. That deal, if it were ever seriously considered, had foundered on the 1973 Mideast war and the Arab oil embargo.

After Desert Storm, however, strategists proclaimed that a new arrangement was in place. "The Saudis have become one of our key bilateral relationships," Richard Haass, the top Middle East adviser on George H. W. Bush's National Security Council, told the *Wall Street Journal* in 1992.

The delusion that the grateful kingdom would be our reliable friend soon gained credence in the oil markets. "As long as we have a nice, friendly regime in Riyadh that is beholden to the United States, there shouldn't be any threat to oil prices or supplies." So said Henry Schuler, director of the energy security program at the Center for Strategic and International Studies, in a 1992 *Christian Science Monitor* article. "Nobody else matters."

The Saudis were indeed pumping a lot of oil. They had become the largest source of U.S. imports, selling the United States 1.8 million barrels a day by the early 1990s. Meanwhile, the West stayed hooked on Arab oil even as the Saudis were buying U.S. military supplies to shore up their own defenses and, possibly, to quell any potential political backlashes. In the two years after Saddam's invasion of Kuwait, Saudi Arabia purchased fully $25 billion in arms and equipment from American manufacturers.

Politicians call it "recycling petrodollars." In reality, it's just plain old influence buying. That was former CIA operative Robert Baer's charge in a perceptive 2003 book, *Sleeping with the Devil: How Washington Sold Our Soul for Saudi Crude*. Baer blasted the corrosive co-dependence of the United States and Saudi Arabia. "The way I look at things," Baer wrote, "it amounts to an indirect, extralegal tax on Americans. Saudi Arabia raises the price of gasoline, then remits a huge percentage to Washington, but not just to anyone. A big chunk goes to pet White House projects; part goes into the pockets of ex-bureaucrats and politicos who keep their mouths shut about the kingdom. And a lot goes to keeping our defense industry humming in bad times."

The Carlyle Group, a private, Washington D.C.-based, multibillion-dollar investment firm, offers a prime example of the incestuous relationships that link Washington insiders, America's business interests, and the oil-producing nations. Carlyle's roster of current advisers and alumni—luminaries like former Secretary of State James A. Baker III, former President George H.W. Bush, former Secretary of Defense Frank Carlucci, former Securities and Exchange Commission Chairman Arthur Levitt, former Clinton White House Chief of Staff Thomas "Mack" McLarty—reads like a who's who of Washington VIPs. The firm's usually clandestine business dealings, many involving the defense industry and government contracts doled out by politicians, have long raised ethical eyebrows.

In October 2004, the group again found itself in an uncomfortable public spotlight. At issue was Carlyle's involvement in a consortium seeking to land business collecting Iraqi debt owed to Kuwait.

The proposed deal revolved around the management of $27 billion of claims against Iraq. What gave the arrangement an especially unpleasant aroma was the involvement of Baker. At the time, Baker was serving as President George W. Bush's special envoy overseeing the Iraqi debt negotiations.

When the news leaked and Baker's potential conflict of interest became known, Carlyle quickly denied that it had ever given final approval to the Kuwaiti deal and promptly withdrew from any participation whatsoever. A Carlyle spokesman admitted that the firm had been considering helping the consortium, but claimed it would have made certain that Baker did not benefit from any of the Kuwaiti business. However, that belated attempt at reassurance missed the point. Given its list of heavyweight political advisers and its business dealings with Middle Eastern oil-producing states and their citizens (Carlyle maintained business ties to the Bin Laden family prior to the events of September 11, 2001), Carlyle and firms like it invite an almost inevitable collision between oil industry priorities and the greater national interest.

Against this backdrop of petrodollar recycling, the U.S. domestic oil industry was once again deep in the doldrums in the early 1990s. By mid-1992, the American Petroleum Institute reported that domestic production had plummeted to 1961 levels. Drilling-related jobs had been reduced by half in the preceding decade. Exploring for costly new crude was seen as so futile that only 596 drilling rigs were working in June of 1992, down from a peak of 4,530 in 1981. Oil executives were clamoring for a national energy policy and lobbying to revoke a 1986 tax on drilling. Thomas Coffman, president of the Texas Independent Producers and Royalty Owners Association, told the *Austin American-Statesman* that new technology could unlock 33 billion barrels of supposedly inaccessible oil still lurking in the reservoirs of Texas, but would not happen without a national energy policy designed to aid industry.

Yet the big international oil companies were flush with cash. Consumer advocates pointed out that whereas prices at the pump rose in lockstep with world oil prices during the bubble created by the Gulf War, they took a lot longer to come down after the bubble popped. Citizen Action, a Washington D.C.-based group, estimated that the war fattened the companies' profits by 20 to 25 percent. And Richard Kessel, executive director of the state of New York's Consumer Protection Board, complained, "Oil company profits were much better than they would have been had there been no invasion."

TROUBLE IN PARASITE

Relations within OPEC soured in the early 1990s as the world economy softened and the illusion of oil scarcity became less believable. The Saudis were strong enough to impose their policy of disciplined production and steady prices on the cartel, but it was popular only with Kuwait and the United Arab Emirates, the members with the largest proved reserves and excess pumping capacity. The other seven voting members (Iraq was suspended during its embargo) were mainly pushing for as much revenue as the traffic would bear. Inevitably, though, most of the members cheated on their assigned quotas, pumping close to their announced capacity and driving prices down. The cheaters profited only slightly more than those who played by the OPEC rules.

Complicating the situation was the potentially huge Iraqi supply that hung over the market. Eventually the United Nations embargo would end, whereupon Iraq's 3 million barrels a day would come back to market. Some day, the other members knew, they would have to cut their quotas to make room for it. More worrisome still was the estimated 6 million barrels a day Iraq was capable of producing at full capacity. Any member who actually cut back before that point would be punished by a further cut when the time came. So most of them kept pumping away. Thus, OPEC had little control over its output.

The sluggish world economy was undercutting demand for petroleum products. By its own logic, the cartel should have been cutting production quotas, but that would have been a futile gesture since most members kept exceeding the quotas already in place. Non-OPEC producers weren't even pretending to reduce output. Those factors combined to drive the price well below the OPEC target of $21. By 1993, when the price averaged only $16, OPEC's total oil revenues had plummeted by two-thirds from their 1980 peak.

The cartel's five largest member nations were all in debt, unable to trim their spending to fit their diminished treasuries. Saudi Arabia, the biggest spender of all, was particularly strapped for cash.

The Saudis had created the world's most lavish welfare state, imposing no taxes on their citizens but offering interest-free home loans, free education and health care, and even cut-rate telephone service. The kingdom watered the desert to export strawberries to France and tulips to Holland. By 1992, it was producing 4 million tons of hugely expensive wheat, 60 percent of it for subsidized export. It even set up commercial fish farms in the desert.

The Saudis had agreed to pay $55 billion toward the cost of the Persian Gulf War. But with its oil revenues decimated, massive spending was imperiling the kingdom's financial health. The kingdom's total cash reserves, which rocketed to $120 billion in the early 1980s, had plunged to $15 billion by 1994.

By now, the Saudis also had to deal with a new occupant of the White House, one not as pliable as his predecessor. As a candidate, Bill Clinton had promised to honor the reality that "some countries and cultures are many steps away from democratic institutions." But he had also pledged to be much more aggressive than Bush in promoting worldwide democracy, which the wary Saudis saw as a threat. Their suspicion deepened when the Clinton administration began pressing King Fahd to make good on the war payments and also on a promise to buy $6 billion worth of aircraft from U.S. airplane manufacturers Boeing and McDonnell Douglas.

Over the years, Saudi Arabia had acquired a number of powerful Washington friends to buffer demands from the White House. It was customary for the Saudis to place former U.S. ambassadors to Riyadh on retainer. They lavished contracts and donations on numerous Washington institutions and organizations. In other words, the Saudis bought and paid for an infrastructure of influence. "Every Washington think tank, from the supposedly nonpartisan Middle East Institute to the Meridian International Center, took Saudi money," wrote Baer, based in part on his direct observations in the Middle East during twenty years with the CIA. "Washington's boiler room—the K Street lobbyists, PR firms, and lawyers—lived off the stuff. So did its bluestocking charities, like the John F. Kennedy Center for the Performing Arts, the Children's National Medical Center, and every presidential library of the last 30 years."

The Saudi banks were loaded with debt, and outside experts said the government would have to borrow at least $30 billion on its own account from international lending institutions over the next few years. The guest workers who handled the chores that Saudis disdained were sending home $16 billion a year, a chronic drain on the Saudi economy. But the government would not cut spending, especially the billions funneled every year to the extended royal family. Moreover, the Saudi princes feared that any attempt to cut subsidies for water, gasoline, electricity, and domestic air travel would trigger a backlash from their already restive subjects.

All told, the OPEC parasite was suffering lean times. The pickings would get even slimmer before its victims charged to the rescue once again. The cartel's 1993 attempt to crack down on quota breaking ended with the total quota being lifted to 24.5 million barrels a day—an implicit acceptance of a good measure of the excess production. Meanwhile, with the world economy recovering from recession and demand for petroleum products rising, the price of oil actually drifted upward from $16 a barrel to a range of $18 to $20, but it was still short of the $21 target price. Then, in 1996, when the members were collectively pumping 26 million barrels a day, or 1.5 million over the quota, the looming problem burst into crisis: Iraq, as feared, returned to the market.

Lifting its six-year embargo in May 1996, the United Nations agreed to let Iraq exchange some of its oil for food to relieve the suffering of the Iraqi people. As much as 700,000 barrels a day would soon be added to the already saturated market, portending a sharp price drop unless other OPEC members agreed to cut their own production levels by an equivalent amount. But no one wanted to sacrifice any revenue. Thus, when OPEC members gathered in Vienna in June, executives of international oil companies courted the Iraqi oil minister while the other delegates haggled bitterly over quotas that most of them knew would be violated in any case.

The prospects may have been grim for OPEC and the fantasy of oil scarcity, but they were bright indeed for the world's economy. If the renewed flow of Iraqi oil could not be offset, many experts predicted that the price would quickly drop back to $16, a boon to consumers everywhere. And since the U.N. had authorized Iraq to sell $2 billion worth of oil every 180 days, a falling price would mean that more barrels would have to be sold to reach that figure. The added supply would push down the price still further, in a serendipitous cycle that would save consumers around the world billions of dollars.

Despite the obvious negative implications for OPEC, the members still could not agree to cut their quotas. "OPEC may still be alive, but it is quite impotent," Nordine Ait-Laoussine, the former oil minister of Algeria who had become an international oil consultant, told the *New York Times*.

Reverting to its role as the cartel's swing producer, Saudi Arabia cut back its own output to make up for much of the resumed flow of Iraqi oil. It leaned on Kuwait and the United Arab Emirates to soak up the rest. Demand for oil began to pick up as an economic boom roared through Asia. A short year later, the price was back up to $20 a barrel. Meeting in Indonesia in 1997, OPEC felt secure enough to agree on a full 10 percent increase in its quota, to a total of 27.5 million barrels a day.

Once again, the increase wasn't quite what it seemed. In reality, the cartel was only legalizing quota cheaters, because OPEC members were already pumping 28 million barrels a day. But the Saudis were confident that the market was firming, and they wanted to raise their own production from 8 million barrels a day to 8.76 million. They knew that most of their fellow members were pumping near presumed capacity, and thus were in no position to exceed higher quotas any time soon.

Elsewhere, the evidence of improving fundamentals seemed solid enough. Non-OPEC producers claimed to have no online excess capacity and no prospect of major additions in the foreseeable future. Production from promising new oil reserves discovered in the Caspian region was said to be at least ten years away. Apart from the Caspian, large discoveries outside the Gulf region were increasingly rare (small wonder, given that little had been invested in exploration).

But once again, confidence was waylaid by reality. This time, though, it was OPEC's confidence. When a financial crash swept through Asian economies and abruptly aborted the region's boom, the effects were felt around the world. Demand for oil dropped— but OPEC's members kept right on pumping. By the middle of 1998, oil was selling for $12 a barrel, a twelve-year low. A desperate OPEC tried both to police its members and to expand the conspiracy by negotiating production cutbacks from non-members. Mexico and Norway indicated they were inclined to go along. After all, every oil-producing nation had a vital interest in keeping the price up. John H. Lichtblau, chairman of the New York-based Petroleum Industry Research Foundation, predicted, "This may be the end of the old OPEC, but a wider organization may take its place that may be more effective."

Lichtblau's forecast proved premature. The cheating within OPEC continued, and Norway decided to opt out of any more production cuts. The price hit a low of $10.38 that year, with oilmen saying it would fall below $10 if OPEC could not produce genuine cutbacks of at least 1 million barrels a day. Oil at $10 a barrel would have been a bonanza for the rest of the world, of course. But for the OPEC parasite, it might have been fatal.

ARASITE FOUND

OPEC reasserted itself in the nick of time. In March 1999, collusion to control supply again became the order of the day. And in yet one more reprise of a now-familiar tune, the West lent OPEC a crucial helping hand.

Just as Lichtblau had observed, interests were converging: Almost everyone in the oil business—producing nations and big petroleum companies alike—now saw the long-term advantage of selling the optimum amount of crude at the highest possible price. For their part, the petroleum companies, tired of suffering under OPEC's thumb, were now ready for their own round of crony capitalism. Low prices had contributed to a 40 percent profit plunge in the global oil industry, not to mention the layoff of hundreds of thousands of workers in 1998. No bottom was in sight. (On the bright side, the low oil prices had stimulated growth and hiring in other industries; in fact, employment showed a net gain when all was said and done.)

Peter Gignoux, manager of the petroleum trading desk at Salomon Smith Barney in London, summed up the prevailing view. "Nothing moves markets like fear," he told the *New York Times*.

"Around the oil markets today . . . all wish OPEC good luck."

The love-fest was mutual. OPEC members were eager to be reconciled with the big companies. The nations that had once thrown out the petroleum giants were now strapped for capital to expand and modernize their industries. Irony abounded when Algeria, Iraq, Iran, Kuwait, and even Saudi Arabia began openly inviting the big petroleum companies to come back, invest money, and share in future profits, if not the equity.

As OPEC ministers gathered in 1999 for their annual meeting in Vienna, Western oilmen were slipping discreetly past bodyguards into hotel suites to meet officials from such pariah nations as Iraq, Iran, and Libya. Sure, they might be under official sanctions, said Oscar S. Wyatt, former chairman of the U.S. energy giant Coastal Corporation. But as he told the *New York Times*, "Somebody has got to keep the contact with these huge oil producers when these sanctions come off. The Americans don't know why they are doing what they've done and how to undo it. We cannot come out of this world without any friends."

Economic conditions now favored the cartel. The Asian financial crisis was easing, demand was again on the rise, and oil prices had recovered to a range of $14 to $15 a barrel. Moreover, there was "a new spirit in OPEC," its president, Algerian oil minister Youcef Yousfi, declared. Ending decades of rivalry and bickering, Saudi Arabia's Crown Prince Abdullah reached a diplomatic détente with Iran's moderate president Mohammed Khatami, agreeing that a higher price would benefit both countries and that the only way to get it was to reinforce the illusion of shortage by truly cutting production. Venezuela's new president, Hugo Chavez, renounced his country's former policy of flat-out pumping in defiance of OPEC quotas, saying it had produced nothing but a ruinous drop in prices and revenues. If new production cuts were decreed, Venezuela would stick to the rules, Chavez vowed.

Indeed, Chavez had taken it upon himself to rally the troops. With oil dipping to $8 a barrel when he came to office in 1998, the man who has been called "Fidel with oil" hopped on a plane to crisscross the world of OPEC nations, preaching internal discipline at every stop. In an interview with the *Bangkok Post*, Chavez took credit for personally engineering production cutbacks and quota keeping. "It is true," he said, "that this effort has been successful in part due to the intensity and persistence of our oil diplomacy." He went on to point out "the necessity, even the obligation, of production cuts in order to defend" the cartel members against an unacceptable economic hit.

Crucially, some key non-member nations would also answer Chavez's call to put "a fair price" on oil via production cuts. Mexico had previously approached OPEC with suggestions of cooperation, and now Norway, Oman, and Russia were interested, too. Before the Vienna meeting, Abdullah and Khatami set up phone calls and meetings among heads of state, bypassing oil ministers and technocrats. The key OPEC nations agreed on genuine cutbacks in their quotas and persuaded the four outsiders to join the deal, in effect becoming *de facto* OPEC members. The "wider organization" that Lichtblau had foreseen a year earlier was becoming a reality.

It was a stunning and devastating turn of events for the world economy. Then-current global oil production of 70 million barrels a day was being cut by 3 percent, or 2.1 million barrels. OPEC members were cutting 1.7 million barrels, with Saudi Arabia once again absorbing the lion's share of 585,000 barrels. The four non-member nations committed to production cuts totaling 388,000 barrels a day.

The pact was expected to lift oil prices to $17 or $18 a barrel. More importantly, it signaled a new sense of discipline. OPEC president Yousfi gloated, "To people who predicted the imminent demise of OPEC, I say, 'Not yet.'"

Abdullah bin Hamad Al-Attiyah, Qatar's oil minister, underscored the potential threat when he said, "The message to world oil markets from oil producers is solidarity, unanimity, and resolve."

Would the producers adhere to their quotas this time? There were open doubts that the limits would be honored, especially by Russia, which had never kept a promise to reduce production. "When the Saudis say they will cut, they do cut," observed consultant Ait-Laoussine. "The Russians are another matter."

It helped that OPEC's most powerful member, Saudi Arabia, made a threat no one could ignore. Seemingly out of nowhere, the Saudis found unused capacity. Claiming it had miscalculated the market in the 1980s and invested heavily to expand production, the kingdom announced that it actually had the capacity to pump 3 million barrels a day more than its quota. Was this mystery crude really part of the 31 million barrels pumped by the cartel in 1979? Had the Saudis been hiding 3 million barrels of slack capacity to wield as a threat when needed? Or was the extra capacity truly new? Had the Saudis, all by themselves, boosted OPEC's overall capacity to 34 million barrels? Wherever the added pumping capacity came from, the Saudis wasted no time in warning that, in case of cheating, they would open their spigots and flood the world with oil. The price would drop calamitously, and every producer would suffer. Far better, the Saudis said, to get in line and stay there.

This time, the threat worked. Illusory or not, supply would now be tightly controlled to hold the price on target. After years of chaos, OPEC had again slipped a noose around the neck of the industrialized world.

8

OLD SCHEMES FOR THE NEW MILLENNIUM

To hear assorted pundits tell it, OPEC members began 1999 so divided that cheating on production quotas would soon resume, driving down prices in the process. The pundits were wrong. In fact, OPEC was poised to greet the new millennium with resurrected schemes to refill its coffers and restore its power. It had a grand design that would help propel the price of crude to more than $57 per barrel by April 2005.

OPEC's grand design was helped along in the intervening years by a compliant friend in the White House, as well as by surging demand in China. (China overtook Japan in 2003 to become the world's second-largest oil-consuming nation behind the United States. Before fears over China's rising consumption become overblown, it is important to note that the 5.8 million barrels per day it currently consumes—only 2 million of which are imported, compared to the more than 20 million barrels of crude oil consumed per day in the United States, of which 10 million are imported—

makes up only a small part of the world's total and should be easily covered by available capacity.)

The cartel's resurgence began with the Vienna Pact of March 23, 1999. The public squabbling that had marred OPEC's previous gathering was absent, replaced by a determined and unified mood. Qatar's oil minister, Abdullah bin Hamad Al-Attiyah, put it succinctly: "1998 was a very hard year for everybody. Everybody learned the lesson, and nobody wants to see oil at $10 a barrel again." Reading between the lines, he seemed to imply that without OPEC's manipulations, oil would find its fair-market level, and that level was quite likely $10 a barrel.

Although the Qatar minister's expressed fear of $10 oil and his nod toward a more disciplined cartel only reinvigorated the skeptics, there were compelling reasons for OPEC's fresh resolve. Low oil prices had forced Persian Gulf states to curb spending at home and abroad. While Gulf state rulers feared that reduced spending on their citizens' welfare might fan political unrest, the U.S. defense industry was forced to grapple in early 1999 with the unhappy news that Saudi Arabia, the biggest American arms customer, would make no major purchases that year. Indeed, Saudi Arabia's currency, the riyal, had come under siege by speculators who hoped to force its devaluation.

Given that threat to the world's richest petrocracy, and with the Faustian bargain hanging in the balance, one can easily picture certain Washington officials and lobbyists quietly cheering as OPEC began its program to cut daily output by 1.7 million barrels. Variations on the tableau would unfold in other capitals of the oil-obsessed world: London (home to British Petroleum), Paris (Total), Moscow (Lukoil), The Hague (Royal Dutch/Shell Group), and Rome (Ente Nazionale Idrocarburi).

OPEC initially said it aimed to raise prices to a range of $17 to $20 a barrel by September 1999. It either fibbed or miscalculated. By September 30, a barrel of crude cost $25. Industry analysts were largely unperturbed and, in yet another misreading, predicted that the price would peak at $28 before tumbling back to around $23 by year's end. Instead, as 1999 ended, oil stood at $25 to $26 a barrel and was poised to move still higher in the early months of 2000. It hit $34.37, a nine-year high, on March 8.

Various factors were working in OPEC's favor to strengthen demand. The U.S. economy was continuing to expand (a remarkable nine-year run that would soon hit a brick wall), as investors both large and small were caught up in the euphoric trading of technology stocks. The United States was riding high, complacent in its unmatched clout.

To be sure, there were some jitters as the millennium approached. American officials warned that terrorists might be plotting an attack on U.S. soil, following the mid-December arrest of an Algerian man caught trying to smuggle bomb-making explosives from Canada through the state of Washington en route to the Los Angeles airport. But most revelers, though apprehensive given the repeated warnings of terrorist plots and Y2K computer-related disruptions, were undeterred on New Year's Eve.

If anything, concerns about the millennium served to boost the price of oil. Some stockpiling occurred in response to the dire predictions of disrupted commerce should older computers fail to interpret "00" as the year 2000, and instead turn their internal calendars back to 1900. "We definitely have the sense homeowners are stockpiling heating oil ahead of Y2K," one energy analyst told the *Wall Street Journal* in mid-November. At the same time, the American Petroleum Institute noted that U.S. oil inventories had declined from the previous month, despite moderate weather.

Executives and economists schooled by big oil companies never-theless saw scant reason for concern. Alan Struth, a former chief economist for Phillips Petroleum who was then with Honeywell Bonner & Moore in Houston, told Bloomberg News that the $25 price in late September was "not that big a deal" in present-day dollars. He said oil would have to climb to $72 a barrel to reach the equivalent of prices in 1982, when the U.S. tumbled into recession. (Despite the regularity with which such comparisons are made, they are patently self-serving, simply a way to explain away reality. A price is a price, and it exists in the present.)

Big oil companies were so confident the price would drop that they had kept their exploration budgets below 1997 levels. Thierry Desmarest, chairman of France's Total, declared in June 2000 that his corporation would not invest in finding any oil that would be unprofitable at $13 a barrel. "If people think the price will stay above $25 a barrel, they will significantly increase their investment in exploration and production, and in another two or three years, we will be facing another crisis," he said. In other words, Desmarest feared that significant new finds might force the price down to around $10 a barrel, as had happened in 1998, a more accurate reflection of oil's true market value than the then-current, cartel-induced spot price of about $25.

By slowing or suspending vigorous exploration in other corners of the globe, the major oil companies furthered the perception that OPEC was the "producer of last resort" and, more ominously, the "reserve of last resort"—erroneous ideas that have kept the oil-dependent masses cowed. That stance played right into OPEC's hands, as did the lack of any critical analysis of OPEC's actions. Not only would its members not face significant competition from new discoveries, but, as always, they were being allowed to operate under the radar, far removed from a critical eye. All in all, a guarantee that the world would stay hooked on OPEC oil.

THEIR STABILITY, OUR TORMENT

By March 2000, however, with gasoline averaging $1.60 a gallon in the United States, consumers demanded action. The Clinton administration quickly launched a one-man missile, Energy Secretary Bill Richardson, to pound OPEC for relief. He was Clinton's most tireless and personable—if unorthodox—diplomat. Known for his straight-to-the-point speech, alligator boots, and fancy cigars, Richardson had been an unusual but effective U.S. ambassador to the United Nations before taking the energy post. And it was Richardson—working on special assignment—who, in 1996, negotiated the release of three Red Cross workers taken hostage in Sudan, and also smoothed negotiations for the freeing of a downed pilot in North Korea. In those years, Richardson dubbed himself the "undersecretary for thugs."

So Richardson wasn't a man to hesitate about placing a direct call to the cell phone of OPEC President Ali Rodriguez-Araque of Venezuela to lobby for higher production quotas, even as the ministers gathered for their scheduled meeting in March 2000. Iranian officials waxed indignant that Richardson had the effrontery to lobby OPEC's ministers for relief—apparently miffed at the thought of giving the victim of a robbery a vote in the matter. "In the 40-year history of OPEC, there has never been a case of the Secretary of Energy calling OPEC ministers in the middle of a meeting," complained Hossein Kazempour Ardebili, Iran's representative on the OPEC board of governors. "We are very upset and disappointed at the external pressure. We don't like it." Note Ardebili's mind-set.

In effect, he was saying that OPEC's price fixing was such a divine right that the fixers' biggest consumer had to be chastised for even seeking an audience with their august selves.

In the years immediately following the first Gulf War, the United States arguably enjoyed its greatest leverage, having rescued Kuwait and shielded Saudi Arabia from Saddam Hussein's designs of conquest. If America had persuaded Saudi Arabia and Kuwait to defect from OPEC, the cartel's power could have been smashed. Instead, the United States was lulled by a booming economy and special interests, thus giving OPEC members ample time to regroup. By March 2000, America was a humble petitioner again, subject to the whims and tirades of OPEC ministers.

Nonetheless, the Saudis were willing to propose a production increase—the first of three such increases that would occur over the next four months. These were not for charitable reasons, of course, but due to political considerations. The Gulf War had proved that a U.S.-led coalition was the ruling family's best protection. Needless aggravation of such allies would be imprudent.

The Saudis proposed manipulating the price back toward $25 from its high of over $34. "We want a stable market, we want a well-supplied market, and we want a market that will be in equilibrium all the time," said Saudi oil minister al-Naimi. His soothing phrases were familiar. Saudi oil princes always don conciliatory masks in a crisis; it usually sedates Washington politicians. Al-Naimi himself is well-versed in U.S. thinking, having earned a bachelor's degree in geology from Pennsylvania's Lehigh University in 1962, followed a year later by a master's degree in geology from Stanford.

The idea of stability may sound soothing to U.S. politicians concerned with keeping voters happy. But when the Saudis are applying the notion to global oil supplies, it has nothing to do with fair prices for consumers. Quite the contrary; stability in this context is merely a way to rationalize higher prices and get powerful leaders and opinion makers to do the OPEC cartel's bidding. Because oil is such an all-encompassing commodity, its owners and their allies comprise a huge cast of favored players—big oil companies, bankers, contractors, investors, equipment makers, pipeline operators, shipping owners, and so on. This global petro-lobby can and often does sway government energy policymakers in ways not evident to the voters and the media. It's crony capitalism at its worst.

Not all the OPEC members, however, are always willing to take the roundabout "stability" route to higher prices. Iran balked at the March 2000 Saudi proposal to temper prices. Nevertheless, the Saudis prevailed, not surprisingly since they had the capacity to supply the larger amounts all by themselves.

OPEC agreed to raise the total quota by 1.45 million barrels a day. Almost immediately, Iran reversed course and went along. This lifted the total increase to 1.7 million barrels. (A continued holdout would have been both useless and expensive, since Iran would have wound up selling less oil at a lower price.) "We are going to keep and preserve our market share," declared Iran's Ardebili. "Beyond that, we will see what happens."

By these actions, the OPEC ministers consented to increase production for the first time since November 1997. President Clinton hailed the OPEC vote in March 2000 as "good news for our economy," but he also exhorted Congress to pass energy measures that would include new tax breaks for domestic oil producers.

Despite the increase in OPEC production quotas, oil prices kept rising. After dropping to $26 in the immediate wake of the March increase, they quickly resumed their climb, hitting $31 three months later. Why? For starters, it turned out that OPEC members had, as usual, been lying about their actual production. Prior to the announced increase, they had quietly overshot their stated quotas by a collective 1.2 million barrels a day. So what was now touted as a rise of 1.7 million barrels was really no more than 500,000 "new" barrels on the market. A second reason for soaring prices was that inventories were low and demand was rising.

The ministers had agreed to impose another automatic production increase if the price topped $28, but that clause in the pact was ignored. Richardson, the goat of the March meeting, held his peace, possibly distracted by the uproar over nuclear weapons data that had disappeared from a vault at the Energy Department's Los Alamos National Laboratory in his home state of New Mexico.

When the OPEC members met again in June 2000, they agreed to another increase of 708,000 barrels. This time, Iran went along quietly, condescendingly praising Washington for its passivity and promising to endorse further automatic increases if the price rose again. "We had a very good atmosphere this time," said Bijan Namdar Zanganeh, Iran's petroleum minister. "In our last meeting, all the members complained of U.S. intervention. We didn't feel external political pressure this time."

Zanganeh also spoke of the goal of stability, using language that seemed as cagey as it was smooth. "We are looking for a stable price, not necessarily high or low," he said. "If the market needs more oil, we will produce it. We have an automatic mechanism for it." He refused to describe this mechanism other than to say it was a gentlemen's agreement.

Gentlemanly or not, the new collusion was aimed at keeping oil-dependent nations in the thrall of OPEC.

BRAZEN BEHAVIOR IN CARACAS

When the June production increase also turned out to be a mirage, the markets predictably pushed prices up again. With the price above $32 as the summer wore on, the Saudis announced a unilateral production increase of 500,000 barrels a day. Apologists raved. "They were getting really antsy about prices not coming down and about their inability to affect market psychology," theorized Roger Diwan, managing director of PFC Energy, a Washington consulting group. "Now, the Saudis have taken the oil bull market by the horns and pulled it down."

Not exactly. With demand for oil still on the rise and U.S. inventories at twenty-four-year record lows, the dip in prices occasioned by the Saudis' action disappeared. By mid-August, oil was right back up to $31.80.

Inevitably, the price of oil became an issue in the 2000 presidential campaign. The Republican candidate was George W. Bush, governor of Texas and son of former President George H. W. Bush, the man who had thrown OPEC a lifeline in 1986 and then saved the Saudis from Saddam Hussein in 1991. Now, Bush the younger was telling voters he could be more effective than Bill Clinton—and, by extension, the Democratic candidate Al Gore—in persuading OPEC to be less greedy.

Clinton resumed his public lobbying for another OPEC quota increase. But still the price rose, hitting a ten-year high of $37.20 after Labor Day. OPEC responded by holding the first summit meeting of its heads of state in twenty-five years. The meeting, which took place in Caracas forty years to the week from the cartel's founding, had been called in late July by the newly re-elected Venezuelan president, Hugo Chavez.

In calling the summit, Chavez made no secret that he wanted

strictly enforced production restrictions to keep the price of oil high. In his inaugural address, he regaled his assembled OPEC brethren by comparing the price of a barrel of oil to the price of a barrel of shampoo, Coca-Cola, mineral water, and assorted other consumer products. To no one's surprise and everyone's delight, Chavez concluded that oil was certainly cheap at the price. But speaking with less candor and more duplicity, the heads of state stressed OPEC's willingness to hold a "constructive dialogue" with the industrialized nations to stabilize oil prices.

If that sounded like an attempt to blame the victim for the crime, that's exactly what OPEC intended to do. It was at this summit meeting that Saudi Arabia's Crown Prince Abdullah complained of OPEC being "unfairly blamed" for high oil prices. He said Western governments should "share the sacrifice" by cutting their taxes on oil—a nonstarter that would have increased gasoline consumption, extended dependence on fossil fuels, and, not coincidentally, fattened OPEC's purse. Whether Abdullah's comments were naïvely off the mark or brilliantly disingenuous, his primary aim was to prolong dependence on Saudi oil.

Meanwhile, OPEC President Ali Rodriguez-Araque, a lawyer and former leftist guerrilla who was also Venezuela's minister of energy, said the industrial nations should increase their refinery capacity in order to bring down oil prices, advice that conveniently ignored the fact that OPEC's artificially induced shortage was the reason for the heightened tensions.

The meeting approached farce—or at least a truly astonishing display of gall—when the heads of state insisted that the international treaty on global warming include a clause to compensate OPEC for any decline the accord might cause in the demand for oil. The treaty—provisions of which were due to be hammered out at a November conference in The Hague—threatened to drive "a stake into the heart of oil production, especially in member countries," said Nigerian president Olusegun Obasanjo. If the world adopts policies "explicitly intended to dramatically reduce the consumption of fossil fuels," he complained, "oil exporting countries would stand to lose more than $20 billion of revenue by 2010."

The best that could be said about this parade of self-serving finger-pointers is that they were spewing out a pile of rubbish in some misguided effort to fill their national treasuries (or perhaps to line some pockets). By this line of reasoning, if an embezzler is apprehended, his victims should be forced to make up for his lost income.

But it was also at this meeting that Crown Prince Abdullah pledged more unilateral production increases, saying Saudi Arabia was "willing and ready" to pump any amount of oil "necessary to stabilize the world oil market." That finally impressed the markets. The price tumbled to just over $30 the next day, and then hovered for several months in a range of $27 to $29.

The first half of 2001 brought a slowdown in the global economy, accompanied by a lessening demand for oil. But OPEC successfully tweaked its supply, keeping it just under what the market could absorb and keeping the price between $25 and $29. And when Iraq briefly pulled its 2.5 million barrels a day off the market to protest a United Nations decision on the Oil-for-Food program, the Saudis pumped just enough extra oil to offset the deficit and hold the price steady.

Oddly enough, the victims of this conspiracy seemed to welcome it. Oil prices were "high yet stable," according to PFC Energy's Diwan. The OPEC nations, he said, "have convinced the market of their ability" to hold the price steady, as if stability alone were worth the huge premium OPEC is able to extract.

Nor did the newly elected George W. Bush, campaign rhetoric notwithstanding, appear alarmed. A friend of the oil industry, he chose to continue the family tradition: Far from leaning on OPEC to restrain its greed, he very nearly praised the cartel as it curbed production to keep oil prices high. "It's very important for there to be stability in a marketplace," Bush said during his first summer in office. "I've read some comments from the OPEC ministers who said this was just a matter to make sure the market remains stable and predictable."

The new president seemed willing to accept the stability of a monopoly's manipulated price—despite the worldwide drain of funds that could have been much more productively invested—so long as prices didn't spiral to unspecified heights. Even when the Bush administration was startled by OPEC's decision in July 2001 to cut crude production a third time, the response was timid. White House officials only expressed their surprise; they did not ask for relief in a meeting with Venezuelan energy officials on July 27, according to *Platt's Oilgram News*. President Bush merely observed that "any rise in energy prices would hurt" the U.S. economy.

The new vice president, former Halliburton chief executive Dick Cheney, agreed with oil minister Rodriguez's specious argument that a lack of refinery capacity was at fault. "The big problem in gasoline today isn't crude," the vice president said in a May 2001 interview on PBS's *Frontline*. "It's the lack of refinery capacity. We haven't built any new refineries in this country in over 20 years." Although some dissent surfaced in the new administration—chief economic adviser Lawrence Lindsey and Federal Reserve chairman Alan Greenspan recommended that the White House put pressure on OPEC to raise production—Vice President Cheney prevailed when it came to shaping the administration's energy proposals. In short order, the administration called for relaxing clean-air standards to facilitate building new refineries and expanding old ones, and President Bush urged exploration on federal lands, including Alaska's National Wildlife Refuge, thus raising environmental concerns without offering the counterweight of a viable national policy to reduce dependence on fossil fuels.

CASHING IN ON FEAR, GRIEF, AND RECESSION

The American psyche was irrevocably altered on September 11, 2001, when nineteen Arab terrorists—most of them Saudis—crashed hijacked jetliners into the Pentagon and the twin towers of New York's World Trade Center, killing more than 3,000 people. The horrors of that day are forever seared into the memories of eyewitnesses, myself included, and those who watched the calamity unfold on live television. The videotaped scenes were played again and again. From coast to coast, it seemed that everyone knew someone who had lost a relative or a friend. From that day, the United States viewed the rest of the world, and especially the Middle East, through the lens of the war on terror.

Yet the nation's response at every level—military, cultural, economic—had to be filtered through the oil market. Strategists in Washington wanted to uproot terror from all its Islamic bases, but they had to balance this goal against the danger that too broad a campaign might trigger uprisings against moderate Islamic governments. "If the United States wants a broad coalition of allies, it needs to have a narrow list of targets," Raad Alkadiri, a Middle East specialist at PFC Energy, told the *New York Times* shortly after the 9/11 attack. "If they have a broad list of targets, they will have a narrow list of allies."

Most Arab rulers were nearly as eager as the Bush administration to smash the Al Qaeda network led by Osama bin Laden, the exiled son of a prominent Saudi family. Yet rulers in the Gulf states feared being seen as too sympathetic to the United States. So key Arab leaders gave their assurances to Washington emissaries behind closed doors: They would not embargo their oil in retaliation for a U.S. attack against bin Laden, and they would supply enough oil to keep the price steady in its current, lofty range. But when Washington suggested that OPEC increase its production quotas to ease the price and help cure the recession, the cartel balked at the economic risk, fearing the kind of price collapse that followed its 1997 Jakarta decision to raise production quotas by 10 percent.

In any case, the terrorist attack's immediate impact on the oil markets was little more than a flutter. Within two weeks, the price had stabilized at just below $26. And within two months, an internal OPEC crisis gave Washington the price break it wanted. In early November, the cartel encountered a breach in its "wider alliance" with Angola, Mexico, Norway, Oman, and Russia.

Back in July 2001, with the recession still shrinking the world economy, OPEC conferees meeting in Vienna had ordered another price-propping, million-barrel cut in the daily production quota, effective September 1. But the non-OPEC partners in the coalition reacted in the old-fashioned, pre-solidarity way. They raised production, cashed in on the high price, and grabbed a bigger share of the market. It was the first real threat to the grand plan begun in 1999 to restore OPEC to preeminence.

Responding with the menace of a Mafia don, the cartel offered a deal that non-OPEC producers would be scared to refuse. Another 2 million barrels daily must be siphoned out of the market, OPEC said, and it was willing to absorb three-fourths of the cut.

But it would not act unless the non-OPEC producers held back 500,000 barrels a day of their own output. If they didn't do their part, the market would effectively be flooded, thereby touching off an open price war.

"Of course, it will hurt our economy," said Chekib Khelil, Algeria's oil minister. "But it will hurt non-OPEC producers, too. We are not trying to put anybody on their knees," he added, with a straight face. "We [just] want other producers to share in the pain if they are going to share in the benefits."

Caught in the crossfire, the markets were sent reeling as the price of oil plunged to a two-year low of $17.45 a barrel. Angola, Oman, Norway, and Mexico quickly signaled submission. But Russia, now the world's second-largest oil exporter, was openly defiant, promising only a token cut of 30,000 barrels a day.

Both sides dug in for the fight. Speaking off the record, an OPEC official played the card of political upheaval in the Middle East. The West should watch out if the oil price fell below $15, because that would force major cuts in Arab governments' welfare spending, which could spark the overthrow of friendly regimes. But Russian president Vladimir Putin, who had been pursuing better relations with Washington, riposted that a little Middle East turmoil wouldn't end the world. Russia's huge new oil fields in the Caucasus region, he boasted, could displace a destabilized Middle East as the West's alternative source of energy.

The price war lasted just a few weeks before Russia capitulated, quietly agreeing to a cut of 150,000 barrels per day. True to form, Russia could not resist a little fudging and soon began exceeding its quota, but not enough to depress the market severely. Six months later, in April 2002, with the world economy rebounding and violence escalating in the Middle East, the price was again approaching $28 a barrel.

MANY THANKS FOR ROBBING US

Although the United States had ousted the Taliban government from Afghanistan and was trying to stabilize the country and capture bin Laden, the war on terror had only just begun. Washington was rumbling with talk that the next move would be to rid Iraq of Saddam Hussein. As the talk grew louder and the Bush administration's intentions in Iraq became unmistakable, nervous jitters swept the oil markets.

Trying to maintain the charade of scarcity but still discourage competition, OPEC's ministers sought to reassure nervous markets. At their September 2002 meeting, with the price at $29.50, they left production quotas unchanged while characteristically affirming their readiness to pump more at the first sign of short supplies or price spikes. Even an attack on Iraq, they made plain, would not trigger an embargo. "If there is a supply disruption, we will satisfy the demand in the market, whatever the reason," promised Algeria's Khelil.

What no one ever seemed to notice was the emptiness of the promises. How many times had OPEC vowed to tamp down any price spikes and how many times had prices continued to spike?

Some ministers helpfully pointed out that "coordinated cheating" had effectively raised the quotas already, with member countries quietly agreeing to overproduce their assigned limits by nearly identical percentages in order to keep the price from rising too high. A spike in prices at this critical moment would have been politically embarrassing for OPEC, given its relationship with the Bush administration. By November, however, the cheating had, in OPEC's opinion, gotten out of hand; the price had drifted down to just over $25.

There were two theories to explain the drop. Leonidas P. Drollas, chief economist for the Center for Global Energy Studies, a London consulting firm, held that OPEC's members had been overproducing all year and simply wanted to make more money when the price began to drop. But another European analyst argued, off the record, that it was part of the cartel's strategy in the windup to war. "OPEC wanted to get the base price of oil down so it wouldn't spike so high if war broke out," he said.

But by January 2003, the price had climbed to $30. Commentators claimed the price was inflated by a "fear premium" of $5 to $6, a wholly self-serving, OPEC-touted rationale for excessive pricing that, this time, was supposedly induced by the prospect of a prolonged absence of Iraqi oil. Experts warned that the outbreak of war could drive the price to $35 or even $40, at least until buyers were reassured that producers were pumping enough and supply lines were working.

Clearly, the grand illusion still had its believers: Despite all the billions of barrels of oil beneath the deserts, the world somehow accepted the notion that OPEC oil was in short supply, or, more incredibly still, that the loss of Iraq's relatively meager contribution could substantially disrupt supply.

That same month, when a revolt against Hugo Chavez and his attempts to control the oil sector cut off the flow of Venezuela's oil, the cartel raised its quotas again and pledged to keep pumping as much as necessary until Venezuela came back into the market. All this was, of course, just part and parcel of OPEC's practiced stage-craft. The cartel was as effective as the mob in persuading its victims how much they needed its protection.

And, like the mob, the oil-producing nations' persuasive powers made for big paydays. At winter's end, the Saudis would be pumping 9 million barrels of oil a day at hugely elevated prices, raking in an estimated $1 billion a week. The royal clan stood to make still more once Iraq's oil vanished from the market, and they used the kingdom's spare pumping capacity to fill the gap. Nonetheless, the aggrieved princes complained that their efforts to preserve stability were underappreciated.

Before long, though, the Bush administration would smooth those ruffled royal feathers by continuing to fill the U.S. Strategic Petroleum Reserve even after oil prices had begun to rocket higher, and by also expressing its gratitude to OPEC and the Saudis for all they had done to keep the price stable. As a reward, the White House even promised to avoid tapping the reserve unless OPEC was unable to pump enough oil to meet any shortfall in supplies. Having handed OPEC a blank check to continue its manipulations, the president might just as well have handed over the key to Fort Knox.

9

IRAQ'S REAL VICTORS

After the second Gulf War, it's worth asking, who was the victor in Iraq?

Try OPEC.

In literal terms, of course, OPEC is not one of the myriad combatants now striving to control Iraq. But if you ask who is snatching victory out of chaos, my candidate is OPEC. At no cost in blood or treasure whatsoever, OPEC has effectively wound up as the *de facto* master of Iraq's oil, a vast reserve second only to Saudi Arabia's—and one that the Saudis must effectively control if they are to maintain their own grip on pricing. That Iraq's oil is constantly sabotaged is no big problem for OPEC. It merely gives the cartel another way to confuse bettors in the global shell game that is the oil business.

The measure of this coup is that the cartel, faced with ever increasing numbers of non-OPEC competitors and treading a path of declining market share and lessening influence over world prices, has nonetheless managed to retain enormous clout. It has done so, in large part, by getting a grip on the oil of Iraq, its recently returned eleventh member nation. OPEC has demonstrated its political power and ability to control prices in a region containing most of Earth's oil reserves. By no coincidence, world oil prices have risen more than 90 percent (at this writing) since the invasion of Iraq, reaching levels never before recorded.

How this happened is a tale of American illusion, Iraqi hope, and OPEC opportunism. The story opens with the U.S. invasion in 2003. When the air war started on March 20, traders were convinced that Saddam would be defeated in short order and that Iraq's oil structure would suffer little damage.

Indeed, the first battle was blessedly brief. Sweeping north from Kuwait, American and British troops overcame a blinding sandstorm and pushed rapidly toward Baghdad, while Iraqi forces melted into the civilian population. It took the coalition forces only twenty-six days to seemingly conquer a country 80 percent the size of France. America's second, slimmed-down Iraqi war was hailed as a triumph for the Rumsfeld doctrine—named for U.S. Secretary of Defense Donald Rumsfeld—of using minimal troop strength and maximum firepower. Iraqis were expected to be ecstatic about their liberation from a demonic dictator, and some citizens of Baghdad did gleefully join the victorious troops in toppling a giant statue of Saddam Hussein.

A month later, outfitted as a Navy fighter pilot and beamed around the world speaking from an aircraft carrier, President Bush declared victory in Iraq. At that euphoric moment, the price of oil was still around $28 a barrel. But in the next few weeks, it shot up by more than $2.

Did oil's price levitation have anything to do with OPEC's vote on April 24 to slice 2 million barrels a day off of its production as of

June 1? Nonsense, said the Saudi oil minister, Ali al-Naimi, who stressed that the cartel would do everything it could to get the price back down to around $25 a barrel. But even though Iraqi production was beginning to show signs of life, oil prices remained near the top of the price band. Still, at their June meeting, OPEC delegates said they saw little reason to change the cartel's target production ceiling of 25.4 million barrels a day.

Al-Naimi's assurances notwithstanding, over the next few months, the price never came within shouting distance of $25, and stayed instead in the $30-to-$32 range. It drifted back near $28 in September, still above the supposedly maximum target and also considerably higher than the below-$20 price many observers had expected following the speedy end of the Iraq war. As it happened, the price failed to decline for a very good reason: OPEC never took any steps to increase production.

A failure to quickly resume Iraqi exports as expected also contributed to the price pressure. U.S. officials had assumed that exports would begin to flow within weeks after the fighting stopped, and that rising oil revenues would pay for much of Iraq's recovery and reconstruction. As the whole world knows by now, that official optimism was way overblown. To the surprise of the Americans, Iraq's oil industry turned out to be in abysmal shape.

When Iraq's oil revenues plummeted during the six years of the United Nations-imposed embargo, Saddam bemoaned the hardship placed on his country's citizens, especially the children. Responding to his pleas, the U.N. agreed to an Oil-for-Food exchange starting in 1996 that allowed Iraq to issue vouchers for limited purchases of oil by foreign buyers. The money received was supposed to be used for humanitarian aid. Instead, Saddam saw a colossal business opportunity.

According to a recent CIA report, Saddam personally chose the voucher recipients, including at least four U.S. companies (Bayoil, ChevronTexaco, El Paso, and ExxonMobil) and Texas oilman Oscar S. Wyatt, who alone received 74 million barrels. (Wyatt, who had once criticized the shortsightedness of those who ignored outlaw nations, apparently resold the oil at a profit of $23 million.)

Various European oil companies got in on the deal, too, and all of Saddam's chosen blockade busters made so much money that he demanded large kickbacks. Investigators believe Saddam used the cash windfall to buy an array of military equipment and build more palaces for his pleasure and enjoyment. So much for the starving children.

For years Saddam had been plundering Iraqi oil industry profits, leaving such decay that any return to normal output was expected to require billions of dollars of new investment. The problems were compounded when the U.S. Army failed to prevent postwar looting, thus enabling thieves to strip the oil infrastructure of practically everything that could be carried. Worse still, Iraqi insurgents began targeting the industry and its workers, both foreign and domestic. Day after day, saboteurs assassinated oil officials, destroyed generators, torched wells, and blew up pipelines. No sooner did repair crews restore one rupture than attackers struck elsewhere, grinding away at what was left of the infrastructure. Exports were repeatedly slowed or stopped. In Iraq itself, once-abundant gasoline no longer sold for $1 a gallon—assuming there was any to be sold. By September of 2003, Iraq was exporting just 1.8 million barrels a day, compared to the 2 million barrels sold under the Oil-for-Food program before the war, and a far cry from the 6 million barrels that would be needed to meet the Bush administration's pre-war forecast of postwar Iraqi revenues.

A WHIP FOR THE TORMENTOR

It was hoped that the situation would be temporary. It might get worse before it got better, American officials thought, but surely, with the help of the smartest Texas oilmen that dollars could buy, the industry would soon be back on track.

Regardless of the correctness of their assumptions, now was the time to strike a blow at OPEC itself. The U.S. strategists could have done the world a great service by persuading Iraq to disavow this conspiracy against the world economy. With the United States in total control of Iraq's oil industry, it could have and should have seized the moment to rein in OPEC. All it would have taken was a decree from Paul Bremer, the coalition viceroy, removing Iraq from the cartel and thus depriving OPEC of the leverage provided by Iraq's vast reserves. That bold step would have weakened the cartel's future market power considerably.

But the Bush administration was leery of any action so overt (and so seemingly reasonable). It shied away from any admission that the war had, even in part, been fought to gain control of a resource vital to the U.S. national interests and beneficial to the world economy. Bush officials insisted that nothing could be further from the truth. The president was adamant that he acted only to abolish tyranny, spread the blessings of democracy, and wage the war on terrorism.

To help with the mission, former Shell Oil CEO Phil Carroll was named chairman of a committee that was supposed to give nothing more than advice to the Iraqi Oil Ministry. Declaring himself no proconsul, Carroll said the committee would have no veto over any Iraqi decisions, particularly those involving contracts to restore and develop the industry. As for the oil cartel, Carroll promised no unseemly pressure from Washington.

Nevertheless, the Shell alumnus is said to have personally encouraged the U.S.-appointed Iraqi oil minister to get involved with OPEC. He hinted at his true position on the morning of May 29, 2003, when he told a CNBC interviewer: "Iraq was a founding member of OPEC, and the truth is that Iraq will find its way into OPEC." And as the April 2005 *Harper's* related, the Bush administration and the American oil industry actually wanted Iraq to resume an active role in OPEC. Indeed, no lesser light than Vice President Dick Cheney pushed for an OPEC-friendly policy for Iraq, according to Edward Morse, whom the magazine described as "one of the men to whom Washington turns to obtain the views of Big Oil." Morse, a veteran in the energy sector whose experience spans business, government, academia, and publishing, is currently executive advisor to Hess Energy Trading Company. He is also, *Harper's* said, a close associate of Rob McKee, Carroll's successor in Iraq.

Why would the administration favor OPEC over the economic interests of U.S. citizens? Because, as *Harper's* explained, the State Department has gone out of its way to accommodate Saudi Arabia and Russia, both of which benefit from peddling their oil at outrageously high OPEC prices. It's no secret that the Saudis are primarily interested in maximizing their oil profits, and they can't do that if Iraq floods the market with its oil. So to maintain their control over pricing, they have to keep a lid on production. Getting Iraq back into the OPEC circle was one way of doing that. Promoting insurgency could be another way of keeping Iraq from reaching its full potential as an oil producer if the bloodletting scares off needed foreign investment.

Disturbing though it may be to contemplate, one has to wonder if it is just coincidence that many of the Iraqi insurgents have ties to Saudi Arabia. James Bennet, writing in the May 15, 2005, *New York*

Times, expressed puzzlement over the goals and strategy of the insurgents, noting that they have shown "little interest in winning hearts and minds among the majority of Iraqis, in building international legitimacy, or in articulating a governing program or even a unified ideology or cause beyond expelling the Americans. They have put forward no single charismatic leader, developed no alternative government or political wing, displayed no intention of amassing territory to govern now." Indeed, the insurgents seem bent on obliterating popular support by the indiscriminant murder of civilians. Hardly a winning strategy for gaining control of the country.

But perhaps the goal is not to gain control of the country, just to destabilize it. Could it be that, under the guise of jihad against Americans, an all-out effort is being waged to keep Iraq in turmoil in order to thwart normal economic development and keep oil-producing capacity at a bare minimum? Might the ultimate goal be to maintain the OPEC status quo so as not to jeopardize existing producers, notably Saudi Arabia and Kuwait? The Saudis have been notably silent on the subject of the insurgency.

Dick Cheney basically runs U.S. energy policy, says Morse. The vice president "thinks that security begins by . . . letting prices follow wherever they may." Even, apparently, if those trumped-up prices threaten the economic stability of the United States. So Iraq was allowed to take its old seat as a voting member of OPEC. This was more than just another token of the Bush administration's esteem for the cartel, it was one more example of the oil-dependent Western victim gladly handing a whip to its tormentor.

None of this, of course, detracts from the heroic efforts of our young men and women in uniform. Far from it, for they are constantly in harm's way because of the continuing insurgency. By and large, they have performed with enviable excellence in a hellish situation.

OPEC wasted no time in cracking that whip across the backs of oil consumers. When the oil price briefly dipped below $28 a barrel, the ostensible top band of the target range, the cartel swung into action. At its September 2003 meeting, OPEC pared back its production quota by 3.5 percent, thus nudging the price back above the ceiling.

The ministers claimed they were only looking ahead to future market conditions, and cited rising non-OPEC oil production in the face of a sluggish world economy. "We saw more supply than the market needed," said Obaid bin Saif al-Nasseri, chief delegate of the United Arab Emirates. "Any lack of action could have been very negative for prices."

Many outside observers had a different take. Mehdi Varzi, a private energy consultant in London, said that OPEC was flexing its muscles. He said OPEC's message to Washington was clear: "You can send a delegation to OPEC, but we control the oil price."

Even Anibal Octavio da Silva, head of the non-OPEC Angolan delegation, observed dryly that "forecasts of supply and demand suggest there is no need for an immediate cut in supply."

Needed or not, OPEC continued to pinch consumers. In the months that followed, OPEC would reduce the quota two more times, withdrawing a total of 3.9 million barrels a day from world production.

A CONSPIRACY BUFF'S DREAM

Ever generous when it comes to the oil cartel, the Bush administration registered no protest. In fact, as mentioned, it made another huge contribution to OPEC by promising not to push prices down by pumping oil from the nation's Strategic Petroleum Reserve

(SPR), an enormous stash of more than 600 million barrels that constitutes the world's biggest supply of emergency crude oil.

The reserve oil is buried in 3,000-foot-deep salt caverns along the Gulf of Mexico. Workers shoot water at high pressure into the caverns to make holes in the salt for storing oil barrels. Geologic pressures make the barrels leak-proof, and maintenance is cheap— only 10 percent of the cost of storing oil in surface tanks. Oil companies love the SPR, and no wonder: When they fill the reserve with oil pumped from federal land, the government waives its normal royalty fees, thus boosting the companies' profits.

The SPR was conceived after the 1973 Arab oil embargo as a significant diplomatic tool and embargo-stopper. Only presidents are allowed to tap it, customarily when a major oil shortage causes runaway prices and a genuine national crisis. But instead of drawing out oil from the SPR, President Bush did the opposite: Stubbornly adhering to a plan conceived in the aftermath of 9/11, he increased the reserve from 611 million barrels to 700 million at the same time OPEC was cutting output quotas, a move over which Michigan Senator Carl Levin and other critics could only shake their heads. Calling the president's actions "illogical and counterproductive," Levin went on to suggest to an Associated Press reporter that "the administration should listen to common sense."

President Bush's action invited U.S. oil companies to divert domestic oil from the market to the stockpile, and they quickly did so. As a result, Levin pointed out, the policy not only pushed oil prices still higher as the market supply tightened even further, but it also increased American dependence on foreign oil because U.S. companies had to go abroad to fill the gap created by pumping domestic oil into Louisiana salt caverns. Not to mention that salting away domestic oil at rising prices unnecessarily worsened the federal budget deficit, since U.S. oil companies were effectively selling their oil to the government at inflated, cartel-determined prices well above what would have prevailed in a free-market environment. It was the mother of all boondoggles.

As the United States struggled to mop up the Iraqi resistance, fears rose around the world that the conflict might again disrupt the global oil supply. Accordingly, the price climbed still higher, topping $35 a barrel, thus increasing suspicions that OPEC had tacitly raised its target prices. Although the cartel had once pledged to increase production to force the price down if it topped $28, Saudi Arabia's al-Naimi arrived at OPEC's meeting in March 2004 with a plan to cut another 1 million barrels a day of production. He again blamed speculators for the high price, and pronounced that "throwing more oil on the market would be destructive for everybody." Al-Naimi didn't say so, but his definition of "everybody" clearly didn't include the world's long-suffering consumers, who had to scrimp on other needs and wants just to cover their increasingly inflated energy costs.

Predictably, the price of oil became an issue in the 2004 presidential campaign. During the primaries, Senator John Kerry hammered at President Bush for not "putting pressure on OPEC to increase the supplies," and said the U.S. should "not allow those countries to undermine the economies of the world." White House spokesman Scott McClellan remarked blandly that the president's focus was on "the importance of letting the market determine the prices"—as if President Bush, an oilman himself, didn't understand that OPEC, not the market, was setting the price.

According to one nameless OPEC official interviewed by the *New York Times*, the administration calculated that overt pressure on the cartel might backfire, as it had when Bill Richardson, now governor of New Mexico, ruffled OPEC feathers with his aggressive diplomacy. "The administration knows this history," the official said, adding that OPEC officials "are telling them, 'Keep your mouth shut.'"

The administration's kowtow to the Tony Sopranos of petroleum did not pay off. In late March, the same official admitted that the cartel had toyed with the idea of increasing production, but shelved the discussion rather than risk being seen as doing favors for Washington.

The *omerta* policy made for awkward sound bites. "We've made it clear that we're not going to beg for oil," Energy Secretary Spencer Abraham declared bravely when he appeared before the Senate Armed Services Committee in late March 2004 to explain the Bush administration's stance toward OPEC. Of course, there was no need to beg, not when the administration had already given OPEC the key to the vault.

That same month, crude oil prices topped $38 for the first time since the run-up to the 1991 Gulf War. What seemed at the time like a brief episode, more a blip than a sea change, further increased doubts about the wisdom of continuing to fill the SPR. (In retrospect, the price spike was no blip, but rather the beginning of a long-term drift to ever-higher price levels.) McClellan deflected media questions by saying that gasoline prices wouldn't even be an issue if Congress had passed the energy legislation President Bush proposed in 2001. Shortly thereafter, the administration commended OPEC for helping to stabilize prices, and promised not to tap the Strategic Petroleum Reserve so long as OPEC could supply what was needed.

Accommodating OPEC had become an inbred habit. But beyond conveying the clear message that we would willingly tolerate OPEC's price manipulation, President Bush tossed away the perfect chance to use his bully pulpit to protest against high prices. If he had just had the presence to say, "We refuse to buy oil for the reserve at more than $35 a barrel," he could have sent a strong and effective signal of condemnation against the cartel's price manipulations.

Meanwhile, America's underappreciated role as OPEC's protector was neatly symbolized when some thirty-six U.S. Navy and Coast Guard warships were dispatched to ports and oil terminals in the Persian Gulf, safeguarding the 16 million barrels of oil that pass through the Gulf every day. Amy Myers Jaffe, an analyst at the James A. Baker III Institute for Public Policy at Rice University in Houston, estimated that the U.S. military was spending up to $80 million a day to guard OPEC's oil against terrorist attack—another huge subsidy from American taxpayers, and one that added insult to injury by underscoring the nation's abject obeisance to OPEC. A Navy think tank pondered still more expensive measures, including the use of sophisticated sensors and miles-long security fences, anchored in the seabed, to surround offshore oil wells and shipping terminals.

Of course, OPEC's American defenders had good reason to worry: On October 6, 2002, the French-flagged supertanker *Limburg* had been rammed by a small explosives-laden vessel while steaming along in the Arabian Sea off the coast of Yemen. The 299,000-ton *Limburg*, part of a class of ships designated as Very Large Crude Carriers, was loaded with 397,000 barrels of Saudi crude destined for Malaysia when the attack occurred. Much like the bombing of the USS *Cole* in 2000, the explosion blew open the *Limburg*'s side, killed a crew member, and dumped 90,000 barrels of oil into the sea. No one doubted that the Middle East's vital shipping lanes were vulnerable to terrorist attack.

In May 2004, the White House altered its language—and perhaps its policy—to say it was consulting its "allies" in OPEC about the possibility of more production. But al-Naimi shrugged off that idea. "A lot of things will be said in an election year," he said, before adding cryptically that "people in power" knew that the spiraling price of gasoline in the U.S. was unrelated to the supply of oil. Those versed in OPEC-speak knew this riddle presaged a price rise—not because oil was scarce, but because OPEC was playing with loaded dice. And so prices marched inexorably upward as OPEC adopted the Saudi plan to reduce quotas.

Over the crucial summer and fall of 2004, the cartel squeezed the industrialized world harder than ever. Again and again, OPEC and its oil-industry allies rammed prices higher by repeating their good-cop, bad-cop routine to invoke the specter of a world running short of oil. What the world was really running short of, however, was common sense. Plenty of oil still remained to be brought from the ground, but a kind of petro-hysteria fed disbelief. Every time the Saudis pledged to meet market demand, traders seized on some new calamity to cast doubt on the promises. The grim irony was that Americans and consumers around the world were relentlessly being forced into ever greater dependence on OPEC. In this business, as in drug dealing, the customer was always wrong; having lost the power to resist the seller's come-ons, oil users wound up helplessly addicted.

Unfortunately, the Bush administration did virtually nothing to help the U.S. kick its habit. Indeed, it increased the demand for oil by continuing to insist on filling the Strategic Petroleum Reserve. The game played on nonstop until, early in April of 2005, a barrel of oil cost a once unimaginable $57.79.

RUNNING ON EMPTY WITH A FULL TANK

In the OPEC shell game, the squeeze always begins with what sounds like a reassuring move. It was no different in May of 2004, when Ali al-Naimi announced a unilateral Saudi production increase of 800,000 barrels a day. That would bring the kingdom's output to 9.1 million barrels a day, or 1.4 million barrels under what it then insisted was its flat-out maximum capacity of 10.5 million barrels. How credible was the claim? Were the secretive Saudis doing their last-ditch best to succor an oil-starved world? Or were they really hiding vast reserves and/or capacity while pretending to be running on empty—all part of an elaborate ruse designed to manipulate a captive market of nervous suckers? The Saudis themselves would soon answer that question when, like manna from heaven, new capacity and stunning predictions of vast new reserves would appear.

For months, industry wise men had claimed that all OPEC members but the Saudis were already pumping at maximum capacity. None of their customers knew what was true and what wasn't. As explained in previous chapters, all OPEC members' figures are opaque and must be considered suspect until the cartel allows them to be verified (as the G-7 has recently proposed). Nevertheless, OPEC's claims have been accepted as conventional wisdom, thus allowing al-Naimi to speak out of both sides of his mouth. Couched in words of reassurance, his message was really a scary one, probably the effect he intended. On the face of it, ratcheted-up Saudi production seemingly meant that the world's margin of safety in oil production was now less than 2 percent, and all of OPEC's unused capacity was in Saudi Arabia. What is more, oilmen speculated that the latest Saudi increase—and all the remaining capacity—would be heavy, high-sulfur oil that is more difficult and expensive to refine than the classic light Arabian crude.

Needing another spoonful of sugar to appease sour-tongued skeptics, Saudi Arabia suddenly discovered a lot more capacity. Just days after al-Naimi's promise to raise production, unnamed Saudi officials let it be known that they were bringing a whole new field on line over the summer and increasing capacity in another field, thus raising their total pumping limit to 11.3 million barrels a day (although they would still only pump 9.1 million barrels per day). That wasn't all: It was at this point that the Saudis divulged contingency plans that could boost total output to 12 million barrels a day immediately, rising to 15 million within eighteen months if needed. At the very least, this was a remarkable development, given that the Saudis had made no mention of such large-scale expansion over the previous months. It raised an obvious question: What else were they not telling?

Al-Naimi also said he would try to lower the price by pushing for a 10 percent increase in the cartel's production limits at OPEC's June 2004 meeting, thus raising the quota by as much as 2.5 million barrels a day. Market reaction was tepid, since everyone assumed that most OPEC members, except for the Saudis, were cheating on their quotas and already pumping at their announced capacity. It was also obvious that Iraqi's besieged oil industry could not regain its pre-war output any time soon. The Saudis, of course, professed readiness to fill any Iraqi shortfall, causing the Bush administration to react with the fawning gratitude Saudi royals have long expected from their dear friends in Washington.

In another, more ominous signal that went largely ignored, al-Naimi declared himself still in favor of the cartel's $22-to-$28 target range. However, he said, "[T]he market desires a price of $35 because it's frightened of [the price rising to] $50." He then repeated his old saw that the Saudis, too, were "frightened of that price" because it might damage the world economy and propel the search for alternate energy sources. The irony was that oil had been well above $28 almost continually since December 2003, and the cartel had done its part to keep it there.

All this smog had only one purpose: Al-Naimi was preparing the way; when, not if, the Saudis judged the U.S. sufficiently sedated, the price would jump yet again. And if history were any guide, the Americans, or at least their oil companies, would smile and say, "More, sir?" After all, besides their failure to pursue viable energy alternatives, American leaders had also committed our Navy to ride shotgun on OPEC oil shipments across the seven seas, adding billions more dollars on top of the billions America was already paying for the privilege of being snookered on a colossal scale.

So what about the notion of "independence" from foreign oil? Nothing. For U.S. politicians, energy independence was both a politically correct catchphrase and the last thing on their list of serious goals, particularly when American voters felt entitled to burn more oil than four or five other countries combined. America's schizophrenic policy seemed destined to worsen. With China launched on a mega-growth binge, world oil demand was projected to jump 50 percent in the next twenty-five years. If addicted nations lacked the wit and wisdom to invent energy options, the Persian Gulf's petrocracies, squatting on two-thirds of Earth's currently known oil reserves, would be sitting prettier than ever.

ABRACADABRA FROM THE MERLIN OF THE MOMENT

In June 2004, OPEC finally agreed to raise its production quota by 2 million barrels a day. The move had little effect; the price still hovered around $35. As June ended, al-Naimi effectively confirmed suspicions that the oil price target range was being increased when he backed away from the idea of raising quotas by another 500,000 barrels in coming months. "I believe the current prices are fair," he said. "There is no reason to take any measures either to decrease or increase the production."

The price kept rising, topping $40 in July, amid dead silence from the Bush administration. What did the silence signify? Some might have guessed that things were going exceptionally well for Bush friends in both OPEC and the U.S. oil industry. Indeed, the world's largest integrated oil and gas company, ExxonMobil, wracked up record profits of $25.3 billion in 2004, 17.8 percent more than it earned in 2003. Smart investors expected nothing less from an integrated powerhouse like Exxon. Even in hard times, a seamless enterprise (from oil field to refinery to gas pump) has ample opportunity to calculate its profits creatively.

In this instance, Exxon's peers weren't far behind: America's No. 2 oil company, ChevronTexaco Corporation, reported that its second-quarter profit was more than double its year-earlier earnings. It was Chevron's best quarter since the company acquired Texaco in 2001. Wall Street seers predicted an oil industry windfall so long as the crude price stayed up.

By the end of July, the markets were jumpier still. Trouble seemed to explode wherever oil came out of the ground. Iraq's proliferating insurgents sabotaged pipelines in an effort to cut the country's oil exports by more than half. Terrorists attacked oil facilities in Saudi Arabia. Political uproar roiled Nigeria and Venezuela, reducing their oil flows. The Putin government launched a multi-billion-dollar tax claim against Russia's biggest single exporter, Yukos Oil Company, jailing its CEO and kicking down its defenses with resoled KGB boots. Driven by speculating and stockpiling, the oil price ripped past $43, up more than 41 percent in one year. Economists began alluding to another energy shock, blaming high gas and oil prices for a downdraft in U.S. economic growth. Indeed, U.S. consumer spending fell to a three-year low.

The maddening aspect in all of this was the elusiveness of truth: Was the world really running out of oil? Was OPEC secretly hiding its own enormous strategic reserve? Was it actually rigging the rhythms of supply and demand, playing ups and downs like a yo-yo, so that over the long term, oil prices always rose and consumers always paid up in mortal fear of oil famine lurking around the corner? And most galling, if these suspicions had any basis in fact, as I personally believe they did, where were the regulators, the reporters, the watchdogs, the whistle-blowers who could and should have been blowing this mega-scam sky high?

Absent any countervailing force, the oil-devouring nations simply clapped meekly whenever OPEC's Merlin of the moment stepped onstage to tap his crystal ball and issue yet another misleading prophecy. Saudi Arabia's Ali al-Naimi, for example, repeated his well-honed contention that speculators were to blame for runaway oil prices. "There is enough oil on the market," the minister said. "The fundamental things are okay. Inventories are filled and infrastructure is in a good condition."

Long conditioned to the kingdom's petro-gibberish, the market dismissed it. Traders shrugged off the claim of new capacity coming on line, and concluded that since the Saudi system was only 500,000 barrels a day below its ceiling (or so they believed), those 500,000 barrels would be low-quality crude. Even the International Energy Agency, an adviser to twenty-six industrialized nations, accepted this dubious view, warning that the lack of emergency capacity pointed to "critical" market conditions by year-end.

What happened next? As if al-Naimi had muttered "abracadabra," the price of oil jumped another dollar on the New York Mercantile Exchange, hitting $44.34 on August 3, the highest since trading began in 1983. (And that's when Indonesian oil minister Purnomo Yusgiantoro, as related in Chapter 2, got so bollixed up in "the facts" concerning whether the Saudis or some other OPEC member had any spare pumping capacity, and how quickly it could be tapped.)

Clearly, someone was having trouble keeping the story straight. A long-time observer of the Saudi dog-and-pony show couldn't help but wonder if the kingdom's reigning powers weren't playing the oil futures market. That suspicion would be reinforced in December, when al-Naimi issued back-to-back contradictory statements ahead of a meeting of OPEC members, first saying he saw no need to change production quotas, then reversing himself to opine that OPEC did need to stabilize the market.

The most damning piece of evidence, however, would come on Sunday, December 12, after oil prices shocked the manipulators by falling sharply even though the cartel had, in fact, voted to reduce production by 4 percent. Traders, it seemed, expected cartel members to ignore the guidelines just as they had so many times before. Al-Naimi responded with this astonishing prediction to *Arab News*: "Watch what happens tomorrow. I tell you prices will go up tomorrow." And on the appointed Monday, after some unusual gyrations, the price did indeed rise. The only way al-Naimi could have predicted the price move with such assurance was if he or OPEC or its agents were playing (and manipulating) the oil futures market. If it were indeed the case that OPEC can manipulate the market at will, as it apparently did on December 13, 2004, then how often has the market been manipulated by OPEC and its allies before and since? What portion of OPEC's vast resources—gleaned from hapless oil consumers—are used to manipulate prices in what is supposedly an open market?

As ever, the truth of these matters is anyone's guess. But one fact was indisputable in 2004: There was no shortage of oil. In the United States, gasoline inventories were on the rise, and even some of OPEC's apologists were beginning to suspect the truth, as when a Citigroup analyst wondered how gasoline prices could possibly be up 50 percent from the previous year when inventories showed an additional 8.3 million barrels.

ESCAPING OPEC IS ANOTHER MATTER

The explanation, if anyone would listen, was clear and simple: OPEC's members continued to pump more than their quotas—but just under what the market needed—from fields that were larger than they admitted, all while proclaiming their intent to keep the markets fully supplied.

At the same time, though, they were inflating the price by creating anxiety over a future pinch. Watching the market's blind reaction, the OPEC ministers must have been nudging each other and chortling.

With relentless gasoline-price hikes eroding other consumer spending, and the Federal Reserve pinning the blame for a slowing economy on the oil-price run-up, energy policy now loomed even larger as an issue in the presidential campaign. John Kerry, who insisted on increasing automobile mileage standards and becoming independent of Middle East oil, drew solid applause with a line in his stump speech: "I want America's security to depend on America's ingenuity and creativity, not the Saudi royal family." But some of his advisers, in the timorous oil industry tradition, were said to fear that his stand was unrealistic and might offend Arabs whose cooperation was needed. In essence, however, Senator Kerry's proposals were little different from the president's. He may have worded things differently, but he brought nothing new to the table.

Talk is cheap in the limited discourse of a presidential campaign. Nevertheless, Washington energy consultant Roger Diwan admitted that Kerry was at least heading in the right direction. "The only thing that matters," Diwan said, "is increasing fuel efficiency, because if you can't control demand, you will never have an energy policy."

PHONY HEROES OF PRICE STABILITY

Later in August, the Paris-based International Energy Agency added to the confusion surrounding OPEC's public pronounce-ments about new fields and increased capacity. An IEA spokesman said the cartel was striving so hard to contain prices by raising output that its "sustainable spare production capacity" had shrunk to 600,000 barrels a day. If accurate, the IEA figures meant OPEC customers were left with a supply buffer of less than 1 percent, compared with about 8 percent in 2002. If accurate, the IEA figures also meant the Saudis had been blowing smoke in May when they said they would increase capacity to 11.3 million barrels per day over the summer, much less that they could bump it up to 12 million if necessary.

At about the same time, apparently unfazed by the confusion over their pronouncements, the Saudis said they were now pumping 9.3 million barrels a day. They pledged to tap surplus capacity of 1.3 million barrels if required—still well below the previously advertised 11.3 million barrels. The price of near-term oil futures contracts kept rising, hitting a record $48.70 a barrel in New York on August 19, as traders again questioned the validity of Saudi claims.

As the oil price skittered upward, OPEC's allies cheerily interpreted it as a more or less heroic struggle for market stability. Rising prices in the face of Saudi reassurances, even though OPEC had continued to resist any formal change in output ceilings, were "a very bullish sign from the market," according to Thomas Bentz, senior oil analyst with BNP Paribas in New York. "Everyone knows OPEC's reached full capacity."

The world's media joined the chorus. A long article in the *New York Times* on August 14 painted OPEC as a helpless giant, unable to pump enough oil to keep the price below its $28 ceiling, but also afraid that a post-Hussein Iraq would pump too much oil and bring prices down.

Had anyone looked closely at the International Energy Agency's August report, they would have found reason to be less worried about shortages. The IEA projected world oil demand at 84 million barrels a day, and said that total world output in July was already 83.5 million barrels. It said OPEC members were pumping 29 million barrels daily and could add 500,000 more, while non-OPEC exporters would increase their daily capacity by 1.2 million barrels. In addition, industrial nations had emergency reserves totaling 1.4 billion barrels, not to mention the private, uncounted stores scattered around the world and the stockpiles maintained by oil companies. The total of 4 billion barrels would provide a cushion well beyond the official estimate of five-and-a-half months. In sum, the world could expect spare pumping capacity of about 1.4 percent—tight, but nowhere near scary. And if you added the newly announced Saudi capacity, the excess came to 2.8 percent. Where was the crisis?

PLAYING THE CONSUMPTION CARD

A cool, brief touch of realism intruded on the markets on August 25, 2004, when the U.S. Energy Information Administration reported that American drivers had responded to the sky-high price of gasoline by using less of it than expected over the summer. Gasoline inventories totaled more than 205 million barrels nation-wide, near the top of a five-year range. The oil price dropped by some $2 a barrel in response to this show of consumer discipline.

Even if Americans cut back on their gasoline consumption more by necessity than choice, the summer of 2004 provided a tantalizing glimpse of what the administration might have accomplished with a clear, focused policy to rein in oil consumption.

Refusing to stock the petroleum reserve with any oil priced above $35 a barrel, for instance, would have reduced daily demand by 100,000 barrels. That may not sound like much when total U.S. demand is more than 20 million barrels a day, but prices at the margin are highly sensitive, so such a reduction would have cooled the market and cut the price by far more than its proportions would indicate.

The opposite happened, of course. The Bush administration couldn't find its tongue, and prices went up, up, up after early-fall market reports pointed to a 380,000-barrel-a-day decline in OPEC's August output.

Hold on a minute. Hadn't the cartel made loud pledges to boost production in order to bring prices down? Yes, but pledges were one thing, and follow-through was quite another. OPEC producers could barely count their windfall profits.

When OPEC ministers finally agreed to raise production quotas, traders shrugged it off as a symbolic formality. They stuck fast to their credo that the cartel, which was now producing roughly 30 million barrels a day, had hardly any unused capacity left and no control over the market.

One analyst suggested that OPEC ministers were deluding themselves about their ability to impact oil prices. And economist Leo Drollas, at the London Center for Global Energy Studies, predicted that the OPEC quota increase was "not going to help the market at all. It's a PR exercise to prove to the consumer that OPEC actually likes them."

SHORTAGES AS DESERT MIRAGES

The pessimistic judgment of the cartel's capacity was dubious at best, since it rested on the assumption that OPEC had not increased its pumping capacity for a quarter of a century. But it was accepted wisdom in the industry, nonetheless, and therefore prices continued to rise. Purnomo Yusgiantoro, OPEC's president, kindled the price fire when he said publicly that the target price band "has to be adjusted," and it "should be upward, not downward." The cartel put price adjustment on the agenda for its December 2004 meeting. (The topic was indeed addressed at that meeting, but no formal action was taken. Still, several ministers lobbied for a price band between $30 and $35 a barrel, and some suggested that the floor had already been raised to $32, at least informally.)

And so it went. There was no shortage of oil, even by the IEA's reckoning. In mid-September, the agency reported that "supply is running ahead of demand and stocks are building." Yet, by the end of the month, the price would surpass $50. Any excuse seemed to justify a price uptick. "Noise gets prices," remarked Lawrence J. Goldstein, president of the PIRA Energy Group consulting firm.

"If you hear something, you have to react to it and then find out if it's true or not."

For its part, OPEC was just going through the motions of pretending to drive the price down, reveling in the general view of its helplessness. "Prices are moving independently from whatever OPEC decides," said Nordine Ait-Laoussine, a former OPEC president turned industry consultant. "OPEC can't do anything more today." In early October, the price hovered between $50 and $55.

Hysteria, as we know, rules in this shell game. Billions of barrels of oil are within reasonable reach, and the notion of a shortage, whether now or in the future, is nothing but a desert mirage. But OPEC created the illusion that its members carefully nurture, and the hysteria plays right into the cartel's hands.

OPEC TIGHTENS THE SCREWS

The remainder of 2004 and the beginning of 2005 played like a broken record. The price eased off its October highs, but remained well above both year-earlier levels and OPEC's still officially unchanged target price—thanks to a million-barrel-a-day production cut that took effect on January 1. Prior to the cartel's agreeing to reduce production, Ali al-Naimi insisted that "we have done everything to moderate the price . . . and it will probably moderate more" as fears of shortages lessen.

In reality, OPEC was tightening the screws, trying to define the limits of tolerance among its customers by threatening further production cuts at any and every sign of price weakness. Incredibly, the cartel encountered little resistance, let alone outrage, from the oil-importing nations. The IEA said it thought OPEC was over-reacting to concern about a precipitous drop in prices, and pointed out that $40-plus oil was still very high. Most everyone seemed to accept that OPEC had developed an appetite for the windfall profits brought by record-high oil prices and would do everything in its power to keep the rivers of money flowing.

"All OPEC is doing now is accompanying where the market sees prices going in the future," Paul Horsnell, director of energy research at Barclays Capital in London, told the *New York Times*. "But there's nothing terribly explicit about it"—as if some force other than the cartel were propelling prices higher.

Indeed, Jad Mouawad, the article's author, flatly stated that "OPEC alone is not responsible for high prices." He went on to blame the familiar litany of war, strikes, political upheavals, and hurricanes in places as divergent as Iraq, Nigeria, Venezuela, Norway, Russia, and the Gulf of Mexico. That OPEC had so assiduously worked to create the myth of scarcity and the climate of fear that linked all of these supposedly unconnected events was not a part of the story.

Like just about everyone else, Horsnell and Mouawad had been conditioned to regurgitate OPEC's twaddle as absolute fact. Whereas a year before $30 oil was thought to be outrageous, OPEC now openly defended $40 a barrel and higher with no fear of recrimination.

For their part, the Saudis no longer pretended to worry about the economy. In mid-January 2005, when the price bounced up past $48 and the stock market began to sink, Ali al-Naimi declared that "the price today doesn't seem to be affecting economic growth negatively." If al-Naimi knew that the International Monetary Fund blamed high oil prices when it reduced its forecast for 2004 world economic growth, he apparently dismissed it. Quantifying the connection between oil prices and economic growth, Fred Bergsten, writing in the *Financial Times*, calculated that "every jump of $10 per barrel takes about half a percentage point off annual global growth for several years."

The Saudi oil minister also gave little credence to European Commission president Jose Barroso's pronouncement that $50 oil would brake economic expansion. Al-Naimi's co-conspirator, Chakib Khelil of Algeria, added his two cents worth: Not only was the economy unfazed by the high oil price, he declared, but inflation wasn't affected, either.

Had anyone stopped to think about it, they might have wondered where OPEC's ministers found the nerve to make such pronouncements. After all, only a few short months before, they had sworn that they wanted to bring down the price of oil. Now they fed a new round of rationalizing propaganda to their always-susceptible global patsies. The latest wrinkle was a sob story about how decreasing per-capita oil revenues among the cartel members and loss of revenue from a sinking U.S. dollar were hobbling their economies. (Of course, rising oil prices increase the bulging U.S. trade deficit, which, in turn, further weakens the dollar.) Somehow, the OPEC nations' out-of-control birth rates and economic mismanagement had become the world's responsibility. They shamelessly presented this humbug as justification for unconscionable oil prices.

But while yammering about population growth, dollar depreciation, and the effects of inflation, the OPEC members never once mentioned the price of oil. After sliding back toward $40 in mid-December 2004, it was now up 34 percent from the year-earlier level and had risen a whopping 15 percent just since the beginning of 2005. The dastardly inflation rate, meanwhile, was up all of 2.5 percent during the same period.

THE BAR IS RAISED

Stepped-up terrorist activity ahead of the Iraqi elections sent prices higher in January, while frigid weather in the U.S. and Europe bore the brunt of blame for steadily rising prices in February. Rumblings of a global oversupply of oil stoked fears that OPEC would again reduce overall production quotas at its next gathering. Meanwhile, Iranian oil minister Bijan Namdar Zanganeh, assuming the Saudis' traditional role as the cartel's moderating voice, said he would "prefer to wait to see prices fall below $40" before reducing the supply any further.

Lest anyone be fooled by the seemingly soothing words, however, the price bar was in the process of being jacked up by a whopping amount, anywhere from 43 percent to 73 percent, if later comments by al-Naimi were any indication. Shortly after Zanganeh laid the groundwork for raising the target from $28 to $40, and with oil selling at just under $50 a barrel, the Saudi oil minister declared that the world economy had grown so big that "little fluctuations here and there with oil are not doing so much" damage.

He attempted to justify the obscene prices by saying that OPEC would have to invest more to keep up with the increasing demand for oil. "The world is going to need every barrel we can produce," al-Naimi said. And, apparently, the $338 billion the cartel lifted from consumer pocketbooks in 2004 simply wouldn't cover expenses. Given the virtual absence of protest during all the months of skyrocketing prices, and the total lack of a viable energy policy among the governments of the consuming nations, al-Naimi apparently felt free to shoot for the moon.

Also signing on to the lunar expedition was OPEC Acting Secretary General Adnan Shihab-Eldin, who floated the notion of $80 oil at the beginning of March. He said he couldn't rule out such a spike if production were suddenly disrupted. In short order, the usual cadre of traders, analysts, and media voices leapt to provide the rationale for such an unholy notion. Maybe Iran would cut off production if the United States tried to force it to end its nuclear program. Or maybe continuing violence in Iraq would be the culprit. And what about Russia's meddling, which was impeding its oil production growth?

Kevin Norrish, an analyst at Barclays Capital, wrapped all the troubling possibilities together and advised the firm's investors that "[w]ith low inventory levels plus very little spare crude oil production or refining capacity, the market's ability to absorb supply-side shocks is at its lowest." Toss in a major supply disruption and "even $80 a barrel could look modest."

"Investors were encouraged" by producers saying that high prices were here to stay, according to *New York Times* reporter Jad Mouawad. Now, the OPEC crowd was shamelessly prodding speculators to drive oil prices still higher. Had Mouawad polled consumers who didn't also happen to be investors, he might have found them something other than "encouraged"—unless, that is, they were among the lucky ones who heard a television commentator diligently explain that $80 oil would be equivalent to just $23 a barrel in the 1970s, after taking into account inflation and the value of the dollar. Surely that knowledge eased the worried minds.

A still-plunging dollar, worries about supposedly declining supply, and fears that OPEC might not step up to the challenge kept prices reaching for new highs in March and April, even though crude oil inventories were rising. Venezuela, Qatar, and Algeria came out against raising output, while Nigeria called for other producers to help bring down "excessive" prices. If any OPEC producers answered Nigeria's call, it wasn't apparent in the market. On April 4, the nearby NYMEX futures contract hit a startling $57.79.

True to form, however, news of China's declining consumption was buried in the last paragraph of the Bloomberg News Service story trumpeting the newest NYMEX record. No one seemed to remember that OPEC had made a big point at year-end of how hard-pressed it was to meet its "obligations" in the face of rapidly rising demand from China. The cartel had periodically reminded consumers that it was working hard to keep markets fully supplied, and would quickly step up efforts if prices rose further. But with China's oil consumption dropping 13 percent in the first two months of the year, prices were still roaring ahead! The absurdities were dizzying. A sane person was left to wonder what or who would be the next designated fall guy. Might OPEC blame the market's supply problems on trumped-up rumors that tiny little Luxembourg was planning to ramp up its oil imports?

At bottom, the supposed supply problem was nothing more than a manifestation of business as usual at OPEC—too little concrete information and too much second-guessing. As this book has made abundantly clear, OPEC much prefers to keep people in the dark about all manner of things. Market manipulation is so much easier that way. But no matter if OPEC's production ceiling rises or falls, or if the new price target turns out to be $40, $50, or somewhere in between, this much is certain: Oil-consuming nations will have to run much faster in coming months to clear a breathtakingly higher hurdle.

Perhaps world leaders finally realized just how high the price bar was being set, or maybe it was the irritating impudence of Ali al-Naimi. Whatever the catalyst, the relentless barrage of self-serving remarks from al-Naimi and his OPEC cronies finally rubbed a raw spot on the consuming countries' seemingly impenetrable skins. On February 25, after the Saudi oil minister predicted that oil prices, which had topped $52 in New York the day before, would hover between $40 and $50 a barrel for the rest of the year, previously tongue-tied consuming countries finally found their voices. Within a matter of hours, top officials of the IEA, the European Union, and the U.S. Treasury Department let loose a volley of criticism.

"Oil prices are too high" was the charge that echoed back and forth across the Atlantic. The International Energy Agency's Claude Mandil announced that it was "time to be serious about energy efficiency." Treasury Secretary John Snow pronounced himself "not happy about oil prices one bit," while Peter Mandelson, European Union trade commissioner, declared: "It won't generate confidence in the international economy and the impact of such a price level will be adversely felt, not least by developing country economies."

As heartening as it was to hear this high-profile trio say, "Enough already," it was even more refreshing to read the headline over Mathew Ingram's piece that same day in Toronto's *Globe & Mail*: "It's not the weather; it's OPEC policy that keeps oil prices high." Continuing in that vein of truth, Ingram wrote, "As the price of crude has continued to climb . . . OPEC has rubbed its hands in that unctuous sort of way that undertakers have, as though it is pained about the whole price issue, but has done nothing to stop it. In fact, OPEC leaders have hinted they are pretty happy."

At long last, someone in the news media had bluntly stated the facts.

SOMETHING'S GOT TO GIVE

What does the future hold? As spring came slowly and unevenly to certain parts of the United States, winter-weary consumers were hit with the shocking suggestion that "supply disruptions" might force the oil price past $100 a barrel and bring on a devastating recession. In this context, in a March 31 research note, a Goldman Sachs energy analyst warned of a possible "super-spike" à la the 1970s, when six years of historically high oil prices crushed demand and created a "supply cushion" that eventually ushered in twelve years of below-average prices. The very next day, however, the International Energy Agency weighed in with a suggestion that oil-importing countries could head off such a calamitous price spike by implementing emergency conservation measures.

Still later, well-known investment advisor John Mauldin saw how $100 oil might be the "solution" instead of the "problem." The way he saw it, a super-spike would hasten the day when U.S. and world oil consumers would have to make an all-out effort to develop and use alternate energy sources. That, in his opinion, would be all to the good. Dilly-dallying around at $50 and $60 a barrel had only allowed OPEC to get hooked on ever-bigger profits, Mauldin reasoned. It was an unusual and disturbing opinion, because it touched upon our intransigence and unwillingness to help ourselves before disaster strikes.

According to the Washington-based consulting company PFC Energy, the world now consumes 30 billion barrels of oil a year but discovers only 18 billion new barrels. If the magnitude of this imbalance is accurate—and that's a big if—then presumably it can't go on forever. But, as this book argues, since the world's total reserves remain an enigma wrapped in OPEC secrecy, no one really knows either the true extent of oil reserves or when the turning point will occur, if it has not done so already.

The key to oil sufficiency is, of course, a combination of reducing demand and increasing reserves. The U.S. itself is not doing well on either front. For starters, neither presidential candidate had a workable energy plan. More than one pundit bemoaned the candidates' lack of urgency and failure to address the economic threat posed by high-priced oil. Platitudes and cheap shots over long-dead energy tax initiatives won out over substantive proposals. And despite John Snow's newly irritated demeanor, the Bush administration continues to send mixed messages to OPEC. In early March, for instance, shortly after OPEC floated its $80-a-barrel trial balloon, a less-than-outraged Samuel Bodman, the U.S. energy secretary, told a Senate committee "that the capability of any member of this government to influence members of OPEC is limited." Bodman went on to suggest that he had more important things to worry about. "I have a lot on my plate," he told the panel.

Many Americans were likely to find less on their plates, however, after forking over record high prices for gasoline during the spring season. The average retail price topped $2.28 a gallon in April 2005, surpassing earlier Energy Information Administration projections of $2.15. The situation led Oregon Sen. Ron Wyden to urge the Bush administration to push harder for OPEC price cuts. "OPEC is going to look out for OPEC," Wyden said. "The question is whether this administration is going to stand up for the American consumer."

With our own domestic reserves dwindling, we are presently importing 60 percent of our oil. One-fifth of that comes from the Persian Gulf. By all indications, our Gulf dependence will increase, partly because reserves elsewhere are supposedly being used up faster than those in the Gulf, which currently supplies a quarter of world oil and is thought to have enough in the ground to supply a lot more.

The future appears to be rather bleak, not least because most people in the oil-consuming world, and especially its leaders, have remained incredibly blasé about the consequences of being beholden to an organized group of unprincipled purveyors of our most critical energy source. The next chapter imagines the calamitous economic derailment ahead if our energy policy continues to consist largely of winks and nods, partisan bickering, and, ultimately, tightly crossed fingers.

10

FATE ROLLS THE DICE

The human mind often imagines disaster ahead, then just as often chooses to dismiss it. If it hasn't happened yet, why worry?

But if chance favors the prepared mind, as Louis Pasteur surmised, the corollary, as the title of this chapter suggests, is that fate rolls the dice against those who fail to prepare. That's why the tsunami of 2004 was so utterly devastating. No one was ready for what had never happened before.

In a world that runs on oil, no one has ever seen it priced at $100 a barrel before. So why worry about an OPEC-incited run-up that could crush the global economy? Because fate is sharpening her blade. Time is not on our side. The catalyst could be another terrorist attack. It could be merely a continuation of the market-abetted, hysteria-producing alleged imbalance between supply and demand. Or it could simply be a blatant, no-holds-barred price gouging by OPEC. After all, OPEC has been playing the same game over and over for decades, and rather than stopping it, politicians and bureaucrats in Washington have been little more than accomplices to the crime. The Faustian bargain that George H. W. Bush struck with the Saudis in 1986, introducing a "target price" for oil, gave the producers the upper hand. So why should OPEC stop at $60 or $70 or $80 a barrel?

In hopes of heading off the approaching disaster, this penultimate chapter foresees the future by looking backward from the plausible outcome of events, some of which have already come to pass and some that, as yet, reside only in our imagination. The years are 2006 to 2008.

THE SEEDS OF DESTRUCTION

As the year 2008 drew to a close, the decisive event seemed self-evident: OPEC had decided early in 2006 to use a basket of currencies, not just the dollar, to price its oil, thus sending the real price in Europe and Japan skyrocketing. The ensuing panic eventually drove the price to $100 a barrel and beyond, bringing the world economy almost to a standstill. The oily profiteers of OPEC, panic-mongers nonpareil, created the catastrophe to squeeze still more riches out of a tired old goose. This time, though, they squeezed too hard. The bird perished.

The oil market had been tightening for several years before that fatal day when OPEC knocked the dollar off its pedestal. It all started as just another cycle set in motion by OPEC. After the good times and soft market of the 1990s, when oil averaged just $20 a barrel, the cartel was champing at the bit, anxious to rein in its quota cheaters and increase revenues as the decade drew to a close. The big oil companies and non-OPEC producing nations, themselves hungry for more profits, began cozying up to OPEC on the theory that collusion would hasten the payday for everyone.

Perhaps most significantly, Western governments, led by Washington, not only failed to complain, they actively went along by swapping billions of dollars in tribute to OPEC in the name of "stability," which they defined as an assured oil supply whose price was many times more than what a free market would have justified. This fool's bargain dictated an outcome that increasingly resembled the notorious Stockholm Syndrome, in which hostages fall in love with their captors. Without the victims' naïve cooperation, OPEC could never have pulled off its biggest heist. In the end, we had only ourselves to blame.

The billions of Western dollars flowing to the Middle East were enriching repressive rulers and further enraging resentful masses, and all the while global consumers were becoming highly dependent on OPEC oil. Clearly, it was not in the West's interests to send so much money into one of the world's most volatile regions, to say nothing of the alarming oil dependency. The United States, in particular, was virtually hostage to political stability in an increasingly unstable Saudi Arabia, but its perceptions were dangerously clouded by Saudi secrecy and the human tendency to hope for the best and overlook the worst.

At the same time, the entire Arab world was inflamed by a new generation of Islamic fundamentalists who openly petitioned the Almighty for the destruction of Western society and terrorists who thought it their sacred duty to lend the Almighty a helping hand. Warnings that the vast flow of oil money could be diverted to buying weapons of mass destruction went unheeded. Official eyes were blindly focused on the building supply crisis.

Oil production in the United States had long since peaked, forcing the world's thirstiest consumer to import 62 percent of its supply. Meantime, reliance on OPEC and a curious complacency among world governments, led by the United States, had stalled exploration. No new oil discoveries of any consequence had been reported for at least four years.

Demand certainly didn't stall, though. American SUVs gulped ever-bigger portions of gasoline. China's industrial explosion soaked up 6.4 million barrels of oil a day, and India wasn't far behind. The International Energy Agency predicted that total world demand would reach nearly 84 million barrels a day by the middle of the decade, but wary analysts worried that even that gargantuan number was too little. Tracing the trend lines, some also fretted over a potential drop in production even as demand mushroomed. The word *chaos* crept into industry analyses.

More immediate was the danger that OPEC was cooking its production numbers, keeping traders on edge and ripe for panic buying whenever there was a glitch in the supply lines—whether from a Texas refinery fire or insurgent activity in Iraq.

Demand was fairly easy to gauge; supply was something else. No one really knew how much oil was actually available on any given day. OPEC's members kept their numbers as veiled as their chador-wearing women. By concealing actual output and spare capacity, they forced the market to trade on emotion rather than verifiable data. Veteran oilmen sent spies to try to nail down the facts, but even they were confounded by OPEC spin and contradiction. As for oil prices, well, they bounced up and down, but always wound up higher than ever. Never mind that any supply disruptions were mostly transitory and the system had ample reserves to weather them. The market was on a one-way street heading north.

Consumers everywhere found themselves with big holes in their wallets as the oil price continued to climb to $60 and beyond.

No one was immune. Oil inflation was like a flu epidemic, spreading person-to-person until the contagion infected millions. Commuters suddenly forced to pay $2.50 and higher for a gallon of gas began to brown-bag their lunches, pinching restaurants and sandwich shops in the process. Those Americans who could still afford a vacation took shorter trips, putting a major dent in the tourist industry. Trucking companies hauling everything from wines and spirits to furniture to automobile parts imposed a hefty surcharge on shippers, who passed it on to their customers, who then passed it further down the line to the retail buyer if they could. Eventually, someone had to eat the extra costs. The crunch forced many independent truckers to sell their rigs, playing havoc with both cross-country and local shipping. Higher fuel costs sent the U.S. Postal Service deeper into the red and threatened the survival of rival package shippers FedEx and UPS. Fuel price turbulence knocked already shaky airlines for another loop. With the break-even point for airlines a distant memory at $31 a barrel, and carriers already operating with skeleton staffs, sharp fare boosts were the only option. Traffic spiraled into a tailspin, and one airline after another declared bankruptcy.

Until disaster struck, most Americans had given little thought to the widespread consequences of OPEC's machinations, or, for that matter, to the lack of a comprehensive national energy strategy. But oil is vital to everything from plastic picnic forks to printer's ink to asphalt. Manufacturers raised prices across the board, and potholes went unfilled in city streets around the nation. At first, municipal and factory employees lost overtime, then they were laid off or fired outright. Foodstuffs of every kind—from beef in the butcher case to fresh fruits and vegetables in the produce aisle to milk and cheese in the dairy section—reflected the higher costs incurred by growers and shippers. Those who couldn't bear the soaring prices did without.

Runaway prices on just about everything took the Federal Reserve by surprise. Determined to keep interest rates low and lulled by their own assurances that inflation was somnolent, U.S. Federal Reserve governors were ill-prepared for the economic crisis. The Fed belatedly boosted interest rates a full 2 percentage points. The heretofore-unheard-of move jammed on the economic brakes so swiftly and so sharply that you could almost smell the stink of melting tire rubber. Suddenly higher mortgage rates stopped would-be home buyers dead in their tracks and cast a pall over the building industry. The real-estate market crashed almost overnight, wiping out billions of dollars of paper profits and putting holders of adjustable-rate mortgages and home-equity loans in peril; most owed far more money than their now depreciated homes were worth in a rapidly falling market. Foreclosures and tax-default auctions became common, consumer spending dried up, and soon the entire world was in a recession.

As for the stock market, well, no one was hurling themselves out of windows on Wall Street, but many distraught investors surely considered that option. The stock market had basically been going sideways throughout much of the run-up to $50 oil, but when the price for this basic commodity galloped toward $60 and beyond, the stock averages nosedived. It was a nightmare revisited for those who had taken a beating in the tech-stock meltdown at the beginning of the decade. Transportation and home-building stocks suffered the first big hit, but soon companies in virtually every sector were reporting skyrocketing energy costs and sharply reduced earnings, if not actual losses. Panicked by visions of freezing homes, stalled cars, and shuttered workplaces, investors began dumping even blue-chip names like GE and Procter & Gamble in a frenzy of fear. With the economy buckling under the weight of its exploding oil bill, it became clear that no company was safe.

Like barometric pressure before a hurricane, the value of the U.S. dollar had also been falling steadily against other major currencies. In other times, a drooping dollar would have given a lift to U.S. exports made cheaper for foreign buyers. Not this time. Exports were in free fall as high oil prices also crushed foreign economies, making it impossible for buyers abroad to buy U.S. goods at any price. Hardest hit were the developing nations with fledgling industries and energy-inefficient factories. Imported oil prices ballooned their costs at the same time export markets dried up, crushing young businesses that lacked the resources to ride out the crisis. Japan, too, was vulnerable, as higher prices smothered the fragile shoots of an economy slowly coming back to life after a thirteen-year drought. Only Japan's efforts to wean itself from oil—by 2004, its steel industry had switched entirely to coal to heat forges, and nuclear power generated a third of the country's electricity—prevented another collapse. Even the Chinese economic miracle soured as manufacturers had to pay 65 percent, 80 percent, and even 100 percent more for their rapidly rising oil imports. Given the enormity of China's overseas trade, their forced export and import cutbacks rippled through the global economy, further depressing already struggling trading partners, especially South Korea and Japan.

In Europe, exploding fuel costs derailed efforts by the French to rein in budget deficits as demanded by the European Union. Forced into a corner, the government had to cut popular public programs, thus inciting riots in the streets and efforts to bring down the government. Similar scenes played out across the capitals of Europe, where generous social-welfare programs, long taken for granted but no longer affordable, had to be axed.

Not everyone suffered, though. OPEC and non-OPEC producers alike raked in windfall profits, as did American natural-gas producers whose business soared when homeowners abandoned high-priced heating oil. Ford and Toyota welcomed a burst of orders for thrifty new hybrid vehicles, offsetting the slump in SUV sales. For the umpteenth time, energy-conservation prophets awoke from hibernation and saw the future blowing in the wind (and the sun and biofuels and other alternative sources of energy).

Even so, the global economy apparently had nowhere to go but down. Bad news far overshadowed the good. This was particularly the case in Iraq, where the insurgency had intensified after the country's historic elections in January 2005, defying Washington's optimistic predictions. Falling Iraqi oil exports, while relatively insignificant to the world total, were psychologically huge in pushing prices ever higher. Venezuela's production remained almost normal, but every political demonstration against the Chavez regime, as well as the regime's progressively anti-American utterances, rattled the oil market. Nor did the gush of funds quell the rebel forces in Nigeria; continued violence disrupted the African country's oil production and gave already spooked traders one more reason to bid up prices. The world oil price, which had long since passed $70 a barrel, continued to lurch upward.

Then the governments of China and India became mired in an escalating competition to lock up long-range oil supplies to protect their industries. Each had been quietly buying oil and gas fields, building pipelines, and exploring investments in oil-producing countries. Now they raised the pitch in a bidding war for long-term contracts, each trying to freeze the other out and accepting punitive escalator clauses that threatened to lift oil prices to unimagined levels.

Traders began stockpiling oil to try and stay ahead of the game.

In a replay of earlier "oil shocks," customers stored oil in every available container. Some large companies used expensive tankers as floating warehouses, thus crimping the tanker supply and driving shipping rates still higher.

Anti-Western sentiment in the Middle East intensified as Iraq devolved into civil war and the Israeli-Palestinian conflict continued on its same bloody path. With Iraqi oil exports halted by the insurgency and the market price hurtling toward $80, terrorists—probably bankrolled with excess oil profits—blew up a tanker carrying Kuwaiti oil in the Persian Gulf, destroying the ship and killing most of its crew. Tanker captains began refusing to load at Mina al-Ahmad, cutting into Kuwait's exports. The Saudis said they would pump more oil to make up for the loss. They did, but the price rose anyway.

Then terrorists managed their first truly damaging raid in Saudi Arabia, hitting the huge Ras Tanura oil refinery and the nearby loading facility at Sea Island. This time, the usual mortar and rocket-propelled grenade attack was reinforced with an even-deadlier chemical weapon, resulting in heavy Saudi casualties. Significant amounts of the oil money sloshing around the Middle East had long ago found its way to Osama bin Laden, who used it this time to murder hundreds of his fellow Saudis. The damage to the facilities was repaired within two weeks, but this new evidence of Saudi vulnerability was a major blow to confidence. The oil price left $80 behind as it continued its upward thrust.

The deciding blow came when OPEC announced what sounded like a technical reform. Abandoning its tradition of pricing oil in U.S. dollars, the cartel announced in 2006 that it would switch to a basket of currencies comprising the euro, yen, and dollar. Since the value of the dollar had been plummeting for years, the new arrangement would produce larger and more reliable profits for OPEC. Unfortunately, real oil prices in Europe and Japan would also rise abruptly, worsening the global recession.

The price jumped to $85 a barrel. Gut-wrenching fear gripped the markets. From Beijing to Bremen, from Delhi to Detroit, all the hedging tricks of savvy oil traders lost their punch. Was the world's oil fuel gauge finally pointing to empty? Civilization itself seemed to be dangling over an oil barrel. Desperate to lock in $85 oil, traders scoured the earth for any conceivable source of petroleum— hidden and forgotten, stolen and hoarded, pumped or still underground. And in their mad scramble, the now virtually unhinged treasure hunters drove the price higher and higher, until by year's end, it shot past $100 a barrel.

And still it kept going, to $101, $102.25, and $103.50. At that level, the world economy could only sink further. In the United States alone, the annual toll was $730 billion. The shock swiftly circled the globe, hammering industries, idling billions of workers, destroying businesses, and driving people everywhere into misery.

A DIFFERENT (HAPPY) ENDING

The story doesn't have to end this way, however. We are not without options in the battle to break the OPEC cartel and thereby prevent the calamity this chapter envisions. Indeed, the pages immediately ahead lay out a number of steps we can take now to fend off disaster and put us on the path to energy self-reliance. If we are committed enough to this goal, and determined enough in our desire to break OPEC's stranglehold once and for all, we can look forward to a future bright with promise and prosperity.

11

SPELLING DOOM FOR OPEC

The world has been far too long in OPEC's clutches, thanks to muddled, misguided, and wholly ineffective government policies aimed at influencing supply while largely ignoring demand. As a result, we have ended up subsidizing a parasite that survives only by feasting on our lifeblood, and financing terrorists who use our money to threaten our very existence.

But it's not too late to save our economies and our children's future (not to mention our self-respect) by freeing ourselves from the cartel's grasp and regaining control of our own economic destiny. We can begin our liberation by openly embracing a clear, two-pronged policy designed to destroy the cartel.

First, we must cut back on world energy usage by taking steps to control demand (just as OPEC works to control supply), thereby lowering the price of oil and depriving OPEC of its obscene profits.

Second, we must become energy self-reliant so as to break the cartel's back once and for all.

Our march to freedom must start with the simple recognition that we have a problem. I firmly believe that free markets work best, and I am not espousing government control. But the United States and other world leaders must stop kowtowing to OPEC, especially to Saudi Arabia, and publicly acknowledge that the current price of oil is not a free-market price. Rather, the price is unfairly set and manipulated by OPEC and its allies. Like any other commodity in a free market, oil should be priced at a level that reflects its actual low cost of production—$1.50 or less a barrel for Arabian oil—plus a reasonable profit margin. It should not be priced at the extortionist levels currently prevailing.

Having twice come to the aid of the Saudis and Kuwaitis—first in 1991, when we ended the threat of an Iraqi invasion, and again twelve years later, when we deposed Saddam Hussein—the United States is entitled to demand some quid for its quo. We and our Western allies should insist that the Saudis and Kuwaitis turn over genuine figures on their reserves and production capacity, which would deflate the hysteria factor and help bring the price in line with actual costs.

To immediately demonstrate our resolve and send a powerful message to the cartel that its manipulations will no longer be tolerated, the U.S. government should make judicious use of the Strategic Petroleum Reserve to damp down price spikes in the oil market and smooth out temporary supply shortages. A hue and cry will go up from domestic oil producers, which also enjoy inflated profits as a result of OPEC's manipulation. Their friends in Washington will mount a bare-knuckled fight to maintain the status quo and the revenue streams it brings, while asserting the strategic importance to our national interests of a profitable domestic industry. But the costs of tolerating the present situation have become too great. It would be far better, and cheaper, to break OPEC's chokehold and develop a program to preserve the domestic industry as a government-subsidized part of the petroleum reserve.

All of this will require great courage on the part of our leaders. And no one is better equipped to lead the fight than George W. Bush, a former oilman who understands the business. By standing up to OPEC and regaining our energy self-reliance, the president could secure enormous economic benefits for this country and the world, while also returning America to its role as a true world leader, not just a militarily superior world cop. Our national policies could be grounded in principle and concern for the world's good as well as our own, without being distorted by the need to safeguard our supply of oil. George W. Bush could assure his place in history as the man who broke the back of OPEC and the malign governments it has supported, while also putting the United States and much of the rest of the world on the road to lasting peace and prosperity.

The United States alone has the power and wherewithal to go up against the massive wealth and influence of the oil industry and its allies. It alone can put the OPEC cartel out of business. Indeed, the playing field will never be leveled without forceful intervention by our government.

Nevertheless, the economic effects of high-priced oil and the global threat of terrorist acts funded by egregious oil profits affect all nations, so the battle should be joined by all. What is more, a concerted global effort would snuff out the OPEC menace much more rapidly, lessening the potential for further damage to be inflicted around the world. Therefore, the administration must bring both major importers and less-developed nations into the fight.

So what is stopping us? Nothing more than our own complacency and lack of determination, both of which should be sorely tested by OPEC's increasingly gluttonous and hostile behavior. This chapter lays out the various weapons we have in our arsenal—ranging from releasing oil from the Strategic Petroleum Reserve, to the pursuit of alternative energy sources and the adoption of a voucher-based gas-distribution program, to taking legal action in world and domestic courts and supporting innovative ways to influence the demand side of the energy equation by becoming more efficient users. In combination, these efforts can deliver the knockout punch to the cartel.

Here are the steps we must pursue, one by one:

Tap the Strategic Petroleum Reserve.

The most immediately available weapon the president could wield to counter precariously high oil prices is the 700 million-barrel stash of oil salted away in Texas and Louisiana. By opening the spigots and letting some of that oil wash into the markets, the rising tide of prices could be turned back.

Given that oil is a fungible commodity, portions of the accumulated buffer stocks held by the G-7 nations (on top of the U.S. reserve, the other six members hold an additional 700 million barrels) should be made available to the marketplace as and when oil prices reach predetermined levels. The reserves could either be sold or lent to refiners or other oil consumers, to be replaced as and when prices fall back. Economist Stephen Hanke has argued in a *Wall Street Journal* article that lending reserves to oil companies or other consumers would reduce the price of oil by at least $10 per barrel and probably more. Importantly, such action would also provide a powerful counterweight to OPEC's highly successful policy of holding back production as a way to keep consumer-held inventories extremely lean. A release of reserves by a united G-7 would send a powerful message to OPEC, but, if necessary, the U.S. should act unilaterally.

Veteran oil analysts are convinced that hedge funds and other financial-market players are partly responsible for the continuing run-up of crude oil futures contract prices. A "bubble" some call it, because the expanding price is not a consequence of lack of supply. Rather, the price is inflating on OPEC-inspired rumor and irrational fear of relatively inconsequential events. The ensuing volatility created by such behavior attracts additional investors who are simply trying to make a buck on the price gyrations. It's a process that can easily become self-reinforcing.

But it wouldn't take much to knock the wheels off this bus. Even *threatening* to sell some of the SPR's oil could have a big impact on market psychology by increasing the risk and thus driving speculators to the sidelines. Actually releasing a modest amount of oil, as President George H. W. Bush did in 1990, would have an even greater impact, sending a clear signal to both the futures markets and the OPEC producers that the administration will no longer stand idly by while U.S. consumers are subjected to price gouging.

Explore alternative energy sources.

Alternative energy is an old idea whose time is now. The world has a long and glorious history of switching from one fuel source to another as conditions warrant. In seventeenth-century England, for instance, deforestation and poor infrastructure made wood uneconomical as a fuel source and forced a shift to coal. Coal powered the Industrial Revolution before giving way to oil in the late nineteenth and early twentieth century. Now it's time for the world to look again for viable alternatives.

Several possibilities have grabbed attention, from natural gas to cleaner-burning coal to solar and wind power to tidal generation and hydrogen cells. Technology is rapidly advancing on several fronts. And, as mentioned previously, there are billions of barrels of oil locked in the tar sands of Canada and Venezuela, waiting for the technology that will one day profitably mine them. But at this juncture in world history, nuclear energy offers the most easily available, economical, and virtually non-polluting alternative to fossil fuels.

Already the main source of energy in France—nuclear power generates 80 percent of that country's electricity—its principal obstacle in the United States is political foot-dragging on the problem of nuclear waste disposal. Congress has allowed the waste-disposal issue to simmer on the back burner for fifty years. If American leaders could be made to see energy as an immediate issue of national security, new nuclear plants could be coming off the drawing boards in short order. The Tennessee Valley Authority (TVA) already has three such plants in the planning stages.

Because of concerns about radioactive waste, the benefits of nuclear energy seldom get a fair hearing. To begin with, it's relatively cheap and enormously efficient. A 2000 report in the magazine *Foreign Affairs* put the average cost of producing a kilowatt hour of electricity from nuclear energy at just 1.9 cents, compared to 3.4 cents per kilowatt hour produced from natural gas. And whereas 1 kilogram of oil can generate 4 kilowatts of electricity, 1 kilogram of uranium fuel can generate 400,000 kilowatts of electricity (or more than 7 *million* kilowatts if the uranium is recycled).

Nuclear energy is a lot less stressful on the environment, too, despite the uproar over disposal of solid nuclear waste. Unlike power plants burning coal and oil, nuclear plants must include costly systems to prevent the escape of radioactive materials. Nor do they spew out any other harmful pollutants into the atmosphere— no sulfur dioxide, no nitrogen oxides, no particulate matter of any kind. Accordingly, nuclear power causes no lung damage from breathing in harmful emissions, no vegetation destruction from acid rain, and no global warming. Seen in this light, the higher initial cost of nuclear-generation facilities, as compared to fossil fuel-burning plants, fades when the external costs of health and environmental damage are factored in. If coal, gas, and oil-burning plants had to make the same upfront investments to prevent pollution, they would cost a lot more to build than nuclear plants do.

Some of the spent fuel from nuclear power generation can, as suggested above, be reprocessed for reuse. In the United States, however, recycling hasn't been an option since 1977, when President Carter banned it for fear the material could be used to build renegade nuclear weapons. The International Atomic Energy Agency doesn't entirely dismiss the possibility of such proliferation, but it believes that proper inspection procedures can prevent it.

Ironically, recycling spent fuel reduces the volume of nuclear waste that must be disposed of. Other countries, like France and Great Britain, have seen no reason to prohibit reprocessing in the first place. They have come up with engineering solutions to dispose of their smaller volumes of waste. Admittedly, the waste is highly radioactive, but proponents contend that it can be safely disposed of in multi-layered containers and will gradually lose its toxicity over time (a long time, to be sure).

Nuclear power generation has long been burdened by safety and security concerns, heightened by the Three Mile Island incident in Pennsylvania in 1979 and Russia's Chernobyl explosion in 1986. But nuclear accidents are remarkably few. When they have occurred, human error is usually to blame. In the Chernobyl tragedy, both human error and a poorly designed Russian reactor were at fault; the reactor lacked a containment structure, a design that never would have passed muster in the West.

France, which lacks oil reserves, long ago concluded that nuclear power was its best bet for attaining energy self-sufficiency. Confident of their scientific and engineering expertise, the French have shown the way to what could become an OPEC-free future.

A growing number of governments around the world, including China, are bent on increasing their nuclear reactors. Westinghouse Electric, a Pittsburg-based company owned since 1998 by British Nuclear Fuels, has submitted a proposal to build four nuclear power plants for a Chinese government-run company. And, in February 2005, Westinghouse won a "preliminary commitment" from the U.S. Export-Import Bank for up to $5 billion of financing to support its bid. China has clearly confronted these issues and has decided on the efficacy of nuclear energy, and our import bank is helping them proceed. Why not here? Why not now?

In 2002, the Bush administration tested the same waters, urging a group of U.S. utilities to develop a new generation of reactors by the end of this decade. Given OPEC's increasingly predatory nature, it's time for the administration and the energy industry to mount a public relations campaign to bring skeptical Americans onboard the nuclear bandwagon. One might argue convincingly that nuclear energy can become our first and most effective line of defense against nuclear catastrophe—a scenario that becomes ever more probable as we continue sending boatloads of money to unstable regimes riven with fundamentalist extremists seeking out weapons of mass destruction to be pointed at us. Using European and Asian countries as models, the proponents of nuclear energy can reassure Americans about the safety and security of nuclear power generation.

Control gasoline demand.

Getting a nuclear program, or any other alternative-fuel

program in place, is going to take a while. But there's something we can do in the meantime to reduce our energy consumption, drive down the price of oil, and deprive OPEC of some of the billions of dollars it steals from us every year. We can begin almost immediately to put OPEC out of business by instituting a fair and sensible plan for a voucher-based gasoline-distribution program, such as one based on an idea floated several years ago by economist Alan Day Haight of Bowling Green State University. Haight's plan would build on the fact that most driving is discretionary, and would encourage car pooling and the use of public transportation.

Whoa there, you're probably thinking, I don't want anyone telling me I can't buy as much gas as I want. Ah, but here's the beauty of this approach: You *can* buy whatever amount you choose, so long as you're in possession of the proper gas purchase permit (GPP). GPPs would come in the form of magnetic debit cards embedded with a national quarterly target of per-consumer gasoline consumption. Drivers whose allotted amount of gas didn't meet their needs could buy part or all of someone else's allotment— perhaps through classified ads, online bulletin boards, gas station-sponsored markets, and so forth.

Like the Bush administration's so-called cap-and-trade Clear Skies initiative, which allows less-polluting power companies to sell emissions credits to heavier polluters, this plan would let heavier gasoline consumers buy the rights to what less-thirsty consumers cannot use. And unlike an across-the-board gasoline tax, which would make the anti-any-tax folks howl while unfairly punishing the poor and geographically disadvantaged (those people in rural areas who must travel long distances and have no mass transportation options), the GPP approach would give all Americans a chance to join together in the fight against OPEC without unduly burdening anyone.

Such a plan would prepare us for a genuine energy crunch, should one come, and give all of us a new sense of self-respect and the feeling that we are taking control of our own destiny again. Just the mere proposal of a demand-control program would begin to drive down sales of SUVs and give impetus to public transportation plans. Actual passage of the measure would dramatically alter the world's perception of Americans as profligate and self-indulgent consumers.

For the average driver, the GPP distribution plan would not increase gasoline costs. A consumer would pay the same out-of-pocket cash per gallon, and the government wouldn't get its hands on any more of the taxpayers' dollars. It is a more efficient way of distributing energy because it employs market incentives to allow heavier gasoline users to get what they need without increasing the overall consumption of energy. Haight conceived the notion of using magnetic debit cards not out of worry over our dependence on OPEC, but out of concern about the part fossil fuels play in exacerbating the greenhouse effect. It's an idea, however, that can certainly do double duty.

Demand-control measures need not be draconian to make a big impact; reducing national gasoline use by a small percent would be equivalent to all the oil we now buy from OPEC. Once in place, such a mild distribution regime would likely rally Americans to the cause. During World War II, people planted Victory Gardens and traded unneeded rationing points to do what they could on the home front to support the troops overseas. Given what we now know about OPEC's methods and the diversion to anti-Western groups of significant portions of the profits the cartel milks from us, a committed president and his administration could sell the GPP as a way for Americans to help fight the terrorist threat. It is the least we could do when American servicemen and women are giving their lives to the same cause. Who wouldn't want to pitch in?

Put OPEC on trial.

Beyond finding alternative energy sources and instituting demand-control measures, there are legal avenues we could pursue in our quest to break the OPEC cartel. The United States Justice Department could begin the attack right here at home. Oil prices are transparently governed by collusion; OPEC makes no pretense that its regular meetings are for anything but setting quotas to manipulate the price. There is an international equivalent of antitrust law in the rules of the World Trade Organization that prohibits its members from setting quantitative restrictions on imports and export. The WTO flatly bans conspiracies to rig markets and permits us to go after all parties to such a conspiracy, including companies with interests in the United States. The mere announcement of such a policy would rapidly change a good deal of behavior.

We and our allies should press the WTO to recognize that OPEC is an open affront to its rules. The organization should enforce those rules and encourage the free exchange of commerce, the goal around which it was formed and the goal it still espouses. In leading this fight, the United States would win the gratitude not just of the Western world, but of all the emerging nations that now pay extortionate prices for the oil they need for their burgeoning new factories.

Antitrust action must also extend to the non-OPEC producing nations that have been cooperating with the cartel in recent years. We should push them to stop withholding production at OPEC's cue, and, in turn, we should encourage them to use technology to extend the lives of their present oil reservoirs, and to do more exploration for new sources of oil.

OTHER VOICES, OTHER THOUGHTS

As we contemplate the most effective ways to put pressure on OPEC and erode its power, we can take a great deal of guidance from the newly published and eminently sane report, *Winning the Oil Endgame*, written by longtime energy expert Amory B. Lovins and his colleagues at the Rocky Mountain Institute in Colorado. The report, which emphasizes energy-conservation measures in combination with alternative sources, is fast becoming a rallying flag for an unlikely alliance of businesspeople, government officials, intellectuals, and environmentalists.

No one has worked harder than Lovins to devise ways out of the oil morass. He is a phenomenon in his own right: As an infant, he disdained to speak until, at the age of two, he could produce entire sentences. He was admitted to Harvard at sixteen and was an Oxford don at twenty-one. He won a patent at eighteen and published his first physics article around that time. He joined Friends of the Earth in London, where he set to work writing thoughtful articles on energy policy. In 1976, he wrote a prescient article in *Foreign Affairs* contending that improved energy efficiency would permit the Gross National Product to grow faster than energy consumption. It was an idea that most experts, shell-shocked by the 1973 Arab oil embargo, had failed to grasp. But history proved Lovins right: Between 1977 and 1985, U.S. oil use fell 17 percent while GDP grew by 27 percent.

In 1982, Lovins co-founded the Rocky Mountain Institute in Snowmass, Colorado, to focus on energy policy. The institute has grown to forty full-time employees working with a $6 million annual budget. Never "anti-establishment," Lovins has always worked with the private sector and the government, preferring incentive-driven market solutions to sanctions or government fiats. His approach wins friends on both sides of the government-business divide.

The good news, according to Lovins, is that we already have the technology needed to replace oil as an energy source. Even better, the alternative sources will cost less than oil, so the conversion will produce an actual profit. "It's better than a free lunch," he quipped not long ago. "You get paid for eating it." By his institute's reckoning, an investment of just $180 billion over ten years could keep the economy going at full speed, with fuel-cost savings of $70 billion a year by 2025. That means the whole investment—less than half of the $285 billion Americans spent on transportation fuel in 2000 alone—would pay for itself in less than three years. By 2040, Lovins asserts, we could stop importing oil altogether, and ten years later the economy would be using oil only as a raw material for plastics.

The promise of a profitable conversion is a theme common to several proposals by other energy specialists and such mainstream business publications as *Fortune* and *Business Week*. The best proposals also stress that we will reap social and political rewards at home and abroad if we finally end our oil co-dependency.

More dubious solutions that have been floated would rely on buying additional oil from non-OPEC sources, drilling in our own Arctic National Wildlife Refuge, or raising taxes at the pump. All of these are merely Band-Aids for the short run. None would be a long-term solution, and none would enable us to regain our energy self-reliance.

Lovins also cautions against expecting a single form of energy to replace oil. Natural gas, for instance, might seem to be an attractive alternative to oil, but switching our dependency to gas would run the risk of yet another cartel, since 62 percent of the world's currently known natural gas reserves are concentrated in five countries: Russia, Iran, Qatar, Saudi Arabia, and the United Arab Emirates. Russia and Iran together control 45 percent of those reserves.

Fortunately, American ingenuity has never relied on a single resource or incentive to achieve a goal. Here are the broad strokes of what the Rocky Mountain Institute says we must do to regain our energy self-reliance:

Use oil more efficiently.

The United States doubled the efficiency of its oil use after the Arab oil embargo of the early 1970s, and we can do it again. From 1975 to 2003, the oil needed to produce a dollar of real Gross Domestic Product was cut in half. However, cars and light trucks, which devour one-third of the oil consumed annually, have been getting less efficient over the past two decades. That trend must be reversed—and it can be if smart technology, design, and manufacturing are combined to produce compelling products.

Winning the Oil Endgame argues that fuel efficiency can be doubled with an investment of just $12 per barrel of oil used. Since that is only a quarter of the price we are paying now, the profits would be almost immediate. Hybrid cars, for instance, are more expensive than conventional models, but the savings they offer pay back their added cost in just three years. This means that government incentives, while they would be helpful, are not essential for success.

We don't need to revert to rickshaws. But we can learn a trick from the racing bicycles that have carried Lance Armstrong to six wins in the Tour de France. Armstrong's bikes are designed and manufactured by a U.S. company, Trek Bicycle Corporation, that introduced its first carbon fiber composite road bike in 1986. Since then, it has produced an astonishing succession of ever-lighter, ever-stronger bikes. Armstrong won the 2004 race on a Trek carbon frame that weighed only 2.09 pounds, a third less than the 3.17-pound frame he rode just the previous year.

The same phenomenon could—and should—occur in the auto industry. Lighter-weight materials such as carbon fiber, new steel alloys, and advanced polymer composites not only have the advantage of cutting fuel consumption, but would actually reduce risk of injury in a crash, as auto safety expert and physicist Leonard Evans noted in a paper for the Society of Automotive Engineers' World Congress in 2004. Evans should know; he spent thirty-three years in research at General Motors. If Detroit could design lighter-weight vehicles with no compromise of safety, size, and performance, consumers would surely welcome the fuel-efficient models, just as they have rushed to buy Toyota's hybrid Prius.

Similar savings can be achieved by lightening heavy trucks and airplanes, and we have barely scratched the surface in making homes, office buildings, and factories fuel-efficient. Lovins's own home, which doubles as the headquarters of the Rocky Mountain Institute, was built in the mountains a few miles from the ski slopes at Aspen and endures winter temperatures that reach 40 below zero. But it has no furnace. What it does have is a passive solar heating system and rooftop solar cells that save 99 percent of the usual heating costs and 90 percent of the bill for electricity, with no loss of comfort.

On a challenge from the research director of Pacific Gas & Electric, the giant San Francisco utility, Lovins also built an energy-thrifty house in Davis, California, which consumes only 48 percent of the energy used in comparable homes nearby. What is more, the house actually cost $4,490 less to build than comparable houses. The added cost of high-end windows and extra insulation was more than offset by the lack of need for either a furnace or air conditioning.

Get government to help.

Super-efficient buildings and vehicles—like any superior product—need to attract buyers on their own merits. Nonetheless, widespread use could be spurred by creative government incentives for manufacturers and consumers. This means moving beyond the no-win debate over whether government should hike taxes at the gas pump or impose tougher mileage standards on vehicle manufacturers. The best programs always use far more carrot than stick to change behavior.

The Rocky Mountain Institute has a number of sensible ideas about speeding adoption of ultra-efficient vehicles, none of them grossly punitive or tax-increasing. Sales could be spurred, for instance, with government incentives that enable low-income Americans to trade aging gas guzzlers for reliable, super-efficient models at reasonable lease or purchase terms. Temporary federal loan guarantees could help automakers retool, while also assisting airlines in speeding up the replacement of fuel-gulping jetliners with more efficient ones.

Lovins also proposes "feebates"—fees to be paid by buyers of inefficient vehicles that would fund rebates on super-efficient models within each vehicle-size class. The rebates of up to $5,000 would be on the scale of the automakers' current sales incentives. Both fees and rebates would be proportional to the vehicle's deviation from average mileage. Consumers would still enjoy their freedom of choice: You can have an SUV if you insist, but a smaller, relatively efficient Subaru Forester will set you back a lot less than a Ford Expedition, and a hybrid Toyota Escape will get you a rebate. Finally, sales of super-efficient vehicles could be accelerated by smart government procurement policies for military and civilian fleets.

If such programs encourage U.S. citizens to embrace super-efficient vehicles and airplanes, and make more efficient use of energy-saving applications in buildings and factories, Lovins projects a potential 29 percent reduction in expected oil consumption by 2025.

Conservation doesn't require austere measures or toiling by candlelight. Lovins's Colorado house sports a greenhouse and a hot tub. And Food Lion, the giant supermarket chain headquartered in Salisbury, North Carolina, reduced its energy usage by 5 percent in 2002 with a couple of hardly draconian measures. The chain installed better-insulating doors on freezers and added sensors to turn off lights in bathrooms and loading docks when they weren't in use. Elsewhere, United Technologies shaved $100,000 from the electricity bill of a single facility simply by turning off computer monitors each night. As company executive Judith Bayer confessed to *Business Week* in 2003, "It's embarrassing that we didn't do it earlier."

Cut use of natural gas by half.

Natural gas is not as abundant or cheap as it used to be. In fact, gas prices were more volatile than those for oil from 2001 to 2003. We should strive to use gas more efficiently in our homes and commercial buildings, and the techniques for doing so are well-established and profitable enough that only laziness can explain the lack of widespread use. For example, more efficient use of gas-fired electricity output, especially at peak demand, could save 8 trillion cubic feet of natural gas every year, cutting gas and power bills by $55 billion.

Eventually, according to Lovins, 10 trillion cubic feet of gas could be conserved each year, and the ensuing reduced demand would lead to lower prices for the gas actually used. The Rocky Mountain Institute estimates that by 2025 we could replace one-third of our non-transportation oil with saved natural gas, substituting it for industrial fuel oil and petrochemical feedstocks. Lovins maintains that, over the long run, the more profitable use for the saved gas would be to convert it into hydrogen, which could then displace most of the oil still being consumed.

Develop a viable biofuel program.

We know that a large-scale program to make fuel from farm products can work. For more than a quarter-century, Brazil has been using cheap sugar cane to make ethanol that now fuels 4 million cars. The ethanol program provided nearly 700,000 jobs in 2003, and reduced Brazil's oil imports by $50 billion from 1975 through 2002. We also know that industry will adapt to the new reality. In mid-2003, General Motors and Volkswagen began selling Brazilians "total flex" cars that can use any pure or blended fuel, from 100 percent ethanol to 100 percent gasoline.

But in the United States, what passes for a biofuel program is really a boondoggle to subsidize big farmers and agribusinesses that grow corn. The costly process of converting corn into ethanol provided just 2.8 billion gallons of fuel in 2003, roughly 2 percent of the 136.4 billion gallons of gasoline consumed in the U.S. that year. Without the subsidies now provided, corn-based ethanol would cost $0.52 more per gallon.

The Rocky Mountain Institute contends that switchgrass and woody crops like hybrid willow and poplar are better suited for producing energy in the United States. With recent advances in biotechnology, liquid fuels made from these harvested crops and farming and forestry waste could cost far less than gasoline, and replace 25 percent of our oil use in 2025. Other economic and social benefits would result as well, since biofuels contain almost no trace metals, sulfur, or aromatics to pollute the air. Also, switchgrass and woody crops need not interfere with food production. Indeed, they would tend to prevent the erosion associated with row crops.

According to the institute, new technology can get twice as much ethanol from the woody crops as corn now yields, and at less cost in both capital and energy. A sounder ethanol program would create 750,000 jobs, many of them in rural areas, and billions of dollars now vanishing into OPEC's coffers would stay within our borders. Even the government would come out ahead: Farm subsidies could be cut as profitable biofuel crops replaced money-losing subsidized grains. Farm income could triple.

Inevitably, biofuels will develop into a major new product line. Giant oil companies like Shell and BP are already eyeing the field. Given the profit potential, Lovins estimates the new industry could attract $90 billion in private investment, reducing or possibly eliminating the need for government funding.

NONE OF THESE EFFORTS WILL BE EASY. But one way or another, change is inevitable. If we don't embrace the challenge of energy self-reliance and try to guide our own destiny, we will be forced into a slower, messier transition by the false shortages, rising costs, and perhaps even wars caused by the present OPEC-controlled arrangement.

In any case, there will be winners and losers. Even for those quick to respond to the challenge, success isn't guaranteed. But the penalty for delay is high and rising. Every dollar added to the price of a barrel of oil costs Americans $7 billion a year, and $4.3 billion of that goes for imports. Oil at $50 a barrel means $87 billion has been added to our annual oil bill just since the end of the $30 average price. That mounting penalty will easily dwarf the $180 billion investment needed over the next decade to escape our oil addiction.

However, the reward for accepting the challenge is even greater. We can save $133 billion every year by 2025, the equivalent of a large permanent tax cut for everyone in the country. By 2040, we can be free of oil imports. Ten years later, oil will no longer be used as a fuel. We can preserve more than 1 million high-wage manufacturing jobs and add 1 million new jobs. Our air will be cleaner, our federal budget deficit will be lower, and our punishing trade deficit will shrink dramatically.

Even better, we will no longer have to pander to OPEC or any other foreign oil producer. We will be free to conduct our foreign policy according to the merits of the issues involved, without fear of endangering our energy supply. At that point, liberated from our addiction to OPEC oil, we can reclaim our traditional role as a nation whose vision and principles are honored worldwide.

EPILOGUE

That we have been so long under OPEC's thumb is both a disgrace and an encouragement. The disgrace has been more than adequately documented in the preceding chapters; the encouragement lies in my own belief that conventional wisdom, such as that which the cartel has so assiduously ingrained in our thinking about the scarcity of oil and the precariousness of our supply, will eventually run its course. The end of the line, the day reality finally overcomes myth and manipulation, will, I believe, arrive sooner rather than later.

Already, as this book documents, a growing number of skeptical voices are questioning the conventional wisdom about OPEC's oil reserves and pumping capacity. Demands for more transparency among the producing nations and calls for oil companies to subject their reserve estimates to external audits are both encouraging signs.

Also heartening are the murmurs of discontent coming from within OPEC itself. For instance, Indonesian oil minister Purnomo

Yusgiantoro, who recently completed a term as OPEC president, has openly expressed doubts about the wisdom of the cartel's aggressive pricing. On February 25, 2005, as most OPEC members appeared to revel in $50 oil and the new breed of Saudi leaders tossed aside the kingdom's long-polished patina of concern about runaway prices, Purnomo bluntly said the oil price was too high. Indonesia, which is one of the smallest producers within OPEC, subsidizes fuel sales at home. In the face of rising domestic consumption, the Indonesian government, too, has been feeling the pinch of skyrocketing market prices. From the outside looking in, it seems as if forty-five years of double-talk and thinly disguised threats are starting to lose their luster, even among some of the less affluent OPEC allies.

OPEC certainly has it in its power to set things right. The cartel could do itself and the world a huge favor by opening up its books and revealing the truth about its actual output and its real reserves, and by beginning to deal with the baksheesh corruption that infects the entire oil export business. Massive corruption allowed Saddam Hussein and his cronies to pocket $21 billion from the U.N.'s Oil-for-Food program through illegal sales, kickbacks, and crafty pricing schemes.

Equally important, the world needs OPEC's help in opening up more Gulf oil fields. Right now, OPEC is swimming in cash from high oil prices. Members show little interest in actually boosting reserves or production as opposed to talking about it.

The cartel's least-interested member is, not surprisingly, its kingpin kingdom, Saudi Arabia. The Saudis have banned outside oil companies ever since they nationalized Aramco in 1980. Given all the military aid, technology, and humble forehead-touching that successive U.S. administrations have bestowed upon the Saudis since 1980—not to mention defending them from Saddam Hussein in the first Gulf War—the kingdom's chilly shoulder is close to insufferable.

The Middle East now contains both Earth's principal oil supply and some of its most unstable countries. With Iraq in flux, Islamic anger rising, and Al Qaeda and its look-alikes flourishing, the United States can't rule out the possibility that malcontents will attempt to overthrow autocratic regimes in countries like Saudi Arabia, Egypt, Iran, and Syria. Under these circumstances, the United States has never had a greater interest in protecting Persian Gulf oil from chaos, to say nothing of striving harder for peace and social justice throughout the region. It would be a remarkable transformation, a miracle, in fact, if the Saudis and other OPEC members truly supported these aspirations and actually opened their books and their oil fields to outside exploration and partnership participation.

The stars may be coming into alignment for just such a miracle. As happened with Sulexco, the sulfur cartel I described in the introduction to this book, the fiction of OPEC may soon collapse under its own weight. When that day comes, it will be one of great rejoicing for consumers everywhere.

SOURCES

Ken Adelman, "Is It About The Oil?" *Oil & Gas Investor*, June 2003.

M. A. Adelman, *Genie Out Of The Bottle* (Cambridge, Massachusetts: MIT Press, 1995).

M. A. Adelman, "The Real Oil Problem," *Regulation*, Spring 2004.

Ali Al-Naimi, "Saudi Oil Policy: Stability With Strength," speech before Houston Forum, Houston, Texas, October 20, 1999 www.saudiembassy.net/1999News).

Mike Allen, "Bush Chides U.S. Allies In Mideast," *Washington Post*, June 30, 2004.

Lizette Alvarez, "Britain Says U.S. Planned To Seize Oil In 73 Crisis," *New York Times*, January 2, 2004.

Edmund L. Andrews, "With Iran Balking, OPEC Nations Plan To Sell More Oil," *New York Times*, March 29, 2000.

Edmund L. Andrews, "Reluctant Iran Falls In Line With OPEC Production Rise," *New York Times*, March 30, 2000.

Edmund L. Andrews, "Oil Prices Surge Past $31 With No Sign Of OPEC Intervention," *New York Times*, June 13, 2000.

James Arnold, "Russia's Threat To OPEC Deal," BBC News Online, November 16, 2001.

Dan Balz, "In Oregon, Kerry Assails Bush On Gas Prices," *Washington Post*, May 19, 2004.

Bhushan Bahree, "Saudis To Raise Output Capacity With New Wells," *Wall Street Journal*, May 24, 2004.

Bhushan Bahree, "Can OPEC Steady The Oil Markets?" *Wall Street Journal* (Europe), June 2, 2004.

Bhushan Bahree, "Oil's Run Is Likely To Keep Fast Clip," *Wall Street Journal*, March 4, 2005.

Neela Banerjee, "Toward Oil Price Stability," *New York Times*, June 25, 2000.

Neela Banerjee, "Saudi Arabia To Raise Oil Production 500,000 Barrels A Day," *New York Times*, July 4, 2000.

Neela Banerjee, "White House Takes A Softer Line Toward OPEC In Hopes Of Getting More Oil Imports," *New York Times*, June 4, 2001.

SOURCES

Neela Banerjee, "OPEC Maintains Output Levels, With Another Look In July," *New York Times*, June 6, 2001.

Neela Banerjee, "Military Plans Must Ensure Oil Flow," *New York Times*, September 24, 2001.

Neela Banerjee, "For OPEC's Captain, U.S. Roots," *New York Times*, November 18, 2001.

Neela Banerjee, "Global Oil Glut Contains Subtle Dangers," *New York Times*, January 2, 2002.

Neela Banerjee, "Mideast And Venezuela Turmoil Sends Oil Prices Into Wild Swings," *New York Times*, April 9, 2002.

Neela Banerjee, "OPEC Keeping Oil Price Down By Increasing Its Production," *New York Times*, November 15, 2002.

Neela Banerjee, "OPEC Is Expected To Agree To Put World Needs Before Quotas," *New York Times*, March 11, 2003.

Neela Banerjee, "Persian Gulf Oil Disruptions Have Already Begun," *New York Times*, March 20, 2003.

Neela Banerjee, "With The War Largely Over, OPEC Fears Oil Price Drop," *New York Times*, April 21, 2003.

Neela Banerjee, "U.S. Official Treads Carefully In Overseeing Iraqi Oil Industry," *New York Times*, May 13, 2003.

Neela Banerjee, "OPEC Unfazed By Prospects For Renewed Flow Of Iraqi Oil," *New York Times*, July 28, 2003.

Neela Banerjee, "Oil Prices Set Another Record, Topping $42," *New York Times*, June 2, 2004.

Neela Banerjee, "Oil Prices Fall Below $40, In 5.6 Percent Slide," *New York Times*, June 3, 2004.

Neela Banerjee, "Kerry Goal Of U.S. Independence On Oil Divides Advisers," *New York Times*, August 7, 2004.

Judith Barnett, "A Mind-Bending Venture Into Saudi Gender Politics," *Washington Post*, June 25, 2004.

Sarah Barnes, "Oil Business Sinks In Deepening Hole," *Austin American Statesman*, February 9, 1992.

Robert J. Barro, "With Friends Like OPEC, Who Needs . . ." *Business Week*, May 8, 2000.

James Bennet, "The Mystery Of The Insurgency," *New York Times*, May 15, 2005.

Peter Bergen, "Crude Relations," *Washington Post*, March 14, 2004.

C. Fred Bergsten, "An Action Plan To Stop The Market Manipulators Now," *Financial Times*, March 14, 2005.

C. Fred Bergsten, "Oil Price-Fixing Cartel Must Not Be Tolerated," *Financial Times,* April 8, 2005.

C. Fred Bergsten, *The United States and the World Economy* (Washington D.C.: Institute for International Economics, 2005).

Harry Berkowitz, "The Price of Oil, Prices Same as '90 Despite War Cutoff," *Newsday*, July 31, 1991.

Harry Berkowitz, "World Oil Economics Still Feeling War's Effect," *Toronto Star*, August 5, 1991.

Anna Bernasek, "OPEC Is Back In The Driver's Seat," *Fortune*, July 9, 2001.

Michelle Billig, "The Venezuelan Oil Crisis," *Foreign Affairs*, September/October 2004.

Nancy Birdsall and Arvind Subramanian, "Saving Iraq From Its Oil," *Foreign Affairs*, July-August 2004.

Jon Birger, "It's Energy Prices," *Money*, October 2003.

Ed Blanche, "Will Iraq Quit OPEC?" *Middle East*, July 2003.

Javier Blas, "Saudis Flag Support For Higher OPEC Price Band," *Financial Times*, July 1, 2004.

Javier Blas, "Slick Statements Dominate The Opaque World Of OPEC," *Financial Times*, December 10, 2004.

Justin Blum, "Shortage Fear Unabated, Price Of Oil Rises Again," *Washington Post*, July 31, 2004.

Justin Blum, "Oil Prices Up Despite Saudi Offer," *Washington Post*, August 12, 2004.

Justin Blum, "Price Of Oil Passes The $45 Mark," *Washington Post*, August 13, 2004.

Justin Blum, "Traders Unmoved By OPEC Gesture," *Washington Post*, September 16, 2004.

Justin Blum, "Terrorists Have Oil Industry In Cross Hairs," *Washington Post*, September 27, 2004.

Justin Blum and Nell Henderson, "Oil Continues Upward March," *Washington Post*, September 29, 2004.

Justin Blum, "Oil Cartel Votes To Reduce Output," *Washington Post*, December 11, 2004.

Paul Blustein, "Saudis Plan To Increase Crude Oil Production," *Washington Post*, May 22, 2004.

Paul Blustein, "Attack On Foreign Workers Adds To Oil Sector Worries," *Washington Post*, May 31, 2004.

Paul Blustein, "Oil Prices Reach New Peak As Terrorism Anxieties Jump," *Washington Post*, June 2, 2004.

Paul Blustein, "Oil Prices Dip On Pledges Of More Pumping," *Washington Post*, June 3, 2004.

Paul Blustein, "Oil Pressure Eases, For Now," *Washington Post*, June 4, 2004.

SOURCES

James Boxell, "World Oil Reserves Up 10 Percent, Says BP," *Financial Times*, June 16, 2004.

Robert L. Bradley, *The Mirage Of Oil Protection* (Lanham, Maryland: University Press Of America, 1989).

Keith Bradsher, "Oil Wealth Wasting Away In Indonesia," *New York Times*, March 19, 2005.

Keith Bradsher, "OPEC Leaves Quotas Intact, But Says It Can Pump More," *New York Times*, September 20, 2002.

Britannica.com

David Buchan, "The Oil War: President George W. Bush's Insistence On The Need To Remove Saddam Hussein Is Putting OPEC Under Pressure," *Financial Times*, September 14, 2002.

James Buchan, "If The Chinese Get Off Their Bikes," *New Statesman*, September 18, 2000.

James Buchan, "Sand Trap," *Washington Post*, April 11, 2004.

John Burgess, "OPEC Votes To Cut Its Production 10 Percent," *Washington Post*, February 11, 2004.

H. Sterling Burnett, "The Oil Supply," *San Diego Union-Tribune*, May 28, 2004.

John C. Campbell, "The Middle East—A House Of Containment Built On Shifting Sands," *Foreign Affairs*, Winter 1981-1982.

John Carey, "Taming The Oil Beast," *Business Week*, February 24, 2003.

Ariana Eunjung Cha and Jackie Spinner, "U.S. Companies Put Little Capital Into Iraq," *Washington Post*, May 15, 2004.

Fadhil J. Chalabi, "OPEC: An Obituary," *Foreign Policy*, Winter 1997/1998.

Terence Chea, "Alternative Fuel Activist Has Plan To Eliminate Oil," *Houston Chronicle*, November 21, 2004.

David S. Cloud, "Los Alamos Scientist's Indictment Causes Concern On Damage To National Security," *Wall Street Journal*, December 13, 1999.

Robert Collier, "More Poverty Than Affluence In Oil-Fed Economy," *San Francisco Chronicle*, September 27, 2000.

Lynn C. Cook, "What Really Counts Anyway? SEC Policy On Booking Reserves Is Antiquated And Harmful, Some Oil And Gas Experts Think," *Houston Chronicle*, February 24, 2005.

Terence Corcoran, "The 'Peak Oil' Cult," *National Post*, October 5, 2004.

Robert Corzine, "OPEC Looks For A Long-Term Future," *Financial Times*, December 3, 1997.

Donald Coxe, "A Poor Grasp Of History: Wall Street's Optimists See Too Many Parallels Between The Two Gulf Wars," *Maclean's*, April 28, 2003.

Peter Coy, "A Fragile Reprieve On Energy," *Business Week*, October 6, 2003.

Peter Coy, "The Trouble With Gushing Oil Demand," *Business Week*, April 26, 2004.

David Crawford, "West's Relations With Saudis Face Growing Strains," *Wall Street Journal*, December 7, 2004.

Michael Crowley, "The Oil-For-Food Scandal," *Slate*, December 17, 2004 (slate.msn.com).

Chip Cummins, "Oil Prices Face Slippery Triggers In Futures Market," *Wall Street Journal*, May 18, 2004.

Chip Cummins, "Guard Duty: As Threats To Oil Facilities Rise, U.S. Military Becomes Protector," *Wall Street Journal*, June 30, 2004.

Bob Davis, "Bad Habit: Why The U.S. Is Still Hooked On Oil Imports," *Wall Street Journal*, March 18, 2003.

Kathleen Day, "Record Fine Levied For Riggs Bank Violations," *Washington Post*, May 14, 2004.

Kathleen Day, "Justice Department To Probe Former Examiner At Riggs," *Washington Post*, July 29, 2004.

Bob Deans, "12/23/73: The Day OPEC Changed The World," *Austin American Statesman*, December 19, 1993.

Defense.gov

Christophe Deloire and Christophe Dubois, "A Jihad For Your Penny," *Wall Street Journal*, December 17, 2004.

Neil Dennis, "Oil Jumps On News Of Attack In Saudi Arabia," *Financial Times*, June 2, 2004.

William Diebold Jr., "The United States In The World Economy: A 50 Year Perspective," *Foreign Affairs*, Fall 1983.

Tom Doggett, "Government Sees Record Gas Price Of $2.15," Reuters, March 8, 2005.

Michael S. Doran, "Intimate Enemies," *Washington Post*, February 18, 2004.

Kate Dourian, "Oxy, Partners Sign Libya Upstream Deals," *Platt's Oilgram News*, March 8, 2005.

Christine Ebrahim-zadeh, "Dutch Disease: Too Much Wealth Managed Unwisely," *Finance & Development*, March 2003.

EIA.doe.gov

Daniel Eisenberg, "Oil's New Boss," *Time*, October 9, 2000.

Larry Elliott and Alex Brummer, "The West Put Over A Barrel," *The Guardian*, October 17, 1998.

Larry Elliott, "Chancellor Tells OPEC Oil Market Manipulation Must Stop," *The Guardian*, February 5, 2005.

Mona Eltahawy, "The Wahhabi Threat To Islam," *Washington Post*, June 6, 2004.

EnergyBulletin.net

Edward Epstein, "World Insider," *San Francisco Chronicle*, January 8, 1992.

Anthony Faiola, "Oil Prices Generate Winners And Losers," *Washington Post*, October 3, 2004.

SOURCES

Maswood Farivar, "Oil Shoots Above $41 A Barrel For The First Time," *Wall Street Journal*, July 15, 2004.

Ahmad Faruqui, "Saudi Arabia In The Eye Of The Storm," Global Beat Syndicate, March 1, 2004 (www.nyu.edu/globalbeat/syndicate/faruqui).

John J. Fialka, "Debate Widens Over Most Effective Way To Security Energy Department's Los Alamos Nuclear Site," *Wall Street Journal*, March 15, 2000.

John J. Fialka, "Senate GOP Blasts Absent Richardson At Hearing On Los Alamos," *Wall Street Journal*, June 15, 2000.

James Flanigan, "OPEC Is Cause For Worry But Not Panic," *Los Angeles Times*, August 1, 1990.

Neil Ford, "Which Way For OPEC?" *Middle East*, March 2004.

Neil Ford, "Keeping OPEC Together," *Middle East*, November 2003.

Juan Forero and Brian Ellsworth, "Arms Buying By Venezuela Worries U.S.," *New York Times*, February 15, 2005.

Peter Foster, "Russia Cooks OPEC In Oil," *National Post*, November 21, 2001.

Justin Fox, "OPEC Has A Brand-New Groove," *Fortune*, October 14, 2002.

David R. Francis, "Has Global Oil Production Peaked?" *Christian Science Monitor*, January 29, 2004.

David R. Francis, "Six Key Questions For The Future Of Iraq—And Its Oil," *Christian Science Monitor*, June 24, 2004.

Glenn Frankel, "U.S. Mulled Seizing Oil Fields in 73," *Washington Post*, January 1, 2004.

Thomas L. Friedman, "Connect The Dots," *New York Times*, September 25, 2003.

Thomas L. Friedman, "Cursed By Oil," *New York Times*, May 9, 2004.

Thomas L. Friedman, "Old Rules Still Work," *International Herald Tribune*, May 28, 2004.

FromtheWilderness.com

FTC.gov

Jonathan Fuerbringer, "With Oil Prices Increasing And The Election Season At Hand, The Cry Goes Up For OPEC To Raise Output," *New York Times*, August 17, 2000.

Jonathan Fuerbringer, "Middle East Strife And Its Impact On Oil May Blunt Faith In The Recovery And The Rise Of Share Prices," *New York Times*, April 3, 2002.

Beth Gardiner, "Trouble Follows Thatcher, And So Do British Tabloids," *Washington Post*, September 5, 2004.

Mark Gongloff, "$100 Oil?" *Wall Street Journal Online*, March 31, 2005.

Leah McGrath Goodman, "Crude-Oil Prices Rise Above $40 On Warning Of Terrorist Plans," *Wall Street Journal*, July 9, 2004.

Leah McGrath Goodman, "Crude Futures Hit Two-Month High On Supply Fears," *Wall Street Journal*, January 24, 2005.

Emma Graham-Harrison, "Oil Slips But Holds Over $53," Reuters, March 8, 2005.

Will Grant and Jon Farmer, "The World's Oil Barons," *New Statesman*, December 10, 2001.

William C. Gruben and Sarah Darley, "The 'Curse' Of Venezuela," *Southwest Economy*, May-June 2004.

Janet Guyon, "Billion-Dollar Bet On Russia," *Fortune*, February 23, 2004.

Alan Day Haight, "A New (Keynesian) Looks At Gas Rationing," *Challenge* (Armonk), January/February 1996.

Charles Hall, Pradeep Tharakan, John Hallock, Cutler Cleveland, and Michael Jefferson, "Hydrocarbons And The Evolution Of Human Culture," *Nature*, November 20, 2003.

Saul Hansell, "Riggs National Will Settle Spanish Suit Linked To Pinochet," *New York Times*, February 26, 2005.

Steve Hawkes, "Supply Fears Send Price Of Crude Oil To New High," *Evening Standard*, May 12, 2004.

Patrick Healy, "Bush Stands By Aircraft Carrier Speech," *Boston Globe*, September 27, 2004.

H. Josef Hebert, "Oil Reserve On Political Front Burner," Associated Press, March 30, 2004.

David Hecht, "Why War Zones Love Monopolies," *Fortune*, May 31, 2004.

John Helyar, "Fortunes Of War," *Fortune*, July 26, 2004.

Nell Henderson and Justin Blum, "'Oil Shock' Has Some Economists Worried," *Washington Post*, August 20, 2004.

Stuart Herrington, "Will They Fight?" *Wall Street Journal*, March 12, 2003.

Seymour M. Hersh, "White House And Aramco At Odds On Oil," *New York Times*, February 8, 1978.

Mark Hertzgaard, "Running On Empty," *Washington Post*, June 13, 2004.

Carola Hoyos and Kevin Morrison, "Rise In Oil Prices Fires Debate Among Analysts," *Financial Times*, August 8, 2003.

Peter Huber and Mark Mills, "Oil, Oil, Everywhere . . . ," *Wall Street Journal*, January 27, 2005.

Yousseff M. Ibrahim, "OPEC Dealing With Threat Of An Oil Glut Linked To Iraq," *New York Times*, June 6, 1996.

Youssef M. Ibrahim, "Oil Executives Work The Room At OPEC Meeting," *New York Times*, March 23, 1999.

Youssef M. Ibrahim, "Oil Countries Approve World Cutback of 3 Percent," *New York Times*, March 24, 1999.

Youssef M. Ibrahim, "A Rare OPEC Blend Of Oil And Politics," *New York Times*, March 25, 1999.

SOURCES

Youssef M. Ibrahim, "Cheap Oil Focuses Minds," *New York Times*, March 28, 1999.

David Ignatius, "Homemade Oil Crisis," *Washington Post*, May 25, 2004.

David Ignatius, "Why Gas Prices Are Too Low," *Washington Post*, June 1, 2004.

David Ignatius, "As Oil Prices Boil," *Washington Post*, August 20, 2004.

IMF.org

Ron Insana, "That's Oil, Folks," *Money*, November 2000.

Matthew Ingram, "It's Not The Weather; It's OPEC Policy That Keeps Oil Prices High," *The Globe & Mail*, February 25, 2005.

Iran-Daily.com

David Ivanovich, Bennett Roth, and Michael Hedges, "U.S. Will Try To Avert Iraq Crude Terror," *Houston Chronicle*, January 25, 2003.

Amy Myers Jaffe and Robert A. Manning, "The Shocks Of A World Of Cheap Oil," *Foreign Affairs*, January–February 2000.

Bill Jamieson, "Doomsters Are Wrong—There's Plenty Of Oil," *The Scotsman*, May 21, 2004.

Michael Janofsky, "Oil Industry Blames Regulations For Higher Gasoline Prices," *New York Times*, May 13, 2004.

Mead L. Jensen and Alan Bateman, *Economic Mineral Deposits* (New York: Wiley, 1981).

Darrell Jobman, "New Volatile Plateau Supports Energies," *Futures*, February 2004.

James Jordan and James R. Powell, "After The Oil Runs Out," *Washington Post*, June 6, 2004.

Ross Kerber, "Crude Oil Hits A 13-Year High," *Boston Globe*, May 12, 2004.

Glenn Kessler and Alan Cooperman, "U.S. Says Saudis Repress Religion," *Washington Post*, September 16, 2004.

Robert Killebrew, "Al Qaeda, The Next Chapter," *Washington Post*, August 8, 2004.

Henry A. Kissinger, *The White House Years* (Boston, Massachusetts: Little, Brown, 1979).

Paul Klebnikov, "Hitting OPEC By Way Of Baghdad," *Forbes*, October 28, 2002.

Naomi Klein, "Carlyle Covers Up," *The Nation*, November 15, 2004.

Stephen Koepp, "Marc Rich's Road to Riches," *Time*, October 3, 1983.

Charles Krauthammer, "Tax And Drill," *Washington Post*, May 21, 2004.

Paul Krugman, "Feeling OPEC's Pain," *New York Times*, August 5, 2001.

Robert Kuttner, "The Real Reasons For Your Pain At The Pump," *Business Week*, April 19, 2004.

Greg Langley, "PSC Founder Was There From Beginning," *Advocate*, January 25, 2004.

Alex Lawler, "Oil Demand To Rise To Highest In 16 Years," *China Daily*, May 13, 2004.

Calvin Lee, "China Aims To Tap Canada Oil Sands," *Asian Wall Street Journal*, January 6, 2005.

Walter J. Levy, "Oil And The Decline Of The West," *Foreign Affairs*, Summer 1980.

Walter J. Levy, "Oil—An Agenda For The 1980s," *Foreign Affairs*, Summer 1981.

Dafna Linzer, "Poll Shows Growing Arab Rancor At U.S.," *Washington Post*, July 23, 2004.

Dafna Linzer, "Past Arguments Don't Square With Current Iran Policy," *Washington Post*, March 27, 2005.

Thomas W. Lippman, "Worst Fears On Oil Never Materialized," *Washington Post*, February 26, 1991.

Thomas W. Lippman, "The Crisis Within," *Washington Post*, June 13, 2004.

George A. Lopez and David Cortright, "Containing Iraq," *Foreign Affairs*, July-August 2004.

Amory Lovins, "How America Can Free Itself Of Oil—Profitably," *Fortune*, October 4, 2004.

Gal Luft, "Iran's Oil Sector One Year After Liberation," Saban Center Middle East Memo No. 4, The Brookings Institution, June 17, 2004 (www.brookings.edu).

Michael C. Lynch, "Petroleum Resources Pessimism Debunked In Hubbert Model And Hubbert Modelers Assessment," *Oil & Gas Journal*, July 14, 2003.

Richard Mably, "Oil Up, Iraq Threats Counter Saudi Pledge," Reuters, August 11, 2004.

Neil MacFarquhar, "After Attack, Company's Staff Plans To Leave Saudi Arabia," *New York Times*, May 3, 2004.

Peg Mackey and Francois Murphy, "OPEC Debates Need For Oil Supply Cutbacks," Reuters, December 9, 2004.

John N. Maclean and Michael Arndt, "Bush Orders Sales From Oil Reserves," *Chicago Tribune*, January 17, 1991.

Adnan Malik, "Attack In Saudi Arabia Kills Six," *Washington Post*, May 2, 2004.

Charles C. Mann, "Getting Over Oil," *Technology Review*, January-February 2002.

Joseph Mann, "High Oil Costs, Robust Demand, Supply Woes Add Up To High Gasoline Prices," Knight Ridder Tribune Business News, May 13, 2004.

Timothy Mapes and Patrick Barta, "East Timor, Australia Tap Well Of Resentment Over Access To Oil Fields," *Wall Street Journal*, June 10, 2004.

Julia C. Martinez, "Iraq Invades Kuwait—Saddam's Goal: Higher Oil Prices, More Say In OPEC," *Seattle Times*, August 2, 1990.

SOURCES

Leonardo Maugeri, "Not In Oil's Name," *Foreign Affairs*, July/August 2003.

Leonardo Maugeri, "Oil: Never Cry Wolf," *Science*, May 21, 2004.

Leonardo Maugeri, "Time To Debunk Mythical Links Between Oil And Politics," *Oil & Gas Journal*, December 15, 2003.

John Mauldin, "$100 Oil Is The Solution," *John Mauldin's Weekly E-Letter*, April 2, 2005.

Johanna McGeary, "Inside Saddam's Head," *Time*, March 31, 2003.

Dana Milbank, "Candidates Argue Over Escalating Gasoline Prices," *Washington Post*, May 23, 2004.

Judith Miller, "Three Nations Reportedly Slowed Probe Of Oil Sales," *New York Times*, October 2, 2004.

Ken Moritsugu, "Threat Of Terrorist Attack On Saudi Production Facilities Worries Oil Markets," *Knight Ridder Tribune Business Wire*, June 3, 2004.

Kevin Morrison, "Market 'Shrugs Off' Saudi Call Over Quotas," *Financial Times*, May 12, 2004.

Kevin Morrison, "Saudi Arabia To Boost Capacity To Match Global Demand For Oil," *Financial Times*, February 12, 2005.

Edward L. Morse, "The Coming Oil Revolution," *Foreign Affairs*, Vol.69, No. 5, Winter 1990/91.

Edward L. Morse and Nawaf Obaid, "U.S. And Saudi Policies Fed Oil Price Rise," *International Herald Tribune*, May 26, 2004.

Jad Mouawad, "The Oil Market Refuses To Heed Positive News," *New York Times*, August 12, 2004.

Jad Mouawad, "Oil Above $46 And Far Above OPEC's Calling," *New York Times*, August 14, 2004.

Jad Mouawad, "OPEC Finds Few Options To Put A Lid On Oil Prices," *New York Times*, September 13, 2004.

Jad Mouawad, "OPEC Has Been True To Its Word," *New York Times*, September 16, 2004.

Jad Mouawad, "Irrelevant? OPEC Is Sitting Pretty," *New York Times*, October 3, 2004.

Jad Mouawad, "While U.S. Backslides, France Offers Lessons In Cutting Oil Use," *New York Times*, October 5, 2004

Jan Mouawad, "OPEC May Way Cutting Some Production," *New York Times*, December 7, 2004.

Jad Mouawad, "With Geopolitics, Cheap Oil Recedes Into Past," *New York Times*, January 3, 2005.

Jad Mouawad, "Saudis Shift Toward Letting OPEC Aim Higher," *New York Times*, January 28, 2005.

Jad Mouawad, "In Shift, Riyadh Backs Higher Oil Price," *International Herald Tribune*, January 28, 2005.

Jad Mouawad, "Big Oil's Burden Of Too Much Cash," *New York Times*, February 12, 2005.

Jad Mouawad, "When OPEC Speaks, Not Everyone Listens," *New York Times*, March 18, 2005.

Steven Mufson, "Is Gas At $2 A Gallon An Emergency?" *Washington Post*, May 23, 2004.

Cait Murphy, "Why $3-A-Gallon Gas Is Good For America," *Fortune*, June 28, 2004.

Francois Murphy and Amil Khan, "OPEC Seeks To Quell Doubts Over Oil Cut," Reuters, December 11, 2004.

Hafsa-Kara Mustapha, "OPEC Cuts Output To Maintain Prices," *Middle East*, March 2004.

Craig Nelson, "Israel Had Plan To Kill Saddam In 1992 Charges Considered in '91 Missile Attacks," *Atlanta Journal-Constitution*, December 17, 2003.

Colin Nickerson and Anne Barnard, "Aftermath: Details And New Violence Emerge," *Boston Globe*, December 16, 2003.

Andrew North, "Kuwait 10 Years On," *Middle East*, October 2000.

Timothy L. O'Brien, "Just What Does America Want To Do With Iraq's Oil?" *New York Times*, June 8, 2003.

Timothy O'Brien, "A Washington Bank In A Global Mess," *New York Times*, April 11, 2004.

Terence O'Hara, "Riggs Loss Likely To Be Sizable In Second Quarter," *Washington Post*, August 7, 2004.

Terence O'Hara, "Carlyle Disavows Plan To Get Kuwait Business," *Washington Post*, October 14, 2004.

Terence O'Hara, "Riggs Bank Agrees to Guilty Plea And Fine," *Washington Post*, January 28, 2005.

OPEC.org.

Richard A. Oppel Jr., "Cheney Tax Plan From 86 Would Have Raised Gas Prices," *New York Times*, April 6, 2004.

David B. Ottaway, "Pressure Builds On Key Pillar Of Saudi Rule," *Washington Post*, June 8, 2004.

David B. Ottaway, "U.S. Eyes Money Trails Of Saudi-Backed Charities," *Washington Post*, August 19, 2004.

William Overend, "How L.A. Survived the Gas Crunch, Day by Day," *Los Angeles Times*, June 10, 1979.

Greg Palast, "OPEC On The March; Why Iraq Still Sells Its Oil À La Cartel," *Harper's Magazine*, April 2005.

Thomas I. Palley, "Publish What You Pay: Confronting Corruption and the Natural Resource Curse," Open Society Institute, July 1, 2003 (www.soros.org/initiatives/washington/articles_publications/articles/publishpay_2003).

SOURCES

Christopher Palmeri and Stephanie Anderson Forest, "Who's To Blame?" *Business Week*, July 3, 2000.

Tanya Pang, "U.S. Oil Up Above $43, Watches Ivan, OPEC," Reuters, September 12, 2004.

Peter Passell, "Economic Scene: The Curse Of Natural Resources," *New York Times*, September 21, 1995.

Steven Pearlstein, "Our Puzzling Tolerance For Oil-Price Fixing," *Washington Post*, October 13, 2004.

Eric Pfanner, "OPEC Agrees To Increase Its Oil Production Quotas By 6.5 Percent," *New York Times*, January 13, 2003.

Eric Pfanner, "OPEC Says It Will Cut Output, And Price Of Oil Climbs Sharply," *New York Times*, September 25, 2003.

Michael M. Phillips, "The Economy: U.S. Tries To Gird Iraq For The Perils Of Oil-Cash Glut," *Wall Street Journal*, January 19, 2004.

Aron Pilhofer and Bob Williams, "Big Oil Protects Its Interests," www.PublicnIntegrity.org, July 15, 2004.

E. D. Porter, "Are We Running Out of Oil?" API Discussion Paper No. 081, 1995, American Petroleum Institute.

Bill Powell and Mark Gimein, "Don't Mess With The Saudis," *Fortune*, May 12, 2003.

Jonathan Power, "Nigeria Struggles Against The Curse Of Oil, The Gift That Corrupts," *International Herald Tribune*, January 8, 2004.

Todd S. Purdom, "After 12 Years, Sweet Victory: The Bushes' Pursuit Of Hussein," *New York Times*, December 16, 2003.

Charles A. Radin, "In Retrospect, Few Lessons Of Gulf War Worth Learning," *Boston Globe*, February 21, 2001.

Raj Rajendran, "Oil Drawing Hedge Funds," Reuters, September 30, 2004.

Lois Ramano and Howard Kurtz, "Kerry Assails Bush On Oil," *Washington Post*, April 20, 2004.

Nimrod Raphaeli, "Saudi Arabia: A Brief Guide To Its Politics And Problems," *Middle East Review of International Affairs*, September 2003.

Stanley Reed, "The Saudi's Defend Their Slippery Turf," *Business Week*, January 29, 2001.

Stanley Reed, "Does OPEC Have Sand In Its Eyes?" *Business Week*, July 1, 2002.

Stanley Reed, "A Barrel Of 'Ifs,'" *Business Week*, January 13, 2003.

Stanley Reed, "Is OPEC About To Lose Control Of The Spigot?" *Business Week*, January 20, 2003.

Stanley Reed, "The Other Saudi Arabia?" *Business Week*, October 27, 2003.

Stanley Reed, "Cheap Oil? Forget About It," *Business Week*, March 8, 2004.

Robert Reno, "Big Oil Finds Silver Lining In Desert Storm," *Newsday*, January 20, 1991.

Richard Rhodes and Denis Beller, "The Need For Nuclear Power," *Foreign Affairs*, January–February 2000.

Susan E. Rice, "We Need A Real Iran Policy," *Washington Post*, December 30, 2004.

James Richard, "New Cohesion In OPEC's Cartel? Pricing And Politics," *Middle East Review of International Affairs*, June 1999.

John Roberts, "A Matter Of Definition: How Long Is An Oily Piece of String?" *Energy Economist*, May 1, 2004.

Paul Roberts, "Cheap Oil Is History," *Cincinnati Post*, March 29, 2004.

Walter V. Robinson, "White House Affirms That It Opposes Oil Price Intervention," *Boston Globe*, April 3, 1986.

Walter V. Robinson, "On Oil Prices, Reagan Tailors His Tune To Suit The Audience," *Boston Globe*, July 25, 1986.

Larry Rohter, "OPEC's Unity Is Undercut By The Saudis," *New York Times*, September 29, 2000.

Simon Romero, Steven R. Weisman, and Richard W. Stevenson, "Saudis Push Plan For Cut In Production By OPEC," *New York Times*, March 31, 2004.

Simon Romero, "OPEC Seen Supporting Saudi Move On Oil Price," *International Herald Tribune*, March 31, 2004.

Avshalom Rubin, "The Double-Edged Crisis: OPEC And The Outbreak Of The Iran-Iraq War," *Middle East Review Of International Affairs*, December 2003.

Jim Rutenberg, "A Film To Polarize Along Party Lines," *New York Times*, May 17, 2004.

Agis Salpukas, "Oil's Numbers Game," *New York Times*, December 1, 1997.

Agis Salpukas, "Challenges Inside And Out Confront OPEC," *New York Times*, June 23, 1998.

Anthony Sampson, *The Seven Sisters* (New York, New York: Bantam, 1991).

Robert J. Samuelson, "OPEC In A Better Light," *Washington Post*, February 18, 2004.

Robert J. Samuelson, "The Cartel We Love To Hate," *Newsweek*, February 23, 2004.

"Saudi Oil Minister Says $50 Oil No Threat To Growth," Bloomberg, January 29, 2005.

Richard B. Schmitt and Kathleen Hennessey, "Bank, Big Oil Tied To African Payments," *Los Angeles Times*, July 15, 2004.

E.F. Schumacher, *Small Is Beautiful* (New York, New York: Perennial, 1989).

Nelson D. Schwartz, "Break OPEC's Grip," *Fortune*, November 12, 2001.

Nelson D. Schwartz, "Caught In The Crossfire," *Fortune*, March 8, 2004.

Nelson D. Schwartz, "Why $2.18 Gas May Be A Good Thing," *Fortune*, March 22, 2004.

Nelson D. Schwartz, "Oil's Crude Awakening," *Fortune*, September 6, 2004.

SOURCES

Elaine Sciolino, "The World: America Frets As Its Chums Play Their Own Games," *New York Times*, April 12, 1998.

Gerald F. Seib, "Saudis Are Told U.S. Policy Could Shift Its Policy on Oil," *Wall Street Journal*, April 7, 1986.

Gerald F. Seib and Peter Waldman, "Best Of Friends: U.S.-Saudi Ties Grow, Benefiting Americans But Troubling Some," *Wall Street Journal*, October 26, 1992.

Andy Serwer, "Oil Prices Are Spiking," *Fortune*, June 14, 2004.

Anthony Shadid, "Hussein's Baghdad Falls," *Washington Post*, April 10, 2003.

Moin A. Siddiqi, "Which Way Now For OPEC?" *Middle East*, June 2003.

Moin A. Siddiqi, "Swings & Roundabouts," *Middle East*, February 2004.

Ken Silverstein, "Oil Boom Enriches African Ruler," *Los Angeles Times*, January 20, 2003.

Peter Slevin, "U.S. Resumes Ties With Libya," *Washington Post*, June 29, 2004.

Craig S. Smith, "Saudis Have Been Raking In Oil Money," *New York Times*, March 21, 2003.

Glenn Somerville and Mike Dolan, "Group Of Seven Wants More Oil Output," *Reuters*, October 1, 2004.

John Spears, "Pinning Hopes On The Tar Sand," *Toronto Star*, July 25, 2004.

Megan K. Stack, "The World: Militants Kills 5 Westerners Working In Saudi Arabia," *Los Angeles Times*, May 2, 2004.

Joseph Stanislaw and Daniel Yergin, "Oil: Reopening The Door," *Foreign Affairs*, September–October 1993.

Bruce Stanley, "Oil Prices Seen Staying High," *Washington Post*, May 5, 2004.

Bruce Stanley, "Saudis Assure U.S. On Greater Oil Output," *Washington Post*, May 24, 2004.

David Stipp, "Can This Man Solve America's Energy Crisis?" *Fortune*, May 13, 2002.

Robert Stobaugh and Daniel Yergin, "Energy—An Emergency Telescoped," *Foreign Affairs*, Winter 1981-1982.

Prince Bandar bin Sultan, "The Saudis And Oil Stability," *Washington Post*, August 15, 2004.

James Surowiecki, "The Real Price Of Oil," *New Yorker*, December 3, 2001.

Ginger Szala, "The Great Divide," *Futures*, February 2004.

John Tagliabue, "Sheik Yamani: Architect of OPEC Oil Policy," *San Francisco Chronicle*, April 30, 1986.

John Tagliabue, "Yamani Caught In Political Crossfire . . . ," *Journal Record*, November 4, 1986.

David Talbot, "The Next Nuclear Plant," *Technology Review*, January-February 2002.

Sabrina Tavernise with Neela Banerjee, "Oil Prices Tumble To A 2-Year Low," *New York Times*, November 16, 2001.

Bertie Taylor, "Libya Could Keep Occidental Busy For A Long Time," *Oil & Gas Investor*, March 2005.

Heather Timmons, "Iraq Is Soliciting Bids To Help Determine How Much Oil It Has," *New York Times*, August 4, 2004.

Heather Timmons, "Speculators Place Bets On Oil, Roiling Fickle Energy Market," *New York Times*, August 5, 2004.

Patrick E. Tyler, "Oil Trader Got Millions From ARCO," *Washington Post*, February 15, 1983.

Jerry Useem, "The Devil's Excrement," *Fortune*, February 3, 2003.

Nicholas Varchaver and Kate Bonamici, "Oil's New World Order," *Fortune*, February 23, 2004.

Nicholas Varchaver, "How To Kick The Oil Habit," *Fortune*, August 23, 2004.

Juliette Vasterman, "OPEC Sets June Date To Discuss Oil Output," *Washington Post*, May 23, 2004.

Karl Vick, "The Critical Battle For Iraq's Energy," *Washington Post*, January 15, 2005.

Gonzalo Vina and Reed V. Landberg, "G-7 Calls For Oil Information," *China Daily*, February 7, 2005.

Matthew L. Wald, "Report Questions Bush Plan For Hydrogen-Fueled Cars," *New York Times*, February 6, 2004.

Susan Warren, "Fear Factor In The Oil Industry Is Driver Behind Rising Prices," *Wall Street Journal*, June 3, 2004.

Susan Warren, "Exxon's Profit Rises 39 Percent As Refining Profits Surge," *Wall Street Journal* (Europe), July 30, 2004.

Cybele Weisser, "Experiencing Gas Pains? Just You Wait," *Money*, May 2004.

Jonathan Weisman, "Bush's Handling Of Gas Costs Criticized," *Washington Post*, May 18, 2004.

Jonathan Weisman, "Prices For Oil Head Back To Record Levels," *Washington Post*, May 25, 2004.

J. Robinson West, "Paying The Pumper," *Washington Post*, July 23, 2004.

David White, "Impact Of Costly Oil Could Outweigh Benefits Of Aid And Debt Relief For Poorest African Nations," *Financial Times*, June 11, 2004.

WhiteHouse.gov

Craig Whitlock, "10 Killed In Attack On Saudi Complex," *Washington Post*, May 30, 2004.

Craig Whitlock, "Slayings Spurred Saudi Rescue," *Washington Post*, May 31, 2004.

George F. Will, "Oil: How Bad Do You Want It?" *Washington Post*, June 13, 2004.

Anna Willard, "House Cuts Aid To Saudis From Bill," *Boston Globe*, July 16, 2004.

Bob Williams, "Debate Over Peak-Oil Issue Boiling Over, With Major Implications For Industry, Society," *Oil & Gas Journal*, July 14, 2003.

Scott Wilson, "Saudis Fight Militancy With Jobs," *Washington Post*, August 31, 2004.

SOURCES

Michael Woods, "High Oil Prices Don't Mean We're Running Out Of Crude," *Pittsburgh Post-Gazette*, May 21, 2004.

Daniel Yergin, *The Prize* (New York, New York: Free Press, 1993).

Daniel Yergin, "Oil Prices Won't Depend On Iraq, But On Its Neighbors," *New York Times*, August 25, 2002.

Daniel Yergin, "The New World Of Oil," *Money*, May 2003.

Daniel Yergin, "Challenge And Opportunity In A Transition Economy," *Washington Post*, May 4, 2003.

Daniel Yergin, "Thirty Years Of Petro-Politics," *Washington Post*, October 17, 2003.

Daniel Yergin, "Imagining A $7-A-Gallon Future," *New York Times*, April 4, 2004.

Daniel Yergin, "Why It's Painful At The Pump," *New York Times*, April 4, 2004.

Adam Zagorin, "Are We Over A Barrel?" *Time*, December 18, 2000.

Adam Zagorin, Timothy J. Burger, and Brian Bennett, "Watch The Border," *Time*, March 21, 2005.

Adam Zagorin, Timothy J. Burger, and Brian Bennett, "Zarqawi Planning A U.S. Hit?" *Time*, March 21, 2005.

Leslie Zganjar, "Business Hall Of Fame: M. J. Rathbone," *The Greater Baton Rouge Business Report*, April 6, 1993.

"Annan Concerned At Impact Of High Oil Prices On World Economy," Middle East News Online, September 10, 2000.

"An Opportunity To Reduce OPEC's Role," *Business Week*, October 29, 2001.

"Are We Running Out Of Oil?" National Center For Policy Analysis, January 29, 2003.

"A Shocking Speculation About The Price Of Oil," *The Economist*, September 18, 1993.

"Asia: In The Pipeline; The Oil Wars," *The Economist*, May 1, 2004.

"BP PLC: Russian State Secrecy Laws Raise Issue For Joint Venture," *Wall Street Journal*, June 1, 2004.

"Briefing," *Newsday*, August 5, 2004.

"Bush Will Urge Saudis To Halt Oil Price Slide," *San Francisco Chronicle*, April 2, 1986.

"Bush's Stance On Oil Gives Fuel to Foes," *Newsday*, April 10, 1986.

"Business: Oil's Not Well," *The Economist*, February 8, 2003.

"Business: OPEC And The Voice Of Doom," *The Economist*, September 9, 2000.

"Business: Regime Change For OPEC?" *The Economist*, April 26, 2003.

"Business: Saddam's Charm Offensive," *The Economist*, October 12, 2002.

"Business: Slush Money," *The Economist*, June 29, 2002.

"Business: Wanted: 2 Million Barrels," *The Economist*, March 25, 2000.

"Canada And China Boost Links In Oil And Minerals," *Taipei Times*, January 22, 2005.

"China Says Oil Reserves Are Twice As Big As Expected," *Financial Times*, July 3, 2004.

"Crude Oil May Rise From Record As Global Demand Grows," Bloomberg, March 18, 2005.

"Crude Oil Prices Up," *Washington Post*, June 1, 2004.

"Crude Oil Rises Amid Concern OPEC May Extend Production Cuts," Bloomberg, January 10, 2005.

"Deciding The Tough Ones: A Conversation With M. J. Rathbone," *Nation's Business*, June 1965.

"Delta Blues: Shell Needs To Address Its Failures In Nigeria," *Financial Times*, June 15, 2004.

"Desert Shock: Saudis Are Cash-Poor," *Washington Post*, October 28, 1994.

"Finance And Economics: A Burning Question," *The Economist*, March 27, 2004.

"Finance And Economics: The Devil's Excrement," *The Economist*, May 24, 2003.

"G-7 Calls For Oil Producers To Give Data On Reserves, Output," Bloomberg, February 5, 2004.

"G-7 Wants More Oil Info, Cites Growth Risk," Reuters, October 2, 2004.

"Go Nuclear To Save The Planet," *Sunday Times*, May 30, 2004.

"How Secure Is Saudi Oil?" CNNmoney, November 24, 2004 (http://money.cnn.com/2004/)

"In Retrospect, Few Lessons Of Gulf War Worth Learning, Panelists Agree Effect Of Victory Was Overstated," *Boston Globe*, February 21, 2001.

"In The Aftermath Of The Gulf War, Oil Prices Remain Stable," *Christian Science Monitor*, April 1, 1992.

"International: Falling Out, But Not Yet Apart," *The Economist*, May 22, 2004.

"International: Nigeria's Other Export," *The Economist*, April 24, 2004.

"International: Reforming The Nearly Unreformable," *The Economist*, August 7, 2004.

"Letters," *Chemical Engineering Progress*, October 2000.

"Lifting Oil Curse On World Economy," *Korea Herald*, June 24, 2004.

"Little Risk Seen In U.S. Atom Aid," Reuters, March 17, 2005.

"Nigeria Economy: Oil Wealth Benefits Few," *EIU ViewsWire*, August 27, 2003.

"Now That Prices Are $50/BBL (An Increase Of Almost 60 Percent This Year) And Months Into Surpassing The OPEC's Target 'Band' Of $22/$28/BBL, Saudis Suddenly Find The Capability To Raise Production To 11 Million BBLs/Day," Reuters, October 4, 2004.

"N.Y. Crude Oil Jumps To Record As Yukos Says It May Cut Output," Bloomberg, July 28, 2004.

SOURCES

"N.Y. Crude Oil Rises To Record On Supply Disruption Concern," Bloomberg, July 30, 2004.

"Oil A Curse Or Cure? Obasanjo Visits 'Oil Well No. 1,'" *Middle East News Online*, March 17, 2001.

"Oil Closes At 13-Year High," *Washington Post*, May 12, 2004.

"Oil Down on U.S. Fuel Supply Growth," Reuters, August 4, 2004.

"Oil Fuels Our World," Pantagraph Publishing Co., Bloomington, Illinois, April 21, 1991.

"Oil Gains for 3rd Day," Bloomberg, December 10, 2004.

"Oil Halts Price Slide," Reuters, January 21, 2005.

"Oil Prices Ease To $45 A Barrel," Reuters, January 11, 2005.

"Oil Prices Hit Fresh Record High," BBC News Online, August 3, 2004.

"Oil Prices Rise On Cue From Bush," *Chicago Tribune*, April 3, 1986.

"Oil Rally Stalls," Reuters, March 4, 2005.

"Oil Rises To A Record On Speculation OPEC May Not Meet Demand," Bloomberg, April 4, 2005.

"Oil Slips As Supply Fears Recede," BBC News Online, August 4, 2004.

"Oil Workers To Leave Saudi Arabia," *Washington Post*, May 4, 2004.

"OPEC Has Now Reached Maximum Production Capacity . . . ," EnergyBulletin.net, August 11, 2004.

"OPEC Lobbying Non-Cartel Members," Associated Press, September 17, 2004.

"OPEC Must Close Ranks," *Jakarta Post*, December 2, 1997.

"OPEC Output Increase Sought," *Washington Post*, May 11, 2004.

"OPEC President Retracts Slip Of The Tongue," EnergyBulletin.net, August 4, 2004.

"OPEC Seeks Outside Help On Supply," *New York Times*, September 29, 2003.

"OPEC's Fading Power," BBC News Online, March 7, 2002.

"OPEC Targets Fair Oil Price . . .," *Bangkok Post*, October 29, 2000.

"Pentagon: Troops Nearly Caught Al-Zarqawi," CNN.com, April 26, 2005.

"Political (Snake) Oil," *Wall Street Journal*, May 20, 2004.

"Profile: Hugo Chavez," BBC News Online, December 5, 2002.

"Qaeda Ally May Target U.S. Theaters, Schools," Reuters, March 13, 2005.

"Report Favors Divvying Up Nigerian Oil Wealth," *Houston Chronicle*, August 3, 2003.

"Saudi Arabia Opens Fields Before Plan, Lifts Capacity," Bloomberg, August 4, 2004.

"Saudi Gamesmanship," *New York Times*, June 28, 2000.

"Saudi Oil Minister Addresses IAC In Dallas," www.SaudiNF.com, April 23, 2004.

"Saudi Oil Minister Calls On OPEC To Boost Output," Bloomberg, May 10, 2004.

"Saudi Oil Reserves Could Increase By 77 Percent," *Washington Post*, December 27, 2004.

"Saudi Oil Reserves May Top 461b Barrels," *Iran Daily*, December 28, 2004.

"Saudi Paper Blames 'Zionist Lobby' For Cut In U.S. Aid," BBC Monitoring Middle East, July 21, 2004.

"Shah Urges Saving Oil For Petrochemicals," *Chemical & Engineering News*, January 7, 1974.

"Shell Denies Planning Bid For Giant Iran Oilfield," Reuters, September 19, 2003.

"Special Report: Don't Mention The O-Word—Iraq's Oil," *The Economist*, September 14, 2002.

"Special Report: Still Holding Customers Over A Barrel—OPEC," *The Economist*, October 25, 2003.

"Terrorism And Oil," *Washington Post*, June 3, 2004.

"The Changing Shape Of Inflation," *Business Week*, March 8, 2004.

"The End Of The Oil Age," *The Economist*, October 23, 2003.

"The Fall Of Riggs," *Washington Post*, July 21, 2004.

"The Saudi Syndrome," *New York Times*, January 1, 2005.

"The Shadow Of Change," Economist.com, May 7, 2003.

"U.K. Government Calls For Action On Oil Prices," M2 Presswire, October 4, 2004.

"U.S. Dependence On Mideast Oil Held Increasing," *Los Angeles Times*, March 12, 1987.

"U.S. Oil Industry Is 125 Years Old," *Morning Call*, August 27, 1984.

"U.S. Oil Prices Reach A New Record High," Reuters, August 4, 2004.

"U.S. Security, Way Of Life Hang On Stable Oil Flow As Politicians Plot America's Energy Future, National Defense, And Environmental Concerns Rank High," *Christian Science Monitor*, August 29, 1991.

"U.S. Stocks Drop, Sending Dow Average To Biggest U.S. Stocks Drop," Bloomberg, January 13, 2005.

"U.S. Stocks Fall On Oil Prices," Bloomberg, January 21, 2005.

"U.S. To Continue Filling Oil Reserve," Reuters, August 9, 2004.

"Venezuela Arms Purchases From Russia An Ominous Development," *Miami Herald*, February 19, 2005.

"Venezuela Rebuffs U.S. On Arms Deal," Reuters, February 12, 2005.

"Venezuela Remains Price Hawk," *Toronto Star*, May 13, 2004.

"Why Are Oil Prices So Strong?" *Irish Times*, May 12, 2004.

"Why We're At OPEC's Mercy," *Business Week*, October 2, 2000.

"Will The Oil Run Out?" *The Economist*, February 10, 2001.

"World Watch," *Wall Street Journal*, March 24, 2003.

"World Oil Reserves Up 10 Percent, Says BP," *Financial Times*, June 16, 2004.

"Yukos Raises Yugansk Reserves Estimate Fivefold," Reuters, September 17, 2004.

INDEX

Abdel Nasser, Gamal, 87
Abdullah, Crown Prince, 34, 137, 157–58, 170–71
Abraham, Spencer, 189
Adelman, Morris, A., 19
African Explosives & Chemical Industries (AECI), xix
Ahlbrandt, Thomas, 21
Ait-Laoussine, Nordine, 154, 159, 203
Al Qaeda, 26–27, 174, 245
al-Assad, Hafez, 95, 109
al-Attiya, Abdullah bin Hamad, 27, 159, 162
al-Aziz, Abd, 62
Al-Bakka, Dhiaa, 42
al-Naimi, Ali, 13, 32, 34, 3–7, 145, 166, 181, 188, 191–97, 203–6, 208–9
al-Nasseri, Obaid bin Saif, 186
al-Zarqawi, Abu Musab, xiv
Alaska's National Wildlife Refuge (ANWR), 173, 235
Alkadiri, Raad, 173
Allbritton, Joe L., 67
alternative energy sources, xxi, 31, 107, 113, 121, 139–40, 175, 220, 226–30, 233–35
Amerada Hess, 11, 70
American Petroleum Institute, 150
American Society of Newspaper Editors, 132
Anglo-Iranian Oil Company, 79

Arab News, 197
Aramco, 17, 26, 86, 96, 244
Archbold, John, 4
Ardebili, Hossein Kazempour, 165–67
Armstrong, Lance, 236
Art News, xvii
Association for the Study of Peak Oil and Gas, 9, 22
Atlantic Richfield Company (Arco), 119
Austin American-Statesman, 150

Baer, Robert, 148, 153
Baker, James A. III, 149
Bangkok Post, 158
Barclays Capital, 204, 207
Barroso, Jose, 205
Bateman, A. M., 6
Bayer, Judith, 239
Bayoil, 182
Bennet, James, 184–85
Bentley, Roger W., 9
Bentz, Thomas, 200
Bergsten, Fred, 204–5
Bibi-Aybat, 83
"Big Oil", 42, 164, 167, 184, 214
Bin Laden family, 149
bin Laden, Osama, xiv, 63, 174, 176, 221
bin Sultan, Prince Bandar, 35, 68
biofuels, 220, 240–41
Bloomberg News Service, 12, 164, 208

BNP Paribas, 200
Bodman, Samuel, 211
Boeing Company, 125, 152
Boston Globe, 133, 147
Bowling Green State University, 231
BP, 28, 79, 241
Bradley, Robert, 84
Bremer, Paul, 183
Brimstone Export Ltd., xx
British Nuclear Fuels, 230
British Petroleum, 79, 85, 87, 162
British Raj, 78
Brown, Gordon, 11
Bu-Hulaiga, Ihsan, 11
Buckley, Priscilla, vii
Buckley, William F. Buckley, Jr., vii
Bush, George H. W., 40, 127–28, 131–34, 141, 147, 149, 152, 169, 214, 227
Bush, George W., xii, 25, 35, 39–41, 149, 161, 169, 172–73, 180, 184, 187–90, 195, 199, 225
Bush administration, 70, 172, 176, 178, 182–86, 189, 191, 193, 195, 201, 211, 231
Business Week, 235, 239

California Institute of Technology, 20
Cambridge Energy Research Associates, 10, 138
Campbell, Colin, 6, 15, 20
Canada's tar sands, 10, 16, 228
Carlucci, Frank, 149
Carlyle Group, 148–49
Carpenter, Donna, vii
Carroll, Philip J., 41, 183–84
Carter, James E., 116–17, 121–22, 229
CBS News, 116
Center for Global Energy Studies, 176–77
Center for Public Integrity, 39
Center for Strategic and International Studies, 60, 148

Central Intelligence Agency (CIA), xiv, 83, 92, 113, 148, 153, 182
Chavez, Hugo, 59–60, 157–58, 169–70, 177, 220
Cheney, Dick, 130, 172, 184–85
Chernobyl, 229
ChevronTexaco, 22, 79, 182, 195
Children's National Medical Center, 153
Christian Science Monitor, 40, 148
Churchill, Winston, 78
Citigroup Global Markets, 39, 198
Citizen Action, 150
Clear Skies initiative, 231
Clinton administration, 152, 165
Clinton, William J., 40, 152, 167, 169
Club of Rome, 5–6, 104
Coastal Corporation, 157
Coffman, Thomas, 150
Cold War, 80, 88, 95–97, 105
Coming Oil Crisis, The, 6–7
Compagnie Francaise de Petrole, 79
ConocoPhillips, 10–11, 41
Consumer Protection Board (State of New York), 150
Cooper, Kyle, 39
Corporate Average Fuel Economy (CAFE) law, 115
Coyle, Maurice, vii

da Silva, Anibal Octavio, 186
Davis, Jefferson, 66
De Beers, 105
Deffeyes, Kenneth S., 20
depletionists, 9, 17–18, 20–22, 30
Desert One raid, 122
Desert Shield (see Gulf War II)
Desert Storm (see Gulf War I), 147
Desmarest, Thierry, 164
Detroit News, 132
Deutsche Bank, 40
Diaz, Miguel, 60
Die Zeit, 50
Diwan, Roger, 169, 171, 199

Drollas, Leonidas P., 176–77, 202
Durbin, Richard J., 131
"Dutch disease", 52, 58

Economic Mineral Deposits, 6
Eisenhower, Dwight D., 84, 94, 130
El Paso Oil, 182
Enbridge Inc., 16
energy gap, 6, 114
Energy Information Administration, 211
Energy Journal, The, 23
Ente Nazionale, Idrocarburi, 162
Enventure, 41
environmentalists, 44, 234
ethanol, 240–41
European Commission, 205
European Union, 209, 219
Evans, Leonard, 237
ExxonMobil, 10, 70, 79, 182, 195

Federal Bureau of Mines, 5
Federal Reserve, 172, 198, 218
Federal Express (FedEx), 217
"feebates", 238
Fieler, Paul, 116
Financial Times, 205
Flanigan, James, 139–40
Food Lion, 239
Ford, 220, 238
Foreign Affairs, 5, 138, 228, 234
Fortune, 235
Friends of the Earth, 234
Frontline, 172

gas purchase permit (GPP), 231–32
gasoline hoarding in the U.S., 103, 116
gasoline rationing in the U.S., 104, 108, 116, 226, 231–32
General Electric (GE), 218
General Motors, 237, 240
Genie Out of the Bottle, 19
Gheit, Fadel, 27

Gignoux, Peter, 156–57
Globe & Mail, 209
Golan Heights, 109
Goldman Sachs, 210
Goldstein, Lawrence J., 202–3
Goodstein, David, 20
Gore, Al, 169
Great Civilization, 112
Greenspan, Alan, 172
Group of Seven (G–7), 11, 17, 192, 226
Guardian, The, 97
Gulbenkian, Calouste, 79, 137
Gulf Oil, 79
Gulf War I (1991), xxi, 64, 123, 141–42, 145–47, 150, 152, 166, 189, 224, 245
Gulf War II, xxii, 25, 41–42, 44, 179–85, 188, 190, 224

Haass, Richard, 147
Haifa, Princess, 68
Haight, Alan Day, 231–32
Halliburton, 41, 172
Hanke, Stephen, 226
Harper's, 42, 184
Harvard, 50, 167, 234
Healy, Robert, 133
Heinz, John, 130
Herrington, John, 132
Hersh, Seymour, 113
Hlavacek, Ruth, vii
Honeywell Bonner & Moore, 164
Hoover Institution, 50
Hornsell, Paul, 204
Houston Forum, 145
Hubbard, Michael, 87
Hubbert, M. King, 19–23
Hubbert's Peak: The Impending World Oil Shortage, 20
Hussein, Saddam, 25, 41, 64, 87, 102–3, 111, 122–23, 138–39, 141–43, 147–48, 166, 169, 176, 180, 181–82, 200, 224, 244, 245

INDEX

hybrid cars, 220, 236–38
hybrid willow and poplar, 240

Imperial Chemical Industries (ICI),
xix
Ingram, Mathew, 209
International Atomic Energy Agency
(IAEA), 229
International Energy Agency (IEA),
38, 113, 196, 199–200, 202–3,
209–10, 216
International Herald Tribune, xxii,
57–58
International Monetary Fund (IMF),
11, 204
Iran-Iraq War, 14, 122–23, 135, 138
Iranian Hostage Crisis, 117, 121
Iraq Petroleum Company, (IPC), 79
Iraq Petroleum syndicate, 79
Iraqi Governing Council, 42
Iraqi insurgency, 25, 184–85, 220–21
Iraqi Oil Ministry, 41, 183

Jablonski, Wanda, 85–87, 89–90, 137
Jaffe, Amy Myers, 5, 190
James A. Baker III Institute for
Public Policy, 190
Jensen, Mead L., 6
Joffe, Josef, 50
John F. Kennedy Center for the
Performing Arts, 153

Kareri, Simon P., 69–71
Kashagan, Kazakhstan, 8
Keating, Kenneth, 88
Kennedy School of Government, 147
Kern River, California, 8
Kerry, John, 188, 198–99
Kessel, Richard, 150
Khatami, Mohammed, 157–58
Khelil, Chekib, 34, 175–76, 205
Khomeini, Ayatollah Ruhollah, 113,
115, 119
King Fahd, 125, 127, 133–34, 137, 152

King Fahd Academy, 63–64
King Faisal, 97, 108–9
King Saud, 86
Kissinger, Henry, 95, 97, 104,
108–10, 113–14, 137
Koran, 63
Kruschev, Nikita, 88
Kuwait, Iraq's invasion of, 139–41,
148

Laherrère, Jean, 15, 18, 20, 22
Lake Maracaibo, 58
Lehigh University, 166
Lenin, Vladimir, 77
Levin, Carl, 187
Levitas, Mike, vii
Levitt, Arthur, 149
Lichtblau, John H., 155–56, 158
Limburg, 190
Lincoln, Abraham, 66
Lindsey, Lawrence, 172
London Center for Global Energy
Studies, 202
Long, Huey, 89
Lopez, Kathryn Jean, vii
Los Alamos National Laboratory,
168
Los Angeles Times, 70, 116, 139
Lovins, Amory B., 234–35, 237–40
Lowry, Rich, vii
Lukoil, 162

Maadi, 86–87, 90
Mandatory Oil Import Program, 84
Mandelson, Peter, 209
Mandil, Claude, 209
Manning, Robert A., 5
Marathon Oil, 11, 70
Marshall Plan, 50, 80
Martz, Larry, vii
Massachusetts Institute of
Technology, 19
Mattei, Enrico, 88
Mauldin, John, 210

McClellan, Scott, 188–89
McDonnell Douglass, 152
McKee, Rob, 41–42
McLarty, Thomas "Mack", 149
Meir, Golda, 95
Meridian International Center, 152
Middle East Economic Survey, 108
Middle East Institute, 152
Mirage of Oil Protection, The, 84
Mobil, 79, 86, 96
Morse, Edward, 184–85
Mouawad, Jad, 204, 207
"Mr. Five Percent", 79, 137

National Review Online, vii, xxii
National Review, vii
National Security Council, 147
natural gas, xix–xx, 47, 52, 58, 104,
    227–28, 235–36, 239–240
Nature, 6
New York Mercantile Exchange
    (NYMEX), 26, 28, 37, 43, 124–26,
    197, 207–8
New York Times, vii, xxi, 22, 27, 43,
    91, 113, 116, 154, 156–57, 173,
    184–85, 188, 200, 204, 207
Nixon, Richard M., 84, 95–98, 102,
    108–9
"noble fuel", 106
non-conventional petroleum, 9,
    15–16
Norrish, Kevin, 207
nuclear power, 219, 228–30

O'Reilly, David J., 22
Obasanjo, Olusegun, 57–58, 171
Occidental Petroleum Company, 11,
    92–93
Odierno, Major General Raymond,
    25
oil
    connections to terrorism, 112, 190
    cost of production, 16, 81, 145, 224
    embargo, 98–99, 101–2, 109, 141

hoarding   (stockpiling),   116,
    118–20, 163, 195, 200, 220
largest consumers of, 161
negative effects of, 47–73
production data, 30
reserves, 5–6, 8–18, 23, 27, 30–32,
    41, 48, 59, 79–81, 94, 107, 112,
    124, 137, 139, 145, 151–52, 155,
    180, 183, 192, 194, 200, 210–11,
    216, 224, 226, 230, 236, 243–44
"inflation–adjusted price of", 35,
    164
industry, political influence, 39–40
shock of 1973, 38, 78, 95, 98–99,
    102, 111
shock of 1979, 115
shock of 1986, 126
U.S. import limitations (quotas),
    84, 94, 130
U.S. price controls, 102
Oil & Gas Journal, 21
Oil-for-Food program, 72, 142, 154,
    171, 181–82, 244
Okaz, 65
OPEC (Organization of Petroleum
    Exporting Countries)
    connections to terrorism, xiv, xvi,
        61–65, 112, 185
    formation of, 91
    infighting, 101, 157
    influence on non-OPEC producers,
        136, 155, 174–75
    media complicity with, 42–45
    member states, xii
    mission, 91
    officially becomes a cartel, 124, 146
    oil embargo, xxi, 38, 98–99, 101–6,
        108–9, 141, 147, 187, 234, 236
    origins of, 77–91
    potential damage from, 214–22
    price control, 93
    quotas, 6, 29, 31, 33–34, 36–37, 43,
        124–25, 134–36, 139, 146, 151,
        153–55, 157–59, 161, 165,

167–69, 174–77, 186–87, 191, 193–94, 197–98, 201–2, 206, 214, 233

propaganda from, xxii, 12–13, 25–27, 29–37, 107

target price of oil, 36–37, 107, 134, 136, 146, 153, 188, 195, 202–3, 214

U.S. complicity with, xiii, xxi, 38–42, 113, 115, 127–43, 156, 161, 183

U.S. protection of, 190

U.S. shortsightedness about, 94, 101

Open Society Institute, 66

Oppenheimer & Company, 27

Orinoco belt, 16, 59

Otong, 71

Oxford, 234

Pacific Gas & Electric, 237

Palley, Thomas, 66

Page, Howard, 89–91

Party of God, 112

Pasteur, Louis, 213

Perez Alfonso, Juan Pablo, 54, 58, 82, 85–87, 90, 92, 115, 137

Petroleum Intelligence Weekly, 86

Petroleum Industry Research Foundation, 155

Petroleum Week, 85

PFC Energy, 169, 171, 173, 210

Phillips Petroleum, 164

Pickens, T. Boone, 16

Pinochet, General Augusto, 68

PIRA Energy Group, 202

Platt's Oilgram News, 172

Prius, 237

Prize, The, 4, 86, 120

Procter & Gamble, 218

Project Independence, 108

proved reserves, 6, 9, 12–14, 23, 124, 127, 139, 151

"Publish What You Pay", 66

Purnomo Yusgiantoro, 32–33, 36, 197, 202, 243–44

Putin, Vladimir, 175, 195

Qaddafi, Muammar, 92–93

Ramirez, Rafael, 33, 44

Rathbone, Monroe "Jack", 89–91

Reagan, Ronald W., xvii, 117, 127, 129–30, 132–33

Reagan administration, 131, 136–37

"resource curse", 48–49, 52

Rice University, 190

Rich, Marc, 118–19

Richardson, Bill, 165, 168, 188–89

Riggs Bank, 65–72

Rockefeller, John D., xiii

Rocky Mountain Institute, 234–40

Rodriguez-Araque, Ali, 165, 170, 172

Rouhani, Fuad, 91

Royal Dutch/Shell Group, 30, 57, 79, 162

Rumsfeld doctrine, 180

Rumsfeld, Donald, 180

Sachs, Jeffrey, 50

Sadat, Anwar al–, 95, 109

Salamon Smith Barney, 156

Sammons, Cindy, vii

Samuel Kier's Rock Oil, 4

Saudi Arabia, religious oppression in, 62

Schuler, Henry, 148

Schumacher, E.F., 104–5

Science, 6

Scientific American, 6

Scott, Lieutenant General James Terry (retired), 147

Securities and Exchange Commission (SEC), 9–10, 30, 149

Senate Armed Services Committee, 189

September 11, 2001 (9/11), xii, 40, 68, 149, 173, 187

Seven Sisters, 38, 78–94, 96–98, 110–11, 146

Shah of Iran, 87, 94, 103, 106–8, 111–15, 118, 137
Sharp, Philip, 132
Shaybah oil field, 145
Shell Oil, 19, 30, 41, 116, 120, 183–84, 241
Shihab-Eldin, Adnan, 206–7
Shnayerson, Robert, vii
Sieminski, Adam, 40
Simon, William, 108
Six-Day War (1967), 94, 102
Sleeping with the Devil: How Washington Sold Our Soul for Saudi Crude, 148
Small Is Beautiful: Economics as if People Mattered, 104–5
Snow, John, 209, 211
Society of Automotive Engineers' World Congress, 237
Socony-Vacuum, 79
solar power, 227, 237
Soros, George, 52, 66
Stalin, Josef, 83
Standard Oil, xiii, 4
Standard Oil of California, 79, 86, 96
Standard Oil of New Jersey, 79, 86, 89–91, 96
Stanford University, 166
Stanislaw, Joseph, 138
State Oil Marketing Organization (SOMO), 42
Stockholm Syndrome, 215
straight-liners, 21
Strategic Petroleum Reserve (SPR), 40, 141, 178, 186–87, 189, 191, 224, 226–7
Struth, Alan, 164
Subaru, 238
Sulexco, xviii, 245
switchgrass, 240–41

Taliban, 176
Tariki, Abdullah, 82, 85–88, 92
Tennessee Valley Authority (TVA), 228

Teodoro Obiang Nguema Mbasogo (Obiang), 69–72
terrorism, 26, 61–65, 112, 190, 195
Texaco, 79, 86, 96, 110, 195
Texas Independent Producers and Royalty Owners Association, 150
Texas oil business, collapse, 129
"the devil's excrement", 54, 58
Three Mile Island, 229
Time, xiv
"total flex" cars, 240
Total S.A., 15, 79, 162, 164
Tour de France, 236
Toyota, 220, 237–38
Transparency International, 47
Trek Bicycle Corporation, 236–37

U.S. Department of Energy, 141, 168
U.S. Department of Homeland Security, 27
U.S. Department of Justice, xiii, xv, 233
U.S. Energy Information Administration, 201
U.S. Export-Import Bank, 230
U.S. Geological Society, 5
U.S. Postal Service, 217
U.S. State Department, 62, 71, 147, 184
U.S. Strategic Petroleum Reserve (see Strategic Petroleum Reserve)
U.S. Treasury Department, 209
ultimately recoverable reserves, 15
United Nations (U.N.), 72, 123, 140, 142, 151, 153–54, 165, 171, 181, 244
United Nations Iraqi oil embargo, 140, 142, 151, 153, 181
United Nations Compensation Commission, 142
United Technologies, 239
University of Pennsylvania, xvii
UPS, 217
USS *Abraham Lincoln*, 25

INDEX

USS *Cole*, 190
USS *Enterprise*, 132

Varzi, Mehdi, 186
Vienna Pact (March 23, 1999), 162
Volga-Urals region, 83
Volkswagen, 240

Wahhab, Ibn Abdul, 63
Wahhabism, 62–64
Wall Street Journal, 27, 43–44, 125, 133, 135, 147, 163, 226
War on Terror, 173–74, 176, 183
Warner, Andrew, 50
Washington Consensus, 50–51
Washington Post, 35, 119
Watergate, 109
Watkins, Dr. G. Campbell, 23
Webb-Pomerene Act, xviii
Westinghouse Electric, 230
Wharton School of Finance and Commerce, xvii

wildcatting, 18, 89
Winning the Oil Endgame, 234, 236
Wordworks, Inc., vii
World Bank, 55
World Trade Organization (WTO), xv, 233
Wyatt, Oscar S., 157, 182
Wyden, Ron, 211

Y2K, 163
Yamani, Sheikh Ahmed Zaki, 19, 97, 107–8, 113, 115, 121–23, 125, 132–33, 135–37, 147
Yergin, Daniel, 4, 86, 120, 138
Yom Kippur War (1973), 95
Yousfi, Youcef, 157–59
Yukos Oil Company, 30, 195

Zaganeh, Bijan Namdar, 168, 206

NELSON CURRENT

Nelson Current, the political imprint of Thomas Nelson, Inc., publishes probing, engaging, thought-provoking titles that explore the political landscape with audacity and integrity. With a stable of news-making writers including both veteran journalists and rising stars, as well as *New York Times* best-selling authors such as Michael Savage, Nelson Current has quickly established itself as a clear leader in the ever-expanding genre of political publishing.

Check out other provocative, relevant, and timely books at NelsonCurrent.com.

LIBERALISM IS A MENTAL DISORDER
Savage Solutions
By Michael Savage
1-5955-5006-2

The brilliant best-selling author and sharp, sagacious prophet of the airwaves Michael Savage has been diagnosing America's ills for as long as he's been behind a microphone. Now, in his third and most instructive book, he provides the remedy, offering provocative yet practical ways to reclaim our social, political, and cultural integrity. Savage's third best-selling book sets out a compelling narrative of current trends and events and provides the remedy for freedom-loving Americans to effectively medicate the mental disorder of modern liberalism and restore America's former brilliance.

www.NelsonCurrent.com

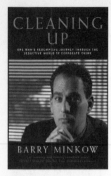

CLEANING UP
*One Man's Redemptive Journey through the
Seductive World of Corporate Crime*
By Barry Minkow
1-5955-5004-6

In this eye-opening book, Barry Minkow, the one-time Wall Street wiz kid who rocked the financial world with one of its biggest scams, tells the riveting true story of how he turned from con to cop, turning his skills to outing crooks and investment scams, and even training FBI agents to do the same. Part autobiography, part exposé, and part wake-up call, *Cleaning Up* is a fast-paced trip into the world of corporate crime, investment scams, pyramid schemes, and accounting fraud where billions of dollars is at stake. It follows Minkow through his multimillion dollar scheme, his stay in prison, and the life-changing events that followed.

THE THIRD TERRORIST
*The Middle East Connection to the Oklahoma
City Bombing*
By Jayna Davis
1-5955-5104-3

Just over ten years after the tragedy in Oklahoma City, this controversial book, which captured the attention of the 9/11 Commission, unscrambles the convoluted and distorted facts about the OKC bombing to present a compelling case that proves Timothy McVeigh and Terry Nichols did not act alone. In fact, according to award-winning investigative journalist Jayna Davis, they worked in tandem with Middle East connections that led directly to Saddam Hussein's personal army. Now available in paperback, this revised edition offers new information covering the Iraq War, the verdict in the Nichols murder trial, and recent confirmation of an Al-Qaeda general's visit to OKC to approve the bombing.

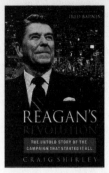

REAGAN'S REVOLUTION
*The Untold Story of the Campaign That
Started It All*
By Craig Shirley
0-7852-6049-8

This is the remarkable story of Ronald Reagan's failed yet historic 1976 presidential campaign—one that, as Reagan put it, turned a party of "pale pastels" into a national party of "bold colors." Featuring interviews with a myriad of politicos, journalists, insiders, and observers, Craig Shirley relays intriguing, never-before-told anecdotes about Reagan, his staff, the campaign, the media, and the national parties and shows how Reagan, instead of following the lead of the ever-weakening Republican Party, brought the party to him and almost single-handedly revived it.

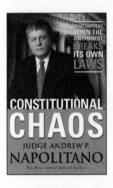

CONSTITUTIONAL CHAOS
*What Happens When the Government Breaks
Its Own Laws*
By Judge Andrew P. Napolitano
0-7852-6083-8

In this alarming book, Fox News commentator Judge Napolitano makes the solid case that there is a pernicious and ever-expanding pattern of government abuse in America's criminal justice system, leading him to establish his general creed: "The government is not your friend." As an attorney, a law professor, a commentator, a judge, and now a successful television personality, Judge Napolitano has studied the system inside and out, and his unique voice has resonance and relevance. Napolitano sets the record straight, speaking frankly from his own experiences and investigation about how government agencies will often arrest without warrant, spy without legal authority, imprison without charge, and kill without cause.

HOODWINKED
How Intellecutal Hucksters Have Hijacked American Culture
By Jack Cashill
1-5955-5011-9

For the last century, many "progressive" intellectuals responsible for shaping the way we think about guns, corporations, the legal system, sex, and even our very history have been completely fabricating the facts. And yet they have been published, praised, promoted, and protected by the cultural establishment who have their own leftist agendas advanced by their liberal lies. This book tells the stories behind the fraud—targeting everyone from Michael Moore to Margaret Mead, Alfred Kinsey to Alex Haley—and proves how their corrosive lies have completely perverted our society, culture, and understanding of the world at large.

BIG FAT LIARS
How Politicians, Corporations, and the Media Use Science and Statistics to Manipulate the Public
By Morris E. Chafetz, M.D.
1-5955-5008-9

Morris Chafetz, president of the Health Education Foundation, has spent decades carefully observing trends in science, government, the legal system, and the media, and now he reveals his unexpected findings in this sharp exposé of the many statistical lies—lies about everything from terrorism to the environment to alcohol and tobacco addiction—that manipulate Americans for the sinister motives of government, the media, corporations, and metertricious lawyers. Clear-sighted and far-reaching, this book will change how you look and listen to the scads of stats that are thrust on us every day.

SPYCHIPS
How Government and Major Corporations Are Tracking Your Every Move
By Katherine Albrecht and Liz McIntyre
1-5955-5020-8

RFID, which stands for Radio Frequency IDentification, is a technology that uses computer chips smaller than a grain of sand to track items from a distance. And as this mind-blowing book explains, plans and efforts are being made now by global corporations and the U.S. government to turn this advanced technology, these spychips, into a way to track our daily activities—and keep us all on Big Brother's short leash. Compiling massive amounts of research with firsthand knowledge, *Spychips* explains RFID technology and reveals the history and future of the master planners' strategies to imbed these trackers on everything—from postage stamps to shoes to people themselves—and spy on Americans without our knowledge or consent.

TAX REVOLT
The Rebellion Against an Overbearing, Bloated, Arrogant, and Abusive Government
By Phil Valentine
1-5955-5001-1

This book is the powerful rallying cry to all Americans to continue to fight against our ever-increasing taxes. Taking a close look at the heroic incident in Tennessee, when citizens converged on the state capitol to protest and repeatedly beat back attempts to pass a state tax, Valentine weaves an inspiring story of how patriotic citizens have stood up to taxes in the past, how many intrepid constituents continue to fight, and how Americans should resist and even revolt against taxes on a state and national level.

www.NelsonCurrent.com

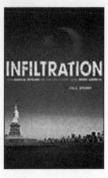

INFILTRATION
*How Muslim Spies and Subversives Have
Penetrated Washington*
By Paul Sperry
1-5955-5003-8

Infiltration explodes the façade of moderation and patriotism that Muslim leaders in America have conveyed in the wake of the 9/11 terrorist attacks. In reality, the Muslim establishment that publicly decries the radical fringe is actually a part of it. The only difference is that they use words and money instead of bombs to accomplish their goals. Now, thanks to Sperry's peerless research, piquant prose, and forthright presentation, their cover is blown as he explains the full scope of the dangerous threat of Islam in America.

CHINA: THE GATHERING THREAT
By Constantine C. Menges, Ph.D.
1-5955-5005-4

In a book that is as controversial as it is meticulously researched, a former special assistant to the president for National Security Affairs and senior official of the Central Intelligence Agency shows that the U.S. could be headed toward a nuclear face-off with communist China within four years. And it definitively reveals how China is steadily pursuing a stealthy, systematic strategy to attain geopolitical and economic dominance within the next twenty years. Using recently declassified documents and groundbreaking analysis and investigative work, Menges explains China's plan thoroughly, exposing their methods of economic control, their secret alliance with Russia and other anti-America nations, and their growing military and nuclear power.

www.NelsonCurrent.com

NELSON CURRENT

A Division of Thomas Nelson, Inc.

What people are saying about Nelson Current books:

BILL O'REILLY
about Judge Andrew P. Napolitano's *Constitutional Chaos*
"This book will open your eyes."

ANN COULTER
about Richard Poe's *Hillary's Secret War*
"This book is required reading."

SEAN HANNITY
about Jesse Lee Peterson's *Scam*
"[A] bold prescription to make America a better place."

RUSH LIMBAUGH
about Star Parker's *Uncle Sam's Plantation*
"[This book] casts a new light on the redemptive power of freedom."

GLENN BECK
about Jayna Davis's *The Third Terrorist*
"When you read this book, you are going to be convinced that it is the truth."

SAM DONALDSON
about John McCaslin's *Inside the Beltway*
"Whether you are a Democrat or a Republican, you will love this book."

NEIL CAVUTO
about Barry Minkow's *Cleaning Up*
"[This] one-of-a-kind story makes for indispensable reading."

GEORGE WILL
about Craig Shirley's *Reagan's Revolution*
"This is an exhilarating story of political daring."

HUGH HEWITT
about Ben Shapiro's *Brainwashed*
"A brilliant new voice for a generation of activists."

MICHAEL MEDVED
about Rebecca Hagelin's *Home Invasion*
"[O]ffers a persuasive, common-sense voice that demands respect—and attention . . ."

ROBERT D. NOVAK
about Tom Coburn's *Breach of Trust*
"This book provides a rare, invaluable portrait of life as it really is on Capitol Hill . . ."